6th Workshop on Balto-Slavic Natural Language Processing (BSNLP 2017)

Valencia, Spain
4 April 2017

ISBN: 978-1-5108-3862-8

BSNLP 2017

**The 6th Workshop on
Balto-Slavic Natural Language Processing**

Proceedings of the Workshop

EACL 2017 Workshop
April 4, 2017
Valencia, Spain

Endorsed by the Special Interest Group on Slavic Natural Language Processing (SIGSLAV)

Preface

This volume contains the papers presented at BSNLP-2017: the Sixth Workshop on Balto-Slavic Natural Language Processing. The Workshop is organized by SIGSLAV—Special Interest Group on NLP in Slavic Languages of the Association for Computational Linguistics.

The Workshops have been convening for over a decade, with a clear vision and purpose. On one hand, the languages from the Balto-Slavic group play an important role due to their widespread use and diverse cultural heritage. These languages are spoken by about one third of all speakers of the official languages of the European Union, and by over 400 million speakers worldwide. The political and economic developments in Central and Eastern Europe place societies where Balto-Slavic languages are spoken at the center of rapid technological advancement and the growing European consumer markets.

On the other hand, research on theoretical and applied NLP in some of these languages still lags behind the "major" languages, such as English and other West European languages. In comparison to English, which has dominated the digital world since the advent of the Internet, many of these languages still lack resources, processing tools and applications—especially those with smaller speaker bases.

The Balto-Slavic languages pose a wealth of fascinating scientific challenges. The linguistic phenomena specific to the Balto-Slavic languages—complex morphology and free word order—present non-trivial problems for construction of NLP tools, and require rich morphological and syntactic resources. This view is also reflected in Serge Sharoff's invited talk on "Pan-Slavic NLP." In the talk, he discusses an ambitious project on language adaptation—ways to adapt tools and resources among closely related languages, such as those in the Slavic group.

The BSNLP Workshops aim to bring together academic researchers and industry specialists in NLP for Balto-Slavic languages. We aim to stimulate research and to foster the creation and dissemination of tools and resources. The Workshop serves as a forum for exchange of ideas and experience and for discussing shared problems. One fascinating aspect of this group of languages is their structural similarity, as well as an easily recognizable lexical and inflectional inventory spanning the entire group, which—despite the lack of mutual intelligibility—creates a special environment in which researchers can fully appreciate the shared problems and solutions.

As a result of discussions at the previous BSNLP Workshops, to help catalyze collaboration, this year we have organized the first SIGSLAV Challenge: a shared task on multilingual named entity recognition. We have built a dataset, which allows systems to be evaluated on recognizing mentions of named entities in Web documents, their normalization/lemmatization, and cross-lingual matching. The Challenge initially covers seven Slavic languages, and it is intended as a first version of an evaluation standard to be expanded in the future.

We received 24 regular submissions, 14 of which were accepted for presentation.

The papers cover a wide range of topics. Two papers relate to lexical semantics, four to development of linguistic resources, and four to information filtering, information retrieval, and information extraction. Four papers cover topics related to processing of non-standard language or user-generated content. One paper describes the Challenge.

Additionally, 11 teams from 10 countries expressed interest in participating in the Named Entity Challenge, of which two teams have submitted results and system descriptions to date, and whose work is discussed during the session dedicated specifically to the Challenge.

Overall, this workshop's presentations cover at least 10 Balto-Slavic languages: Croatian, Lithuanian, Polish, Russian, Rusyn, Slovene, Serbian (via the regular Workshop papers), and additionally Czech,

Slovak and Ukrainian (via the Shared Task Challenge).

This Workshop continues the proud tradition established by the earlier BSNLP Workshops, which were held in conjunction with:

1. ACL 2007 Conference in Prague, Czech Republic,

2. IIS 2009: Intelligent Information Systems, in Kraków, Poland,

3. TSD 2011: 14th International Conference on Text, Speech and Dialogue in Plzeň, Czech Republic,

4. ACL 2013 Conference in Sofia, Bulgaria,

5. RANLP 2015 Conference in Hissar, Bulgaria.

We sincerely hope that this work will help further stimulate further growth of our rich and exciting field.

BSNLP 2017 Organizers

Organizers:

Tomaž Erjavec, Jožef Stefan Institute, Slovenia
Jakub Piskorski, Joint Research Centre of the European Commission, Ispra, Italy
Lidia Pivovarova, University of Helsinki, Finland
Jan Šnajder, University of Zagreb, Croatia
Josef Steinberger, University of West Bohemia, Czech Republic
Roman Yangarber, University of Helsinki, Finland

Program Committee:

Željko Agić, University of Copenhagen, Denmark
Tomaž Erjavec, Jozef Stefan Institute, Slovenia
Katja Filippova, Google, Zurich, Switzerland
Darja Fišer, University of Ljubljana, Slovenia
Radovan Garabik, Comenius University in Bratislava, Slovakia
Goran Glavaš, University of Mannheim, Germany
Maxim Gubin, Facebook Inc., USA
Miloš Jakubíček, Masaryk University, Brno, Czech Republic
Tomas Krilavičius, Vytautas Magnus University, Kaunas, Lithuania
Cvetana Krstev, University of Belgrade, Serbia
Vladislav Kuboň, Charles University, Prague, Czech Republic
Nikola Ljubešić, Jožef Stefan Institute, Ljubljana, Slovenia
Olga Mitrofanova, St. Petersburg State University, Russia
Preslav Nakov, Qatar Computing Research Institute, Qatar
Maciej Ogrodniczuk, Polish Academy of Sciences, Poland
Petya Osenova, Bulgarian Academy of Sciences, Bulgaria
Maciej Piasecki, Wroclaw University of Technology, Poland
Jakub Piskorski, Joint Research Centre, Ispra, Italy/PAS, Warsaw, Poland
Lidia Pivovarova, University of Helsinki, Finland
Alexandr Rosen, Charles University, Prague
Tanja Samardžić, University of Geneva, Switzerland
Agata Savary, University of Tours, France
Kiril Simov, Bulgarian Academy of Sciences, Bulgaria
Inguna Skadiņa, University of Latvia, Latvia
Jan Šnajder, University of Zagreb, Croatia
Serge Sharoff, University of Leeds, UK
Josef Steinberger, University of West Bohemia, Czech Republic
Stan Szpakowicz, University of Ottawa, Canada
Hristo Tanev, Joint Research Centre, Italy
Irina Temnikova, Qatar Computing Research Institute, Qatar
Roman Yangarber, University of Helsinki, Finland
Marcin Woliński, Polish Academy of Sciences, Warsaw, Poland
Daniel Zeman, Charles University, Czech Republic

Invited Speaker:

Serge Sharoff, University of Leeds, UK

Table of Contents

Workshop Program

Tuesday, April 4, 2017

9:00–10:00 **Opening Remarks and Invited Talk**

9:10–10:00 *Toward Pan-Slavic NLP: Some Experiments with Language Adaptation*
Serge Sharoff

10:10–11:00 **Session I: Lexical Semantics**

10:10–10:35 *Clustering of Russian Adjective-Noun Constructions using Word Embeddings*
Andrey Kutuzov, Elizaveta Kuzmenko and Lidia Pivovarova

10:35–11:00 *A Preliminary Study of Croatian Lexical Substitution*
Domagoj Alagić and Jan Šnajder

11:00–11:30 **Coffee Break**

11:30–13:10 **Session II: Development of Linguistic Resources**

11:30–11:55 *Projecting Multiword Expression Resources on a Polish Treebank*
Agata Savary and Jakub Waszczuk

11:55–12:20 *Lexicon Induction for Spoken Rusyn — Challenges and Results*
Achim Rabus and Yves Scherrer

12:20–12:45 *The Universal Dependencies Treebank for Slovenian*
Kaja Dobrovoljc, Tomaž Erjavec and Simon Krek

12:45–13:10 *Universal Dependencies for Serbian in Comparison with Croatian and Other Slavic Languages*
Tanja Samardžić, Mirjana Starović, Željko Agić and Nikola Ljubešić

13:10–14:30   **Lunch**

14:30–16:10   **Session III: Processing Non-Standard Language and User-Generated Content**

14:30–14:55   *Spelling Correction for Morphologically Rich Language: a Case Study of Russian*
Alexey Sorokin

14:55–15:20   *Debunking Sentiment Lexicons: A Case of Domain-Specific Sentiment Classification for Croatian*
Paula Gombar, Zoran Medić, Domagoj Alagić and Jan Šnajder

15:20–15:45   *Adapting a State-of-the-Art Tagger for South Slavic Languages to Non-Standard Text*
Nikola Ljubešić, Tomaž Erjavec and Darja Fišer

15:45–16:10   *Comparison of Short-Text Sentiment Analysis Methods for Croatian*
Leon Rotim and Jan Šnajder

16:10–16:30   **Coffee Break**

16:30–17:20   **Session IV: Shared Task on Multilingual Named Entity Recognition**

16:30–16:40   *The First Cross-Lingual Challenge on Recognition, Normalization, and Matching of Named Entities in Slavic Languages*
Jakub Piskorski, Lidia Pivovarova, Jan Šnajder, Josef Steinberger and Roman Yangarber

16:40–16:50   *Liner2 — a Generic Framework for Named Entity Recognition*
Michał Marcińczuk, Jan Kocoń and Marcin Oleksy

16:50–17:00   *Language-Independent Named Entity Analysis Using Parallel Projection and Rule-Based Disambiguation*
James Mayfield, Paul McNamee and Cash Costello

Toward Pan-Slavic NLP:
Some Experiments with Language Adaptation

Serge Sharoff
Centre for Translation Studies
University of Leeds, Leeds, UK
s.lastname@leeds.ac.uk

1 Introduction

There is great variation in the amount of NLP resources available for Slavic languages. For example, the Universal Dependency treebank (Nivre et al., 2016) has about 2 MW of training resources for Czech, more than 1 MW for Russian, while only 950 words for Ukrainian and nothing for Belorussian, Bosnian or Macedonian. Similarly, the Autodesk Machine Translation dataset only covers three Slavic languages (Czech, Polish and Russian). In this talk I present a general approach, which can be called Language Adaptation, similarly to Domain Adaptation. In this approach, a model for a particular language processing task is built by lexical transfer of cognate words and by learning a new feature representation for a lesser-resourced (recipient) language starting from a better-resourced (donor) language. More specifically, I demonstrate how language adaptation works in such training scenarios as Translation Quality Estimation, Part-of-Speech tagging and Named Entity Recognition.

2 Transfer of Feature Representation

Machine Learning algorithms are limited by the availability of training data. This problem is often addressed by developing algorithms to transfer NLP models across different domains, for example, an opinion mining model trained on IMDb can be transferred to the domain of hotel reviews (Søgaard, 2013). In a similar way, we can assume that a model trained in a donor language can be transferred to a recipient language relying on the fact that both languages come from the same language family.

One of the observations for transferring models across languages is that while the general assumption of similarity holds, the individual features exhibit a slightly different distribution. For example,

Upper baseline (ru)	MAE	0.18
	RSME	0.27
	Pearson	**0.47**

en-ru	$\rightarrow$	en-cs	en-pl
STL	MAE	0.19	0.19
	RMSE	0.25	0.25
	Pearson	**0.41**	**0.46**
Baseline Train: ru Test: xx	MAE	0.20	0.21
	RMSE	0.26	0.27
	Pearson	*0.32*	*0.33*

Table 1: STL for MT Quality Estimation.

in the task of estimating MT quality without reference translations, good MT examples are similar in the feature space describing translation into two related languages, but the exact feature values, such as the Language Model values or the phrase table sizes differ. One way of transferring the feature spaces is via Self-Taught Learning (STL), in which an autoencoder learns to reduce the dimensions of **unlabelled** datasets for the two domains. Then the available **training** set in one domain is transformed using the autoencoder, so that a new prediction model can be equally successful in the source domain and in the new target domain (Raina et al., 2007). As shown in (Rios and Sharoff, 2016), an application of this transformation to predicting the amount of Post-Editing needed to improve raw MT output can produce models which almost reach the accuracy of the original prediction model (Table 1).

3 Transfer of Lexica

Linguistic models can be also transferred through re-using grammatical models trained in a donor language with substitution of the lexicons from a recipient language. For example, a POS tagger can use the transition probabilities from the donor,

Proceedings of the 6th Workshop on Balto-Slavic Natural Language Processing, pages 1–2,
Valencia, Spain, 4 April 2017. ©2017 Association for Computational Linguistics

while the lexical emission probabilities can come from the recipient (Feldman et al., 2006; Reddy and Sharoff, 2011).

Similarly, a traditional MT engine for translation from Ukrainian into English and German can be surpassed by a crude MT pipeline consisting of a direct word-for-word transfer model from Ukrainian into Russian followed by a better resourced model translating from Russian into English and German (Babych et al., 2007). The reason for the success of the pipeline is that the Out-Of-Vocabulary rate is reduced primarily because of the better coverage of the donor lexicon.

Automatic induction of translation lexica between related languages is easier than in the more general case, since in addition to the similarity of the embedding vectors, they often have very similar forms. A reliable lexicon can be produced by combining detection of cognate forms via Levenshtein distance with assessment of semantic similarity via bilingual word embeddings even in the absence of parallel corpora (Upadhyay et al., 2016). One of the problems in transferring the lexica concerns Multi-Word Expressions (MWEs), which tend to differ even for closely related languages. In particular, this concerns fixed-form MWEs without a defined grammatical structure, such as *by and large* or *of course* in English. Such MWEs need to be detected individually in each language and linked to a grammatical model in a donor language via a distributional measure of their similarity to single-word expressions, e.g., *generally* or *definitely* in the examples above (Riedl and Biemann, 2015).

In my talk I have also demonstrated an end-to-end example for transferring feature spaces and lexicons by developing a Named Entity Recognition tagger, which starts with resources available for Slovene and transfers the features derived from a CRF model (Lafferty et al., 2001; Benikova et al.,) to other Slavic languages.

References

Bogdan Babych, Anthony Hartley, and Serge Sharoff. 2007. Translating from under-resourced languages: comparing direct transfer against pivot translation. In *Proceedings of MT Summit XI*, pages 412–418, Copenhagen.

Darina Benikova, Seid Muhie Yimam, Prabhakaran Santhanam, and Chris Biemann. GermaNER: Free open German named entity recognition tool. In *Proceedings of the International Conference of the German Society for Computational Linguistics and Language Technology (GSCL 2015)*, pages 31–38, University of Duisburg-Essen, Germany.

Anna Feldman, Jirka Hana, and Chris Brew. 2006. A cross-language approach to rapid creation of new morpho-syntactically annotated resources. In *Proceedings of the 5th International Conference on Language Resources and Evaluation (LREC 2006)*, pages 549–554, Genoa, Italy.

John Lafferty, Andrew McCallum, and Fernando Pereira. 2001. Conditional random fields: Probabilistic models for segmenting and labeling sequence data. In *Proceedings of the eighteenth international conference on machine learning, ICML*, volume 1, pages 282–289.

Joakim Nivre, Marie-Catherine de Marneffe, Filip Ginter, Yoav Goldberg, Jan Hajic, Christopher D. Manning, Ryan McDonald, Slav Petrov, Sampo Pyysalo, Natalia Silveira, Reut Tsarfaty, and Daniel Zeman. 2016. Universal Dependencies v1: A multilingual treebank collection. In *Proceedings of the 10th International Conference on Language Resources and Evaluation (LREC 2016)*, pages 1659–1666.

Rajat Raina, Alexis Battle, Honglak Lee, Benjamin Packer, and Andrew Y. Ng. 2007. Self-taught learning: Transfer learning from unlabeled data. In *Proceedings of the 24th international conference on Machine learning*, pages 759–766. ACM.

Siva Reddy and Serge Sharoff. 2011. Cross language POS taggers (and other tools) for Indian languages: An experiment with Kannada using Telugu resources. In *Proceedings of the Fifth International Workshop On Cross Lingual Information Access*, pages 11–19.

Martin Riedl and Chris Biemann. 2015. A single word is not enough: Ranking multiword expressions using distributional semantics. In *Proceedings of the 2015 Conference on Empirical Methods in Natural Language Processing*, pages 2430–2440, Lisboa, Portugal.

Miguel Rios and Serge Sharoff. 2016. Language adaptation for extending post-editing estimates for closely related languages. *The Prague Bulletin of Mathematical Linguistics*, 106(1):181–192.

Anders Søgaard. 2013. *Semi-Supervised Learning and Domain Adaptation in Natural Language Processing*. Synthesis Lectures on Human Language Technologies. Morgan & Claypool Publishers.

Shyam Upadhyay, Manaal Faruqui, Chris Dyer, and Dan Roth. 2016. Cross-lingual models of word embeddings: An empirical comparison. In *Proceedings of the 54th Annual Meeting of the Association for Computational Linguistics*, pages 1661–1670, Berlin, Germany.

Clustering of Russian Adjective-Noun Constructions Using Word Embeddings

Andrey Kutuzov
University of Oslo
Norway
andreku@ifi.uio.no

Elizaveta Kuzmenko
Higher School of Economics
Russia
eakuzmenko_2@edu.hse.ru

Lidia Pivovarova
University of Helsinki
Finland
pivovaro@cs.helsinki.fi

Abstract

This paper presents a method of automatic construction extraction from a large corpus of Russian. The term 'construction' here means a multi-word expression in which a variable can be replaced with another word from the same semantic class, for example, *a glass of [water/juice/milk]*. We deal with constructions that consist of a noun and its adjective modifier. We propose a method of grouping such constructions into semantic classes via 2-step clustering of word vectors in distributional models. We compare it with other clustering techniques and evaluate it against *A Russian-English Collocational Dictionary of the Human Body* that contains manually annotated groups of constructions with nouns denoting human body parts.

The best performing method is used to cluster all adjective-noun bigrams in the Russian National Corpus. Results of this procedure are publicly available and can be used to build a Russian construction dictionary, accelerate theoretical studies of constructions as well as facilitate teaching Russian as a foreign language.

1 Introduction

Construction is a generalization of multi-word expression (MWE), where 'lexical variables are replaceable but belong to the same semantic class, e.g., *sleight of [hand/mouth/mind]*' (Kopotev et al., 2016). Constructions might be considered as sets of collocations, but they are more abstract units than collocations since they do not have a clear surface form and play an intermediate role between lexicon and grammar. A language can be seen as a set of constructions that are organized hierarchically. Thus, a speaker forms an utterance as a combination of preexisting patterns.

This view has been developed into Construction Grammar, the theory that sees grammar as a set of syntactic-semantic patterns, as opposed to more traditional interpretation of grammar as a set of rules (Fillmore et al., 1988).

Let us, for instance, consider English near-synonyms *strong* and *powerful*. It is well-known that they possess different distributional preferences manifested in collocations like *strong tea* and *powerful car* (but not vice versa)[1]. These collocations are idiosyncratic and, frankly speaking, should be a part of the lexicon.

On the other hand, it is possible to look at these examples from the constructional point of view. In this sense, the former collocation would be a part of the construction '*strong [tea/coffee/tobacco/...]*', while the latter would be a part of the construction '*powerful [car/plane/ship/...]*'. Thus, collocations like *strong tea* can be considered to be parts of more general patterns, and all collocations that match the same pattern, i.e. belong to the same construction, can be processed in a similar way. This is the central idea of the constructional approach: language grammar consists of more or less broad patterns, rather than of general rules and vast amount of exceptions, as it was seen traditionally.

A constructional dictionary might be useful for both language learners and NLP systems that often require MWE handling as a part of semantic analysis. Manual compiling of construction lists is time-consuming and can be done only for some specific narrow tasks, while automatic construction extraction seems to be a more difficult task than collocation extraction due to the more abstract nature of constructions.

In this paper, we present a novel approach to

---

[1] See (Church et al., 1991) for more examples and discussion on how such regularities may be automatically extracted from corpus.

Proceedings of the 6th Workshop on Balto-Slavic Natural Language Processing, pages 3–13,
Valencia, Spain, 4 April 2017. ©2017 Association for Computational Linguistics

construction extraction using word embeddings and clustering. We focus on adjective-noun constructions, in particular on a set of 63 Russian nouns denoting human body parts and their adjective modifiers. For each noun, the task is to cluster its adjectival modifiers into groups, where all members of a group are semantically similar, and each group as a whole is a realization of a certain construction[2].

Our approach is based on the distributional hypothesis suggesting that word co-occurrence statistics extracted from a large corpus can represent the actual meaning of a word (Firth, 1957, p. 11). Given a training corpus, each word is represented as a dense vector (embedding); these vectors are defined in a multi-dimensional space in which semantically similar words are located close to each other. We use several embedding models trained on Russian corpora to obtain information about semantic similarity between words. Thus, our approach is fully unsupervised and does not rely on manually constructed thesauri or other semantic resources.

We compare various techniques to perform clustering and evaluate them against an established dictionary. We then apply the best performing method to cluster all adjective-noun bigrams in the Russian National Corpus and make the obtained clusters publicly available.

2   Related Work

Despite the popularity of the constructional approach in corpus linguistics (Gries and Stefanowitsch, 2004), there were few works aimed at automatic building of construction grammar from corpus. Borin et al. (2013) proposed a method of extracting construction candidates to be included into the *Swedish Constructicon*, which is developed as a part of Swedish FrameNet. Kohonen et al. (2009) proposed using the Minimum Description Length principle to extract constructional grammar from corpus. The common disadvantage of both studies is the lack of formal evaluation, which is understandable given the complex lexical-syntactic nature of constructions and the difficulty of the task.

Another line of research is to focus on one particular construction type, for example, light

verbs (Tu and Roth, 2011; Vincze et al., 2013; Chen et al., 2015) or verb-particle constructions (Baldwin and Villavicencio, 2002). This approach allows to make a clear task specification and build a test set for numerical evaluation. Our study sticks to the latter approach: we focus on the adjective-noun constructions, and, more specifically, on the nouns denoting body parts, because manually compiled gold standard exists for these data only.

To the best of our knowledge, the presented research is the first attempt on automatic construction extraction for Russian. The approach we employ was first elaborated on in (Kopotev et al., 2016). Their paper demonstrated (using several Russian examples) that the notion of construction is useful to classify automatically extracted MWEs. It also proposed an application of distributional semantics to automatic construction extraction. However, the study featured a rather simplistic clustering method and shallow evaluation, based on (rather voluntary) manual annotation.

Distributional semantics has been previously used in the MWE analysis, for example, to measure acceptability of word combinations (Vecchi et al., 2016) or to distinguish idioms from literal expressions (Peng et al., 2015); in the latter work, word embeddings were successfully applied.

Vector space models for distributional semantics have been studied and used for decades (see (Turney and Pantel, 2010) for an extensive review). But only recently, Mikolov et al. (2013) introduced the highly efficient *Continuous skip-gram* (SGNS) and *Continuous Bag-of-Words* (CBOW) algorithms for training the so-called predictive distributional models. They became a *de facto* standard in the NLP world in the recent years, outperforming state-of-the-art in many tasks (Baroni et al., 2014). In the present research, we use the SGNS implementation in the *Gensim* library (Řehůřek and Sojka, 2010).

3   Data Sources

2 data sources were employed in the experiments:

1. *A Russian-English Collocational Dictionary of the Human Body* (Iordanskaja et al., 1999)[3], as a gold standard for evaluating our approaches;

---

[2]A group may consist of a single member, since a pure idiosyncratic or idiomatic bigram is considered an extreme case of construction with only one surface form.

---

[3]http://russian.cornell.edu/body/

2. Russian National Corpus[4] (further **RNC**), to train word embedding models and as a source of quantitative information on word co-occurrences in the Russian language.

We now describe these data sources in more details.

3.1 Gold Standard

Our gold standard is *A Russian-English Collocational Dictionary of the Human Body* (Iordanskaja et al., 1999). This dictionary focuses on the Russian nouns that denote body parts ('рука' (*hand*), 'нога' (*foot*), 'голова' (*head*), etc.). Each dictionary entry contains, among other information, the list of words that are lexically related to the entry noun (further *headword*). These words or *collocates* are grouped into syntactic-semantic classes, containing 'adjective+noun' bigrams, like 'лысая голова' (*bald head*).

For example, for the headword 'рука' (*hand*) the dictionary gives, among others, the following groups of collocates:

- Size and shape, aesthetics: 'длинные' (*long*), 'узкие' (*narrow*), 'пухлые' (*pudgy*), etc.

- Color and other visible properties: 'белые' (*white*), 'волосатые' (*hairy*), 'загорелые' (*tanned*), etc.

The authors do not employ the term 'construction' to define these groups; they use the notion of *lexical functions* rooted in the Meaning-Text Theory, known for its meticulous analysis of MWEs (Mel'čuk, 1995). Nevertheless, we assume that their groups can be roughly interpreted as constructions; as we are unaware of any other Russian data source suitable to evaluate our task, the groups from the dictionary were used as the gold standard in the presented experiments. Note that only 'adjective + noun' constructions were extracted from the dictionary; we leave other types of constructions for the future work. All the headwords and collocates were lemmatized and PoS-tagged using *MyStem* (Segalovich, 2003).

3.2 Utilizing the Russian National Corpus

The aforementioned dictionary is comparatively small; though it can be used to evaluate clustering approaches, its coverage is very limited.

Thus, we used the full RNC corpus (209 million tokens) to extract word collocations statistics in the Russian language: first, to delete non-existing bigrams from the gold standard, and second, to compute the strength of connection between headwords and collocates. In particular, we calculated Positive Point-Wise Mutual Information (PPMI) for all pairs of headwords and collocates.

It is important to remove the bigrams not present in the RNC from the gold standard, since the dictionary contains a small amount of adjectives, which cannot naturally co-occur with the corresponding headword and thus are simply a noise (e.g. 'остроухий' (*sharp-eared*) cannot co-occur with 'ухо' (*ear*)). In total, we removed 36 adjectives.

After this filtering, the dataset contains 63 nominal headwords and 1 773 adjectival collocates, clustered into groups. There is high variance among the headwords both in terms of collocates number—from 2 to 140, and the number of groups—from 1 to 16. We believe that the variety of the data represents the natural diversity among nouns in their ability to attach adjective modifiers. Thus, in our experiments we had to use clustering techniques able to automatically detect the number of clusters (see below).

We experimented with several distributional semantics models trained on the RNC with the *Continuous Skip-Gram* algorithm. The models were trained with identical hyperparameters, except for the symmetric context window size. The first model (RNC-2) was trained with the window size 2, thus capturing synonymy relations between words, and the second model (RNC-10) with the window size 10, thus more likely to capture associative relations between words rather than paradigmatic similarity (Levy and Goldberg, 2014). Our intention was to test how it influences the task of clustering collocates into constructions. For reference, we also tested our approaches on the models trained on the RNC and Russian Wikipedia shuffled together (with window 10); however, these models produced suboptimal results in our task (cf. Section 6).

As a sanity check, we evaluated the RNC models against the Russian part of the *Multilingual SimLex999* dataset (Leviant and Reichart, 2015). On this dataset, our models produced the reasonable Spearman correlation values 0.42 for window size 2 and 0.36 for window size 10. Thus, we

---

[4] http://ruscorpora.ru/en

consider them suitable for downstream semantic-related tasks.

4 Clustering Techniques

We now briefly overview several clustering techniques used in this study.

4.1 Affinity Propagation

In most of our experiments we use the *Affinity Propagation* algorithm (Frey and Dueck, 2007). We choose *Affinity Propagation* because it detects the number of clusters automatically and supports assigning weights to instances providing more flexibility in utilizing various features.

In this algorithm, during the clustering process all data points are split into *exemplars* and *instances*; exemplars are data points that represent clusters (similar to centroids in other clustering techniques), instances are other data points that belong to these clusters. At the initial step, each data point constitutes its own cluster, i.e. each data point is an exemplar. At the next steps, two types of real-valued messages are exchanged between data points: 1) an instance i sends to a candidate exemplar k a *responsibility* that is a likelihood of k to be an exemplar for i given similarity (squared negative euclidean distance) between embeddings for i and k and other potential exemplars for i; 2) a candidate exemplar k sends to i an *availability* that is a likelihood of i to belong to the cluster exemplified by k given other potential exemplars. The particular formulas for responsibility and availability rely on each other and can be computed iteratively until convergence. During this process, the likelihood of becoming an exemplar grows for some data points, while for the others it drops below zero and thus they become instances.

One of the most important parameters of the algorithm is *preference*, which affects the initial probability of each data point to become an exemplar. It can be the same for each data point, or assigned individually depending on external data.

The main disadvantage of this algorithm is its computational complexity: it is quadratic, since at every step each data point sends a message to all other data points. However, in our case this drawback is not crucial, since we have to cluster only few instances for each headword (the maximum number of collocates is about 150).

4.2 Spectral Clustering

Since the number of clusters is different for each headword, we cannot use clustering techniques with a pre-defined number of clusters, like *k-means* and other frequently used techniques. That is why we employ a cascade approach where the first algorithm defines the optimal number of clusters and this number is used to initialize the second algorithm. The *Spectral Clustering* (Ng et al., 2001) was used for the second step; essentially, it performs dimensionality reduction over the initial feature space and then runs *k-means* on top of the new feature space.

4.3 Community Detection

For comparison, we test *community detection* algorithms (Fortunato, 2010) that take as an input a graph where nodes are words and edges are weighted by their pairwise similarities (in our case, cosine similarities).

The *Spin glass* algorithm (Reichardt and Bornholdt, 2006) is based on the idea of *spin* adopted from physics. Each node in a graph has a spin that can be in q different states; spins tend to be aligned, i.e. neighboring spins prefer to be in the same state. However, other types of interactions in the system lead to the situation where various spin states exist at the same time within homogeneous clusters. For any given state of the system, its overall energy can be calculated using mathematical apparatus from statistical mechanics; spins are initialized randomly and then the energy is minimized by probabilistic optimization. This model uses both topology of the graph and the strength of pairwise relations. The disadvantage is that this algorithm works with connected graphs only.

The *Infomap* community detection algorithm (Rosvall et al., 2009) is based on a random walk model over networks and the Minimum Description Length principle. In this model, each node has a code that consists of two parts: a cluster code and a node code within the cluster. A trajectory of a random walker is described as a concatenation of codes of all nodes on the path. Each time a walker passes from one cluster to another, a new cluster code should be added, which makes the overall description longer; at the same time if a cluster is too big or not connected, the node codes are too long, which is also not optimal. The task is to assign optimal codes to the nodes, so that the overall description length of a random trajectory is minimal.

The algorithm works in an agglomerative fashion: first, each node is assigned to its own module. Then, the modules are randomly iterated and each module is merged with the neighboring module that resulted in maximum decrease of description length; if such a merge is impossible, the module stays as it is. This procedure is repeated until the state where no module can be used. Weights on the edges linking to a particular node may increase or decrease the probability of a walker to end up at this node.

5 Proposed Methods

The input of a clustering algorithm consists of nominal headwords accompanied with several adjectival collocates (one headword, obviously, corresponds to several collocates). For each headword, the task is to cluster its collocates in an unsupervised way into groups maximally similar to those in the gold standard[5]. The desired number of clusters is not given and should be determined by the clustering algorithm.

In this paper, we test 2 novel approaches compared with a simple baseline and with a community detection technique. These methods include:

1. Baseline: clustering collocates with the *Affinity Propagation* using their vectors in word embedding models as features.

2. Fine-tuning *preference* parameter in the *Affinity Propagation* by linking it to word frequencies, thus employing them as pointers to the selection of cluster centers.

3. Cascade: detecting the number of clusters with the *Affinity Propagation* (using collocates' embeddings as features), and then using the detected clusters number in spectral clustering of the same feature matrix.

4. Clustering collocates using *community detection* methods on semantic similarity graphs where collocates are nodes.

Below we describe these approaches in detail.

5.1 Baseline

The baseline approach uses *Affinity Propagation* with word embeddings as features and with default settings, as implemented in the *scikit-learn* library (Pedregosa et al., 2011).

In all our methods—the baseline and the approaches proposed in the next sections—the headword itself participates in the clustering, as if it was a collocate; at the final stage of outputting the clustering results, it is eliminated. In our experiments, this strategy consistently improved the performance. The possible explanation is that including the headword as a data point structures the network of collocates and makes it more 'connected'; the headword may also give a context and to some extend help to disambiguate polysemantic collocates.

5.2 Clustering with Affinity Propagation

We introduce two improvements over the baseline: fine-tuning of the *Affinity Propagation* and using it in pair with the spectral clustering.

5.2.1 Fine-tuning *Affinity Propagation*

Many clusters in the gold standard contain one highly frequent word around which the others group. It should be beneficial for the clustering algorithm to take this into account. There is the *preference* parameter in the *Affinity Propagation*, which defines the probability for each node to become an exemplar. By default, *preference* is the same for all instances and is equal to the median negative Euclidean distance between instances, meaning all instances (words) have initially equal chances to be selected as exemplars.

Instead, we make each word's *preference* proportional to its logarithmic frequency in the corpus. Thus, frequent words now have higher probability to be selected as exemplars, which also influences the produced number of clusters[6].

All the other hyperparameters of the *Affinity Propagation* algorithm were kept default.

5.2.2 Cascade clustering

The clustering techniques that require a predefined number of clusters, such as spectral clustering, cannot be directly applied to our data. Thus, we employ *Affinity Propagation* to find out the number of clusters for a particular headword,

---

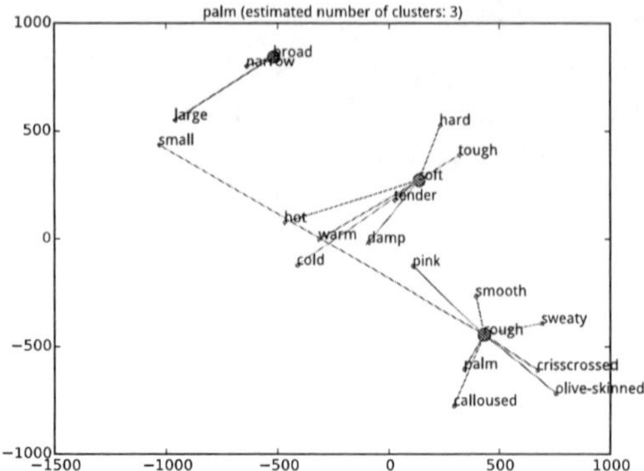

Figure 1: Clustering of the collocates for 'ладонь' (*palm*) by the *Two-Step* algorithm; the measure units on the axes are artificial coordinates used only for the 2-d projection of high-dimensional word embeddings.

and then the clustering itself is done by the spectral clustering algorithm[7] with the default hyperparameters.

We further refer to this method as *Two-Step*. Figure 1 shows a *t-SNE* (Van der Maaten and Hinton, 2008) two-dimensional projection of an example clustering of the collocates for 'ладонь' (*palm*), with 'шершавый' (*rough*), 'широкий' (*broad*) and 'мягкий' (*soft*) chosen as exemplars (large dots on the plot). Note that the Russian data was used to obtain clustering; dictionary-based English translations serve only as labels in this and the following plot.

5.3 Clustering with the Spin Glass Community Detection on Graphs

For comparison with *Affinity Propagation* methods, we use community detection algorithms on semantic similarity graphs. First, a graph is constructed, in which the words (the headword and its collocates) are vertexes. Then, for each pair of vertexes, we calculate their cosine similarity in the current word embedding model. If it exceeds a pre-defined threshold, an edge between these two vertexes is added to the graph with the cosine similarity value as the edge weight.[8]

The *Spin glass* community detection algorithm

---

[7]In our preliminary experiments, we tried to use *K-Means* for the second step, but it performed worse than spectral clustering.

[8]The threshold is automatically adapted for each headword separately, based on the average cosine similarity between pairs of its collocates; thus, in more semantically 'dense' sets of collocates, the threshold is higher.

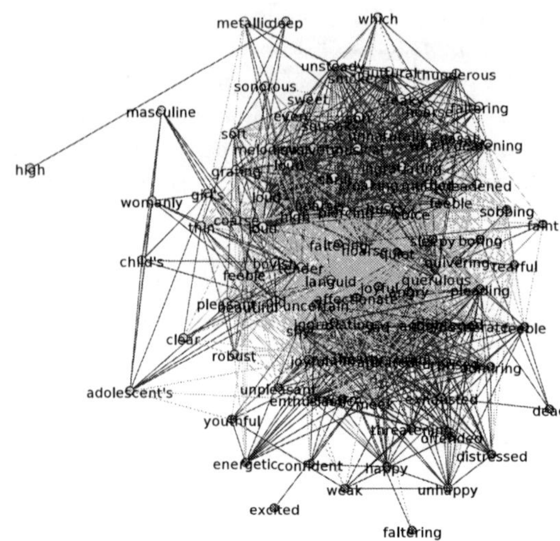

Figure 2: Clustering of the collocates for 'голос' (*voice*) by the *Spin glass* algorithm.

was employed to find clusters in the graph. *Spin glass* cannot process unconnected graphs; thus, if this is the case (about 10-15% of the headwords in the gold standard), we fall back to the *Infomap* community detection algorithm; with connected graphs, it performs worse than *Spin glass*. We use the implementations of the community detection algorithms in the *Igraph* library (Csardi and Nepusz, 2006), and the whole gold standard as a development set to fine-tune the hyperparameters of the algorithms. Figure 2 shows the results of graph clustering for 'голос' (*voice*) headword, with different clusters shown in colors and edge widths representing cosine similarities. The visualization shows that the similarities between words belonging to one cluster are on average higher than those on the inter-cluster edges.

6 Results

We report our clustering performance as macro-average Adjusted Rand Index (Hubert and Arabie, 1985) between the clusterings produced by our algorithms and the gold standard. The Adjusted Rand Index (ARI) is the ratio of correctly classified pairs to all pairs, adjusted for chance. All possible pairs of data points are used to compute ARI; each pair in the gold set may fall either in the same cluster or in two different clusters and the pair is counted as correctly classified if it does the same in the automatically obtained clustering. ARI values range from -1 to 1, where 1 means

Table 1: Clustering evaluation, average ARI and standard deviation

Method	RNC-2	RNC-10	RNCW-2	RNCW-10
Baseline	0.22	0.17	0.17	0.16
StDev	0.27	0.23	0.24	0.24
Spin glass	0.22	0.22	0.18	0.18
StDev	0.28	0.30	0.27	0.28
AffProp	0.33	0.31	0.30	0.28
StDev	0.38	0.37	0.38	0.37
Two-Step	**0.34**	0.33	0.31	0.29
StDev	0.36	0.37	0.37	0.37

perfect correspondence between the gold standard and the clustering; -1 means negative correlation; 0 means the clustering and the gold standard are not related to each other.

We compute ARI individually for each headword and then average over all 63 entries. The Table 1 presents the evaluations results. RNC-2 and RNC-10 stand for the word embedding models trained on the RNC with symmetric window 2 and 10 respectively; RNCW stands for the respective models trained on the RNC and the Russian Wikipedia together. *Spin glass* is the method using communities detection on graphs (Section 5.3), *AffProp* is the single-step *Affinity Propagation* clustering (Section 5.2), and *Two-Step* is our proposed approach of cascade clustering. We also report the standard deviation of the individual headwords ARI for each approach (*StDev*).

As can be seen from the table, the baseline, which is a simple clustering of word embeddings, is difficult to beat. The graph-based community detection algorithm performs on par with the baseline on the models with window size 2 and only slightly outperforms it on the models with window 10. However, using the fine-tuned *Affinity Propagation* makes a huge difference, pushing ARI higher by at least 10 decimal points for all models. Feeding the number of clusters detected by the *Affinity Propagation* into the spectral clustering algorithm (our *Two-Step* approach) consistently increases the performance by one point more. Note that the *Two-Step* method is also considerably faster than the graph-based *Spin glass* algorithm.

It is worth noticing that the larger window models consistently perform worse in this task. It seems that the reason is exactly that they pay more attention to broad associative relatedness between words and less to direct functional or paradigmatic similarity. But this is precisely what is important in the task of clustering collocates: we are trying to find groups of adjectives which can roughly substitute each other in modifying the headword noun. For example, '*beautiful*' and '*charming*' are equally suitable to characterize a pretty face, but '*beloved face*' does not belong to the same construction; however, in the models with larger window size '*beautiful*' and '*beloved*' are very close and will fall into the same cluster.

At the same time, the variance among headwords may be higher than the variance between models. For example, in our experiments, for the headword 'ступня' (*foot/sole*), all four methods—*two-step* and *spin glass* on the RNC2 and the RNC10—yield ARI 0.816 and produce identical results. At the same time, for the headword 'живот' (*stomach/belly*) all four methods produced negative ARI, which probably means that clustering for this headword is especially difficult to predict.

In Figure 3 we present individual headwords ARI for the 4 best performing methods. The headwords in the plot are sorted by the number of collocates. The headwords with less than 10 collocates are excluded from the plot: these smaller entries are more diverse and in many cases yield ARI=0 or ARI=1[9]. It can be seen from the figure that for many headwords ARI from different methods are almost identical and there are clear 'easy' and 'difficult' headwords. The more collocates the headword has the closer are the results produced by different approaches. Similar variability among headwords was observed before in various MWE-related tasks (Pivovarova et al., 2018); we assume that this can be at least partially explained by different abilities of words to form stable MWEs. Nevertheless, it can be seen from Figure 3 that in most cases ARI is higher than zero, pointing at significant correlation between the gold standard and the automatic clustering.

Another interesting finding is that the models trained on the RNC and Wikipedia together show worse results than the models trained on the RNC only, as can be seen from Table 1. Thus, despite

---

[9]However, all 63 headwords were used to compute the average values in Table 1.

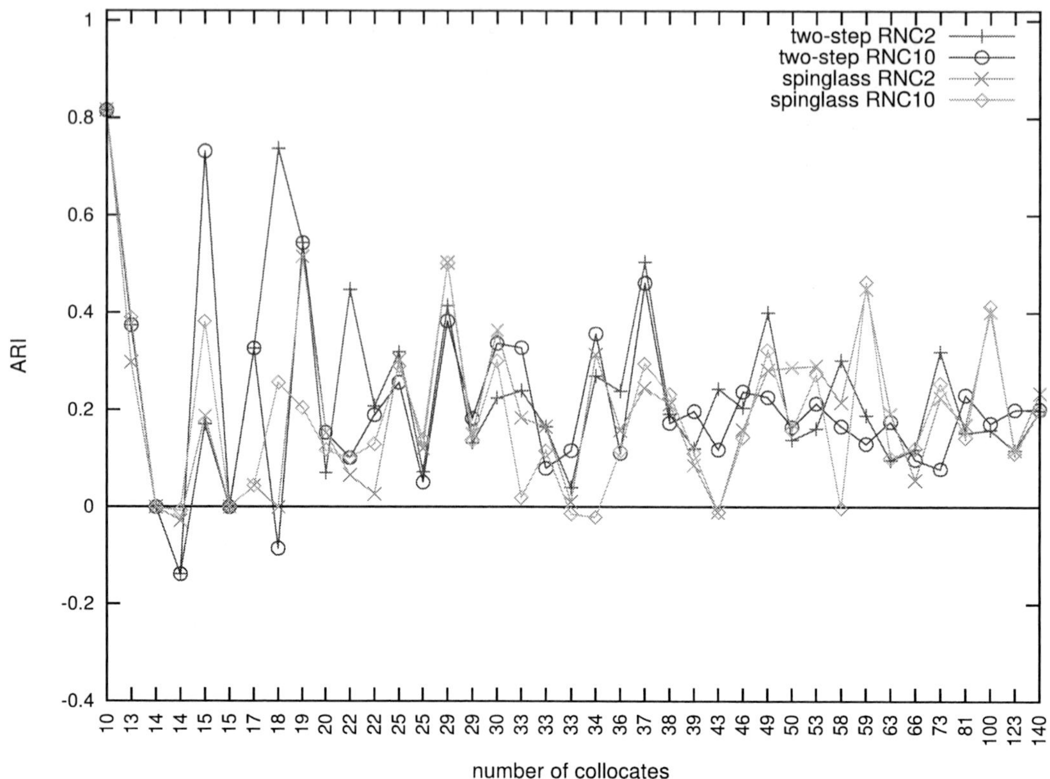

Figure 3: Individual headwords ARI for 4 best-performing methods; the headwords are sorted by the number of collocates.

the fact that the training corpus was more than two times larger, it did not result in better embeddings. This seems to support the opinion in (Kutuzov and Andreev, 2015) that when training distributional models, versatile and balanced nature of the corpus might be at least as important as its size.

Using our *Two-Step* algorithm and the *RNC-2* model, we produced clusterings for all 'adjective+noun' bigrams in the RNC with PPMI more than 1, the corpus frequency of the bigram more than 10 and the frequency of the nominal headword more than 1 000. This corresponds to 6 036 headwords and 143 314 bigrams (headwords with only 1 collocate were excluded). We publish this dataset online together with our gold standard on the home page of the CoCoCo project[10]. For better cross-linguistic comparability, all PoS tags in these datasets were converted to the Universal PoS Tags standard (Petrov et al., 2012).

This clustering was evaluated against our gold standard (*A Russian-English Collocational Dictionary of the Human Body*) as well. We had to work only with the intersection of the gold standard data and the resulting clustering, thus only a part of the gold standard was actually used for the evaluation (59 headwords out of 63, and 966 collocations out of 1758). It produced **ARI=0.38** calculated on all headwords and **ARI=0.31** after we excluded 6 headwords that have only one collocate in this dataset—their evaluation always produces ARI=1, independent of what the clustering algorithm outputs. These results confirm that the proposed algorithm performs well not only on the limited artificial data from the gold standard, but on the real world data.

Note that this is partial evaluation and many bigrams are left unattended. For example, for the headword 'лицо' (*face*), the collocates 'увядший' (*withered*) and 'морщинистый' (*wrinkled*) are grouped together by the algorithm, which is correct according to the gold standard, and these two collocates are used in the evalua-

___
[10]Collocations, Colligations, Corpora, http://cosyco.ru/cococo/

tion to compute ARI. However, in the complete clustering results these collocates are also grouped together with some other words not present in the gold standard: 'сморщенный' (*withered*) and 'иссохший' (*exsiccated*), which is probably correct, and 'отсутствующий' (*absent*), which is obviously wrong. As the dictionary lacks these collocates, they cannot affect the evaluation results, whether they are correct or incorrect. After analyzing the data, we can suggest that the clustering quality of the complete RNC data is more or less the same as it was for the dictionary data, but more precise evaluation would require a manual linguistic analysis.

7 Conclusion

The main contributions of this paper are the following:

1. We investigated MWE analysis techniques beyond collocation extraction and proposed a new approach to automatic construction extraction;

2. Several word embedding models and various clustering techniques were compared to obtain MWE clustering similar to manual grouping with the highest ARI value being 0.34;

3. We combined two clustering algorithms, namely the *Affinity Propagation* and the *Spectral Clustering*, to obtain results higher than can be achieved by each of this methods separately;

4. The best algorithm was then applied to cluster all frequent 'adjective+noun' bigrams in the Russian National Corpus. The obtained clusterings are publicly available and could be used as a starting point for constructional studies and building construction dictionaries, or utilized in various NLP tasks.

The main inference from our experiments is that the task of clustering Russian bigrams into constructions is a difficult one. Partially it can be explained by the limited coverage of the gold standard, but the main reason is that bigrams are grouped in non-trivial ways, that combine semantic and syntactic dimensions. Moreover, the number of clusters in the gold standard varies among headwords, and thus should be detected at the test time, adding to the complexity of the task. However, it seems that distributional semantic models can still be used to at least roughly reproduce manual grouping of collocates for particular headwords.

We believe that automatic construction extraction is a fruitful line of research that may be helpful both in practical applications and in corpus linguistics, for better understanding of constructions as lexical-semantic units.

In future we plan to explore other constructions besides 'adjective + noun'; first of all we plan to start with the 'verb+noun' constructions, since they are also present in the dictionary used as the gold standard. We would also try to find or compile other gold standards, since the dictionary we use is limited in its coverage; for example, the authors allowed only literal physical meanings of the words in the dictionary, intentionally ignoring metaphors.

In all our experiments, we used embeddings for individual words. However, it seems natural to learn embeddings for bigrams since they may have quite different semantics than individual words (Vecchi et al., 2016). It is crucial to determine bigrams that need a separate embedding and/or try to utilize already learned embeddings for individual words[11].

Another interesting topic would be cluster labeling, which is finding the most typical representative of a construction, or a construction name. The *Affinity Propagation* outputs exemplars for each cluster, but these exemplars are not always suitable as cluster labels. For example, for the headword 'ступня' (*foot*) the algorithm correctly identifies the following group of adjective modifiers: ['широкий' (*wide*), 'узкий' (*narrow*), 'большой' (*large*), 'маленький' (*small*), 'изящный' (*elegant*)] with 'узкий' (*narrow*) being the exemplar for this class. However, in the dictionary this group is labeled 'Size and shape; aestetics', which is more suitable from the human point of view. Some kind of an automatic hypernym finding technique is necessary for this task.

Finally, we plan to use hierarchical clustering algorithms to obtain a more natural structure of high-level constructions split into smaller subgroups.

---

[11]We tried additive and multiplicative strategies (Mitchell and Lapata, 2008) to obtain bigram representations from individual word vectors, but for the present moment, they did not yield significant improvements over the baseline.

References

Timothy Baldwin and Aline Villavicencio. 2002. Extracting the unextractable: A case study on verb-particles. In *Proceedings of the 6th conference on Natural language learning*, volume 20, pages 1–7. Association for Computational Linguistics.

Marco Baroni, Georgiana Dinu, and Germán Kruszewski. 2014. Don't count, predict! a systematic comparison of context-counting vs. context-predicting semantic vectors. In *Proceedings of the 52nd Annual Meeting of the Association for Computational Linguistics (Volume 1: Long Papers)*, pages 238–247.

Lars Borin, Linnéa Bäckström, Markus Forsberg, Benjamin Lyngfelt, Julia Prentice, and Emma Sköldberg. 2013. Automatic identification of construction candidates for a Swedish Constructicon. In *Proceedings of the workshop on lexical semantic resources for NLP at NODALIDA 2013*, number 088, pages 2–11. Linköping University Electronic Press.

Wei-Te Chen, Claire Bonial, and Martha Palmer. 2015. English light verb construction identification using lexical knowledge. In *AAAI*, pages 2368–2374.

Kenneth Church, William Gale, Patrick Hanks, and Donald Kindle. 1991. Using statistics in lexical analysis. *Lexical acquisition: exploiting on-line resources to build a lexicon*, page 115.

Gabor Csardi and Tamas Nepusz. 2006. The Igraph software package for complex network research. *InterJournal, Complex Systems*, 1695(5):1–9.

Charles J. Fillmore, Paul Kay, and Mary Catherine O'Connor. 1988. Regularity and idiomaticity in grammatical constructions: The case of let alone. *Language*, pages 501–538.

John R. Firth. 1957. A synopsis of linguistic theory, 1930-1955. studies in linguistic analysis. *Oxford: Philological Society. [Reprinted in Selected Papers of J.R. Firth 1952-1959, ed. Frank R. Palmer, 1968. London: Longman]*.

Santo Fortunato. 2010. Community detection in graphs. *Physics reports*, 486(3):75–174.

Brendan J. Frey and Delbert Dueck. 2007. Clustering by passing messages between data points. *Science*, 315(5814):972–976.

Stefan Th. Gries and Anatol Stefanowitsch. 2004. Extending collostructional analysis: A corpus-based perspective on alternations'. *International journal of corpus linguistics*, 9(1):97–129.

Lawrence Hubert and Phipps Arabie. 1985. Comparing partitions. *Journal of classification*, 2(1):193–218.

Lidija Iordanskaja, Slava Paperno, Lesli LaRocco, Jean MacKenzie, and Richard L. Leed. 1999. *A Russian-English Collocational Dictionary of the Human Body*. Slavica Publisher.

Oskar Kohonen, Sami Virpioja, and Krista Lagus. 2009. Constructionist approaches to grammar inference. In *NIPS Workshop on Grammar Induction, Representation of Language and Language Learning*, Whistler, Canada.

Mikhail Kopotev, Lidia Pivovarova, and Daria Kormacheva. 2016. Constructional generalization over Russian collocations. *Mémoires de la Société néophilologique de Helsinki*, Collocations Cross-Linguistically:121–140.

Andrey Kutuzov and Igor Andreev. 2015. Texts in, meaning out: neural language models in semantic similarity task for Russian. In *Computational Linguistics and Intellectual Technologies: papers from the Annual conference "Dialogue"*, volume 14(21). RGGU.

Ira Leviant and Roi Reichart. 2015. Separated by an un-common language: Towards judgment language informed vector space modeling. arxiv preprint. *arXiv preprint arXiv:1508.00106*.

Omer Levy and Yoav Goldberg. 2014. Dependency-based word embeddings. In *Proceedings of the 52nd Annual Meeting of the Association for Computational Linguistics (Volume 2: Short Papers)*, pages 302–308.

Igor Mel'cuk. 1995. Phrasemes in language and phraseology in linguistics. *Idioms: Structural and psychological perspectives*, pages 167–232.

Tomas Mikolov, Ilya Sutskever, Kai Chen, Greg S. Corrado, and Jeff Dean. 2013. Distributed representations of words and phrases and their compositionality. In *Advances in Neural Information Processing Systems 26*, pages 3111–3119. Curran Associates, Inc.

Jeff Mitchell and Mirella Lapata. 2008. Vector-based models of semantic composition. In *Proceedings of ACL-08: HLT*, pages 236–244. Association for Computational Linguistics.

Andrew Y. Ng, Michael I. Jordan, and Yair Weiss. 2001. On spectral clustering: Analysis and an algorithm. In *Advances in Neural Information Processing Systems*, pages 849–856. MIT Press.

F. Pedregosa, G. Varoquaux, A. Gramfort, V. Michel, B. Thirion, O. Grisel, M. Blondel, P. Prettenhofer, R. Weiss, V. Dubourg, J. Vanderplas, A. Passos, D. Cournapeau, M. Brucher, M. Perrot, and E. Duchesnay. 2011. Scikit-learn: Machine learning in Python. *Journal of Machine Learning Research*, 12:2825–2830.

Jing Peng, Anna Feldman, and Hamza Jazmati. 2015. Classifying idiomatic and literal expressions using vector space representations. In *Proceedings of the International Conference Recent Advances in Natural Language Processing*, pages 507–511. INCOMA Ltd. Shoumen, BULGARIA.

Slav Petrov, Dipanjan Das, and Ryan McDonald. 2012. A universal part-of-speech tagset. In *Proceedings of the Eighth International Conference on Language Resources and Evaluation (LREC-2012)*. ELRA.

Lidia Pivovarova, Daria Kormacheva, and Mikhail Kopotev. 2018. Evaluation of collocation extraction methods for the Russian language. In *Quantitative Approaches to the Russian Language*. Routledge.

Radim Řehůřek and Petr Sojka. 2010. Software Framework for Topic Modelling with Large Corpora. In *Proceedings of the LREC 2010 Workshop on New Challenges for NLP Frameworks*, pages 45–50, Valletta, Malta. ELRA.

Jörg Reichardt and Stefan Bornholdt. 2006. Statistical mechanics of community detection. *Physical Review E*, 74(1):016110.

Martin Rosvall, Daniel Axelsson, and Carl T. Bergstrom. 2009. The map equation. *The European Physical Journal Special Topics*, 178(1):13–23.

Ilya Segalovich. 2003. A fast morphological algorithm with unknown word guessing induced by a dictionary for a Web search engine. In *MLMTA*, pages 273–280.

Yuancheng Tu and Dan Roth. 2011. Learning English light verb constructions: contextual or statistical. In *Proceedings of the Workshop on Multiword Expressions: from Parsing and Generation to the Real World*, pages 31–39. Association for Computational Linguistics.

Peter D. Turney and Patrick Pantel. 2010. From frequency to meaning: Vector space models of semantics. *Journal of artificial intelligence research*, 37(1):141–188.

Laurens Van der Maaten and Geoffrey Hinton. 2008. Visualizing data using t-SNE. *Journal of Machine Learning Research*, 9(2579-2605):85.

Eva M. Vecchi, Marco Marelli, Roberto Zamparelli, and Marco Baroni. 2016. Spicy adjectives and nominal donkeys: Capturing semantic deviance using compositionality in distributional spaces. *Cognitive science*.

Veronika Vincze, Istvan T. Nagy, and Richárd Farkas. 2013. Identifying English and Hungarian light verb constructions: A contrastive approach. In *Proceedings of the 51st Annual Meeting of the Association for Computational Linguistics (Volume 2: Short Papers)*, pages 255–261.

A Preliminary Study of Croatian Lexical Substitution

Domagoj Alagić and **Jan Šnajder**
Text Analysis and Knowledge Engineering Lab
Faculty of Electrical Engineering and Computing, University of Zagreb
Unska 3, 10000 Zagreb, Croatia
`{domagoj.alagic,jan.snajder}@fer.hr`

Abstract

Lexical substitution is a task of determining a meaning-preserving replacement for a word in context. We report on a preliminary study of this task for the Croatian language on a small-scale lexical sample dataset, manually annotated using three different annotation schemes. We compare the annotations, analyze the inter-annotator agreement, and observe a number of interesting language-specific details in the obtained lexical substitutes. Furthermore, we apply a recently-proposed, dependency-based lexical substitution model to our dataset. The model achieves a P@3 score of 0.35, which indicates the difficulty of the task.

1 Introduction

Modeling word meaning is one of the most rewarding challenges of many natural language processing (NLP) applications, including information retrieval (Stokoe et al., 2003), information extraction (Ciaramita and Altun, 2006), and machine translation (Carpuat and Wu, 2007), to name a few. Perhaps the most straightforward task concerned with word senses is word sense disambiguation (WSD), a task of determining the correct sense of a polysemous word in its context (Navigli, 2009). Despite being a straightforward task, WSD has several drawbacks. Most often, it is criticized for relying on a fixed set of senses for each of the words (sense inventory), which – although meticulously compiled by experts – is often of inappropriate coverage or granularity (Edmonds and Kilgarriff, 2002; Snyder and Palmer, 2004). This requirement makes evaluation of WSD models across different applications rather difficult.

An alternative perspective on modeling word senses is the one of *lexical substitution* (McCarthy and Navigli, 2007), a task of finding a meaning-preserving replacement of a polysemous target word in context. For instance, in the sentence "*It took me around two hours to reach Nagoya from Kyoto by coach*", suitable substitutes for the word *coach* may be *van* or *bus*, whereas the substitute *trainer* represents a different sense of the word. Note that such a setup circumvents the need of having a fixed sense inventory, as annotators do not require any kind of resources to come up with a plausible set of substitutes for a word. This seems both more intuitive and far less restrictive than the traditional WSD task. However, the lexical substitution task is still determined by a number of parameters that need to be taken into consideration, as they affect the obtained substitutes in various ways (e.g., variety, count, etc.).

In this paper, we report on a preliminary study of the lexical substitution task for the Croatian language, a first such study so far. We compile a small-scale lexical sample dataset and annotate it using three annotation schemes to gain insights into how they affect the annotations. We analyze the obtained substitutes and report on interesting language-specific details, hoping to facilitate research on this topic for other Slavic languages. Finally, we re-implement one of the best-performing models for English lexical substitution (Melamud et al., 2015b) and evaluate it on our dataset.

2 Related Work

Most work on lexical substitution was done for English (McCarthy and Navigli, 2007; Sinha and Mihalcea, 2014; Biemann, 2012; Kremer et al., 2014). A few notable exceptions include German within the GERMEVAL-2015 (Miller et al., 2015), Italian within the EVALITA-2009 (Toral, 2009), and Spanish within a cross-lingual setup at SEMEVAL-2012 (Mihalcea et al., 2010). Recently, most research on lexical substitution closely relates

Proceedings of the 6th Workshop on Balto-Slavic Natural Language Processing, pages 14–19,
Valencia, Spain, 4 April 2017. ©2017 Association for Computational Linguistics

to the task of learning meaning representations that are able to account for multiple senses of polysemous words (Melamud et al., 2015a; Melamud et al., 2016; Roller and Erk, 2016; Erk et al., 2013).

For the experiments, we adopt the work of Melamud et al. (2015b), who proposed a lexical substitution model based on dependency-based embeddings. Their model is easy to implement, yet it performs nearly at the state-of-the-art level.

3 Dataset Construction

3.1 Data

We took a *lexical sample* approach, in which the experiments are carried out on a predefined set of words. As this is a preliminary study, we decided on using six words: two adjectives, two nouns, and two verbs. We selected these words by taking all the words that have at least three senses and that occur at least 10,000 times in hrWaC, a Croatian web corpus (Ljubešić and Erjavec, 2011). After selecting the words, we extracted 30 contexts (instances) per word from the Cro36WSD dataset (Alagić and Šnajder, 2016), a lexical sample for Croatian WSD. The words we use are: $prljav_A$ (dirty), $visok_A$ (high/tall), $težina_N$ (weight/difficulty), $okvir_N$ (frame), $oprati_V$ (to wash off), and $tući_V$ (to hit/to beat).

3.2 Annotation

Annotation schemes. One insight we wished to gain from this study is how different annotation schemes influence the lexical substitutes obtained through the annotation. We consider three different annotation schemes:

1. SINGLE – In this scheme, annotators are allowed to provide only *single-word expressions* (SWEs) as substitutes. They are also allowed to provide hypernyms if they cannot think of any other suitable substitutes;
2. MULTI – Besides SWEs, annotators can provide *multiword expressions* (MWEs) as well;
3. MULTI3 – Annotators can provide everything as in MULTI setup, but should give their best to come up with *at least three* substitutes.

The motivation for having a separate annotation scheme for single-word substitutes (SINGLE) is based upon an intuition that annotators often do not provide just every substitute they think of, but rather only a couple of those that first come to

their mind. Thus, by allowing the annotators to use MWEs, they could sometimes reach for a more common MWE instead of thinking a bit harder about single-word substitutes. As an example, consider the word *preozbiljan* (too serious) in the following sentence:

(1)   *On je uvijek **preozbiljan** na zabavama.*
     *He is always **too serious** at parties.*

In this case, the annotators might more commonly use the idiomatic phrase *smrtno ozbiljan* (dead serious) than the single-word expression *mrk* (stern).

On the other hand, we use MULTI3 annotation scheme to investigate what substitutes the annotators provide to meet the required number of substitutes. We expect those to be less common near-synonyms or words related to the target word.

Annotation guidelines. Each annotator was presented with a sentence containing a polysemous target word and was asked to provide as many meaning-preserving substitutes as they could think of (in any order). The annotators were also instructed to give the substitutes in a lemmatized form (e.g., *kući* $\Rightarrow$ *kuća*; dative case of *house*). In case of an MWE, they were asked to lemmatize the complete MWE as a single unit instead of doing it on a per-word basis (e.g., *Hrvatskoga narodnog kazališta* $\Rightarrow$ *Hrvatsko narodno kazalište*, instead of *Hrvatski narodni kazalište*; genitive case of *Croatian National Theatre*). The annotators were also told not to consult any language resources during the annotation.

Annotation effort. We asked 12 native Croatian speakers to annotate our data. We split their annotation effort so that each annotator annotates all six words, but using different schemes along the way (two words for each scheme). This resulted in each instance being annotated by four annotators per annotation scheme, and each annotator completing the annotation of 180 instances in total. Each annotator spent around three person-hours on average. Lastly, to account for having only four annotators per instance, we (the authors) manually went through the annotations and corrected typos and wrong lemma forms, a step that took five person-hours.[1] We make our dataset freely-available.[2]

---

[1] We believe that having more annotators per instance could lessen the need of having to correct noisy annotations, as not all annotators would make slips on the same instances.

[2] http://takelab.fer.hr/data/crolexsub

Scheme	Min.	Max.	Avg.	# SWE	# MWE	# PC
SINGLE	0	10	3.92	702	4	27
MULTI	0	13	4.20	687	69	14
MULTI3	0	12	5.93	1003	64	27

Table 1: Dataset statistics. PCs have been counted only within single-word substitutes.

	PA				PAM			
Scheme	N	A	V	All	N	A	V	All
SINGLE	0.32	0.12	0.26	**0.23**	0.44	0.27	0.31	**0.35**
MULTI	0.26	0.17	0.24	0.22	0.39	0.32	0.18	0.29
MULTI3	0.20	0.09	0.29	0.20	0.18	0.16	0.16	0.17

Table 2: Inter-annotator agreement across schemes and POS tags.

4 Annotation Analysis

4.1 Dataset Statistics

After correction, we measure the minimum, maximum, and average number of substitutes across annotation schemes, number of single-word (SWE) and multiword (MWE) substitutes, and number of substitutes where a POS change (PC) occurred, i.e., where substitute's and target word's POS tags are different. We report the numbers in Table 1.

4.2 Inter-Annotator Agreement

We measure the inter-annotator agreement (IAA) using the *pairwise agreement* (PA) and *pairwise agreement with modes* (PAM), following McCarthy and Navigli (2007). PA essentially measures the average overlap of substitutes between all possible annotator pairings across instances. On the other hand, PAM measures the agreement by counting the times a gold substitute mode[3] was included in the annotator substitute set. We report the IAA scores in Table 2. Even though the absolute agreement scores are generally low, we note that they are in line with those of Kremer et al. (2014). From a POS perspective, annotators agreed the most on nouns and disagreed the most on adjectives. Moreover, we note that the MULTI3 scheme has the lowest IAA, possibly because the "coerced" substitutes (especially the multiword ones) have a greater variability. We leave a more detailed analysis of the IAA for future work.

4.3 Observations

We present some preliminary insights into the obtained substitutes, which we think warrant further investigation. Some of the insights are language-specific, while others might be relevant for other languages as well.

Lemmatization. Even though we asked the annotators to provide substitutes in a lemmatized form, it is not obvious whether this is the best approach. Obviously, not lemmatizing the substitutes will inflate the number of proposed substitutes with inflected variants of the same word (across contexts in which the word occurs). On the other hand, lemmatizing each and every substitute may lead to information loss (for example, when lemmatizing adjectives from a superlative into a positive form).

Reflexive pronouns. It is unclear whether the verbs with obligatory reflexive pronouns, e.g., *smijati se* (to laugh) should be treated as MWEs. Currently, we prefer to treat them as SWEs.

Coreference. If a sentence contains the same target more than once, it is often possible to replace one of them with a coreferring pronoun. For example, in the sentence:[4]

(2) *Kako vam se težina nakon dijete ne bi ubrzo vratila na **težinu** prije dijete. . .*
*To prevent your weight after a diet from quickly reverting to **weight** before a diet. . .*

one could provide the pronoun substitute *onu* (one), which would perfectly preserve the sentence meaning (and in fact improve coherence of the text).

Ungrammaticality. Some substitutes may effectively break the sentence grammaticality due to the fact that they replace a multiword expression of which the target word is a part of, rather than merely the target word. As an example, consider:

(3) *. . . koja su započela 22. prosinca u **okviru** operativne akcije. . .*
*. . . which started on December 22 in the **scope** of an operative action. . .*

In this sentence, one may substitute *okviru* (frame/scope) with a preposition *unutar* (within), thus requiring to omit the preposition *u* (in) to preserve overall sentence grammaticality.

---

[3]A *mode* is a single substitute that received the most annotator votes, if such exists.

[4]The translation is slightly ungrammatical to better illustrate the issue.

5 Experiments

5.1 Models

For our experiments, we re-implemented a simple, yet powerful model of Melamud et al. (2015b), one of the best-performing models for lexical substitution. This model posits that a good lexical substitute needs to be both semantically similar to the target word (i.e., paradigmatic similarity) and suitable for a given context (i.e., syntagmatic similarity). To that end, Melamud et al. (2015b) propose four substitutability measures that combine these two concepts in different ways (Table 3). Whereas *Add* measure employs an arithmetic mean, *Mult* measure uses a stricter, geometric mean. Furthermore, they introduce *Bal* variants that balance out the effect of context size. In addition to these models, we use an *out-of-context* (OOC) model as a baseline, which calculates the substitute score simply as a cosine between the substitute's and target word's embedding (also shown in Table 3).

Substitutability measures are calculated using dependency-based word and context embeddings (Levy and Goldberg, 2014), which the authors derived from the original skip-gram negative sampling algorithm (SGNS) (Mikolov et al., 2013). In a nutshell, instead of using models that are based solely on lexical contexts, their model can be trained on arbitrary contexts (in their case, the syntactic contexts derived from dependency parse trees). The rationale behind using dependency-based embeddings is that using only regular SGNS embeddings does not account for substitute's paradigmatic fit in its context.

We train these word-type (lemma and POS-tag) embeddings on hrWaC, a Croatian web corpus (Ljubešić and Erjavec, 2011), using the freely available `word2vecf` tool.[5] We use default parameters: frequency threshold of 5 and negative sampling factor of 15. We did not collapse the relations including prepositions. Before training the embeddings, we discarded all lemmas that appeared fewer than 100 times in the corpus.

5.2 Evaluation

We focus on the SINGLE annotation scheme within our evaluation, as the model we use does not deal with MWEs. To compile the candidate sets for each of the instances, we follow prior work and pool candidates from all substitutes given by the

[5] https://bitbucket.org/yoavgo/
word2vecf

Add	$\dfrac{cos(s,t) + \sum_{c \in C} cos(s,c)}{|C| + 1}$
BalAdd	$\dfrac{|C| \cdot cos(s,t) + \sum_{c \in C} cos(s,c)}{2 \cdot |C|}$
Mult	$\sqrt[|C|+1]{pcos(s,t) \cdot \prod_{c \in C} pcos(s,c)}$
BalMult	$\sqrt[2 \cdot |C|]{pcos(s,t)^{|C|} \cdot \prod_{c \in C} pcos(s,c)}$
OOC	$cos(s,t)$

Table 3: The different substitutability measures for a lexical substitute s of a target word t within a context C.[6]

		Metric	
Models	GAP	P@3	P@5
Add	**0.28**	**0.35**	**0.28**
BalAdd	0.26	0.31	0.26
Mult	0.27	0.28	0.27
BalMult	**0.28**	0.31	**0.28**
OOC	0.26	0.21	0.25

Table 4: Model scores on our dataset.

annotators for a specific target word (i.e., across all target word's instances). This enables us to basically evaluate the model's ability of identifying the viable substitutes and ranking low the ones that bear a sense different of that evoked in a context. Following (Thater et al., 2010), we evaluate the models in terms of generalized average precision (GAP) (Kishida, 2005). GAP is a weighted extension of the mean average precision (MAP) measure, where weights capture how many times the annotators used a certain substitute in a goldset. In line with work of Roller and Erk (2016), we decided not to use the original lexical substitution metrics (*oot* and *best*), but standard P@3 and P@5 scores, which we find more interpretable. We report the results in Table 4.

We observe that the model based on *Add* substitutability measure consistently performs best. Usually, out of the top three substitutes predicted by the model, one of them is correct (P@3 = 0.35). Surprisingly, in terms of both GAP and P@5, the baseline *OOC* model performs comparably well.

To illustrate how the implemented model works, we show the top 10 substitute candidates predicted by *Add* model for one of the occurrences of word *prljav* (dirty) in Table 5. The top candidates perfectly capture the *filthy* sense of this word, whereas

[6] Positive cosine is defined as $pcos(a,b) = \frac{cos(a,b)+1}{2}$.

Sentence (HR)	Sentence (EN)
"Ne diraj me tim prljavim rukama," rekla mu je s prijezirom...	*"Do not touch me with those dirty hands of yours," she told him with contempt...*
Predicted substitutes (HR)	Predicted substitutes (EN)
nečist, neopran, zmazan, uprljan, odvratan, perverzan, mutan, gadan, podmukao, zamazan	*unclean, unwashed, filthy, dirtied, disgusting, perverse, fishy, nasty, scheming, filthy*
Gold substitutes (HR)	Gold substitutes (EN)
nečist, zmazan, zamazan, neopran	*unclean, filthy, filthy, unwashed*

Table 5: Top 10 substitute candidates for instance 6086 as predicted by *Add* model.

the most of the remaining ones depict the *sordid* sense of the word, which is questionable, albeit possible within this ambiguous context.

In general, however, we note that the figures are considerably lower than those obtained for the English lexical substitution task (Melamud et al., 2015b; Roller and Erk, 2016). We speculate that one of the reasons might be the morphological complexity of Croatian. Another, related reason might be the way how word embeddings are trained: we used word-type embeddings instead of word-form embeddings and we did not collapse the relations including prepositions. We leave an investigation of these issues for future work.

6 Conclusion

In this work we tackled the lexical substitution task for Croatian. We compiled a small-scale lexical sample dataset and annotated it using three different schemes. Moreover, we presented interesting insights about the annotations, some of which are specific to Croatian, while others possibly pertain to other (morphologically-rich) languages. Lastly, we re-implemented one of the best-performing models for English lexical substitution and evaluated it on our dataset. A thorough comparison of the annotation schemes, as well as the implementation of a more efficient model that also deals with MWEs are the subject of future work.

Acknowledgments

We are extremely grateful to our 12 annotators for making time to annotate our data. We would also like to thank the anonymous reviewers for their useful and insightful comments.

This work has been fully supported by the Croatian Science Foundation under the project UIP-2014-09-7312.

References

Domagoj Alagić and Jan Šnajder. 2016. Cro36WSD: A lexical sample for Croatian word sense disambiguation. In *Proceedings of the 10th edition of the Language Resources and Evaluation Conference (LREC 2016)*, pages 1689–1694, Portorož, Slovenia.

Chris Biemann. 2012. Turk bootstrap word sense inventory 2.0: A large-scale resource for lexical substitution. In *Proceedings of the 8th edition of the Language Resources and Evaluation Conference (LREC 2012)*, pages 4038–4042, Instanbul, Turkey.

Marine Carpuat and Dekai Wu. 2007. Improving statistical machine translation using word sense disambiguation. In *Proceedings of Conference on Computational Natural Language Learning (CoNLL 2007)*, volume 7, pages 61–72, Prague, Czech Republic.

Massimiliano Ciaramita and Yasemin Altun. 2006. Broad-coverage sense disambiguation and information extraction with a supersense sequence tagger. In *Proceedings of Conference on Empirical Methods in Natural Language Processing (EMNLP 2006)*, pages 594–602, Sydney, Australia.

Philip Edmonds and Adam Kilgarriff. 2002. Introduction to the special issue on evaluating word sense disambiguation systems. *Natural Language Engineering*, 8(04):279–291.

Katrin Erk, Diana McCarthy, and Nicholas Gaylord. 2013. Measuring word meaning in context. *Computational Linguistics*, 39(3):511–554.

Kazuaki Kishida. 2005. *Property of Average Precision and Its Generalization: An Examination of Evaluation Indicator for Information Retrieval Experiments*, volume 2005. National Institute of Informatics Tokyo, Japan.

Gerhard Kremer, Katrin Erk, Sebastian Padó, and Stefan Thater. 2014. What substitutes tell us – analysis of an "all-words" lexical substitution corpus. In *Proceedings of the 14th Conference of the European Chapter of the Association for Computational Linguistics (EACL 2014)*, pages 540–549, Gothenburg, Sweden.

Omer Levy and Yoav Goldberg. 2014. Dependency-based word embeddings. In *Proceedings of the*

52nd Annual Meeting of the Association for Computational Linguistics (ACL 2014), pages 302–308, Baltimore, Maryland, USA.

Nikola Ljubešić and Tomaž Erjavec. 2011. hrWaC and slWac: Compiling web corpora for Croatian and Slovene. In *Proceedings of 14th International Conference on Text, Speech and Dialogue (TSD 2011)*, pages 395–402, Pilsen, Czech Republic.

Diana McCarthy and Roberto Navigli. 2007. SemEval-2007 Task 10: English lexical substitution task. In *Proceedings of the 4th International Workshop on Semantic Evaluations (SemEval 2007)*, pages 48–53, Prague, Czech Republic.

Oren Melamud, Ido Dagan, and Jacob Goldberger. 2015a. Modeling word meaning in context with substitute vectors. In *The 14th Annual Conference of the North American Chapter of the Association for Computational Linguistics: Human Language Technologies (NAACL HLT 2015)*, pages 472–482, Denver, Colorado.

Oren Melamud, Omer Levy, and Ido Dagan. 2015b. A simple word embedding model for lexical substitution. In *Proceedings of the Proceedings of the 1st Workshop on Vector Space Modeling for Natural Language Processing (VSM-NLP 2015)*, pages 1–7, Denver, Colorado.

Oren Melamud, Jacob Goldberger, and Ido Dagan. 2016. context2vec: Learning generic context embedding with bidirectional LSTM. In *Proceedings of Conference on Computational Natural Language Learning (CONLL 2016)*, pages 51–61, Vancouver, Canada.

Rada Mihalcea, Ravi Sinha, and Diana McCarthy. 2010. SemEval-2010 Task 2: Cross-lingual lexical substitution. In *Proceedings of the 5th International Workshop on Semantic Evaluation (SemEval 2010)*, pages 9–14, Uppsala, Sweden.

Tomas Mikolov, Ilya Sutskever, Kai Chen, Greg S Corrado, and Jeff Dean. 2013. Distributed representations of words and phrases and their compositionality. In *Proceedings of the Neural Information Processing Systems Conference (NIPS 2013)*, pages 3111–3119, Lake Tahoe, USA.

Tristan Miller, Darina Benikova, and Sallam Abualhaija. 2015. GermEval 2015: LexSub – a shared task for German-language lexical substitution. *Proceedings of GermEval 2015*, pages 1–9.

Roberto Navigli. 2009. Word sense disambiguation: A survey. *ACM Computing Surveys (CSUR)*, 41(2):10.

Stephen Roller and Katrin Erk. 2016. PIC a different word: A simple model for lexical substitution in context. In *Proceedings of the 15th Annual Conference of the North American Chapter of the Association for Computational Linguistics (NAACL 2016)*, pages 1121–1126, San Diego, California.

Ravi Sinha and Rada Mihalcea. 2014. Explorations in lexical sample and all-words lexical substitution. *Natural Language Engineering*, 20(01):99–129.

Benjamin Snyder and Martha Palmer. 2004. The English all-words task. In *Proceedings of Senseval-3*, pages 41–43, Barcelona, Spain.

Christopher Stokoe, Michael P Oakes, and John Tait. 2003. Word sense disambiguation in information retrieval revisited. In *Proceedings of ACM SIGIR 2013*, pages 159–166, Toronto, Canada.

Stefan Thater, Hagen Fürstenau, and Manfred Pinkal. 2010. Contextualizing semantic representations using syntactically enriched vector models. In *Proceedings of the 48th Annual Meeting of the Association for Computational Linguistics (ACL 2010*, pages 948–957, Uppsala, Sweden.

Antonio Toral. 2009. The lexical substitution task at EVALITA 2009. In *Proceedings of EVALITA Workshop, 11th Congress of Italian Association for Artificial Intelligence*, Reggio Emilia, Italy.

Projecting Multiword Expression Resources on a Polish Treebank

Agata Savary[1] and Jakub Waszczuk[1,2]

[1]Université François Rabelais Tours, France
[2]Université d'Orléans, France
{agata.savary, jakub.waszczuk}@univ-tours.fr

Abstract

Multiword expressions (MWEs) are linguistic objects containing two or more words and showing idiosyncratic behavior at different levels. Treebanks with annotated MWEs enable studies of such properties, as well as training and evaluation of MWE-aware parsers. However, few treebanks contain full-fledged MWE annotations. We show how this gap can be bridged in Polish by projecting 3 MWE resources on a constituency treebank.

1 Introduction

Multiword expressions (MWEs) are linguistic objects containing two or more words and showing idiosyncratic behavior at different linguistic levels (Savary et al., 2015). For instance, at the morphological level they can have restricted paradigms, e.g., in Polish (PL) *zjadłbym konia z kopytami* (lit. *I would eat a horse with its hooves*) 'I am very hungry' can only occur in the conditional mood. At the syntactic level they can: (i) exhibit defective agreement, e.g., in French (FR) in *grands-mères* 'grandmothers' the adjective does not agree with the noun in gender unlike all regular adjectival modifiers, (ii) impose agreement constraints which do not apply to compositional structures, e.g., *to have one's heart in one's mouth* imposes agreement in person between both possessive pronouns and the subject, (iii) block some transformations typical for their structures, e.g., **the bucket was kicked by him*, (iv) prohibit or require modifiers, e.g., (FR) *germer dans le cerveau de quelqu'un* (lit. *to germinate in someone's brain*) imposes a pronominal or nominal modifier of *brain*, etc. At the semantic level, MWEs show a varying degree of non-compositionality, e.g., *to pull strings* is semantically opaque but can be understood compositionally if the components themselves are interpreted in an idiomatic way (*to pull* as 'to use', and *strings* as 'one's influence').

Treebanks in which MWE have been explicitly annotated are highly precious resources enabling us to study such more or less unpredictable properties. They also constitute basic prerequisites for training and evaluating parsers, which should best perform syntactic analysis jointly with MWE identification (Finkel and Manning, 2009; Green et al., 2013; Candito and Constant, 2014; Le Roux et al., 2014; Wehrli, 2014; Nasr et al., 2015; Constant and Nivre, 2016; Waszczuk et al., 2016).

However, few treebanks contain full-fledged MWE annotations, even for English (Rosén et al., 2015). Multiword named entities (MWNEs) constitute by far the most frequently annotated category (Erjavec et al., 2010; Savary et al., 2010). Continuous MWEs such as compound nouns, adverbs and prepositions and conjunctions are covered in some treebanks as in (Abeillé et al., 2003; Branco et al., 2010). Verbal MWEs (VMWEs) have been addressed for a fewer number of languages (Bejček et al., 2011; Eryigit et al., 2015; Seraji et al., 2014), and often restricted to some subtypes only, e.g., light-verb constructions (Vincze and Csirik, 2010).

Lexical MWE resources develop more rapidly than MWE-annotated treebanks (Losnegaard et al., 2016). They already exist for a large number of languages and are often distributed under open licenses. It is, thus, interesting to examine how far MWE lexicons can help in completing the existing treebanks with annotation layers dedicated to MWEs. Our case study deals with four Polish resources: (i) the named-entity annotation layer of a Polish reference corpus, (ii) an e-lexicon of nominal, adjectival and adverbial MWEs, (iii) a valence dictionary with a phraseological component, and (iv) a treebank with no initial MWE annotations.

Proceedings of the 6th Workshop on Balto-Slavic Natural Language Processing, pages 20–26,
Valencia, Spain, 4 April 2017. ©2017 Association for Computational Linguistics

We show how the 3 former resources can be automatically projected on the latter, by identifying syntactic nodes satisfying (totally or partly) the appropriate lexical and syntactic constraints.

2 Resources

The National Corpus of Polish (NCP) (Przepiórkowski et al., 2012) contains a manually double-annotated and adjudicated subcorpus of over 1 million words. Its **named entity layer** (**NCP-NE**), which builds on the morphosyntactic layer (relying in its turn on the segmentation layer), contains over 80,000 annotated NEs, 20% of which are MWNEs. Only the latter were used in the experiments described below. The annotation schema assumes notably the markup of nested, overlapping and discontinuous NEs, i.e., the annotation structures form trees (Savary et al., 2010).

SEJF (Czerepowicka and Savary, 2015) is a grammatical lexicon of Polish continuous MWEs containing over 4,700 compound nouns, adjectives and adverbs, where inflectional and word-order variation is described via fine-grained graph-based rules. It is provided in two forms – intensional (multiword lemmas and inflection rules) and extensional (list of morphologically annotated variants). The latter, generated automatically from the former, was used in our projecting experiments. Tab. 1 shows a sample extensional entry containing a MWE inflected form, its lemma and morphological tag: noun (subst) in singular (sg) genitive (gen) and feminine gender (f).

Inflected form	Lemma	Tag
drugiej połowy	*druga połowa*	subst:sg:gen:f

Table 1: An inflected form of *druga połowa* (lit. *second half*) 'one's husband or wife' in SEJF.

Walenty is a Polish large-scale valence dictionary of about 50000, 3700, 3000, and 1000 subcategorization frames (in its 2015 version) for Polish verbs, nouns, adjectives, and adverbs respectively. Its encoding formalism is rather expressive and theory-neutral, and includes an elaborate phraseological component (Przepiórkowski et al., 2014).[1] Thus, above 8,000 verbal frames contain lexicalized arguments of head verbs, i.e., they describe VMWEs. For instance the idiom highlighted in

example (1) is described in Walenty as shown in Tab. 2. Each component separated by a '+' represents one required verbal argument with its lexical, morphological, syntactic, and (sometimes) semantic constraints. Here, the subject is compulsory and has a structural case (subj{np(str)}), which notably means that it normally occurs in the nominative, but turns to the genitive when realized as a numeral phrase (of a certain type). The subject being a required argument in a verbal frame does not contradict the fact that it can regularly be omitted in Polish, as in (1).[2]

(1) Nie   umiem   w tych   sprawach **trzymać**
     Not   know.SG.PRI in these affairs   hold.INF
     języka   za   zębami.
     tongue.SG.GEN behind teeth.

     (lit. *I cannot hold my tongue behind my teeth in such cases*) 'I cannot hold my tongue in such cases'

The second required argument is a direct object realized as a nominal phrase in structural case, i.e., normally in the accusative but turning to the genitive when the sentence is negated, as in (1). The lexicalized object's head has the lemma *język* 'tongue', should be in singular (sg) and does not admit modifiers (natr). The second complement is a prepositional nominal phrase (prepnp) headed by the preposition *za* 'behind' governing the instrumental case (inst) and a lexicalized non-modifiable (natr) noun with the lemma *ząb* 'tooth' in plural (pl). Walenty's syntax is compact and meant to be easily handled by lexicographers but proved sufficiently formalized to be directly applicable to NLP tasks, such as automatic generation of grammar rules (Patejuk, 2015).

```
trzymać: subj{np(str)}+
  obj{lex(np(str),sg,'język',natr)}+
  {lex(prepnp(za,inst),pl,'ząb',natr)}
```

Table 2: Description of *trzymać język za zębami* 'hold one's tongue' in Walenty

Składnica is a Polish constituency treebank comprising about 9,000 sentences with manually disambiguated syntactic trees (Świdziński and Woliński, 2010). It was created by automatically generating all possible parses with a large-coverage DCG grammar, and then manually selecting the correct parse. It does not contain MWE

---

[1]Walenty and PDT-Vallex for Czech (Urešová et al., 2014) belong to the most elaborate and extensive endeavors towards the description of the valency of VMWEs (Przepiórkowski et al., 2016).

[2]This property is to be distinguished from impersonal verbs, which prohibit a subject, as in *dobrze mu z oczu patrzy* (lit. *looks him from eyes well*) 'he looks like a good person'.

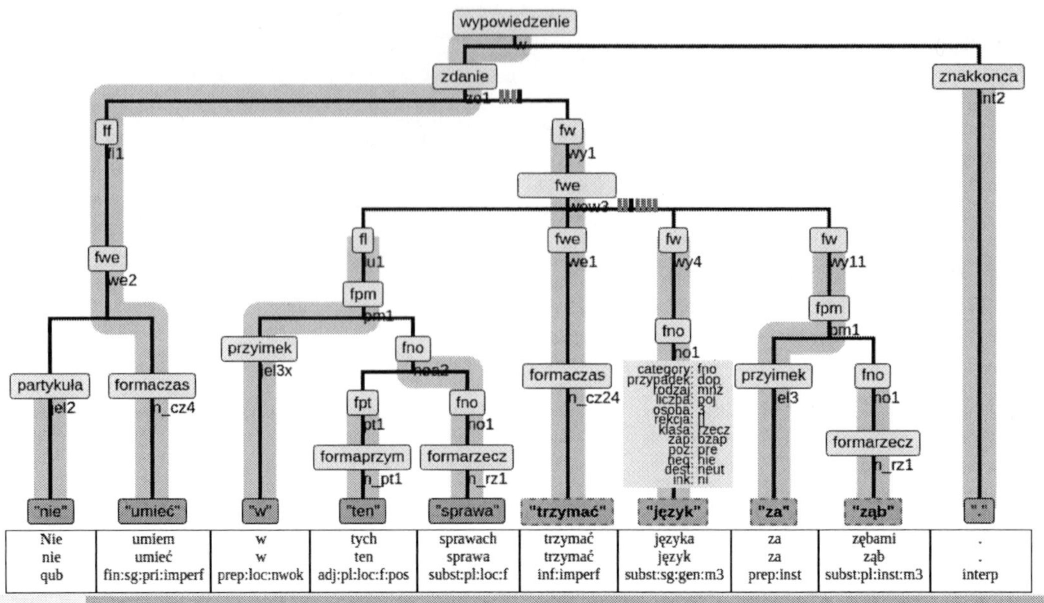

Figure 1: Syntax tree of example (1) in Składnica. The categories denote: `ff` 'finite phrase', `fl` 'adjunct', `fno` 'nominal phrase', `formaczas` 'verbal phrase', `formaprzym` 'adjectival phrase', `formarzecz` 'nominal phrase', `fpm` 'prepositional phrase', `fpt` 'adjectival phrase', `fw` 'required phrase', `fwe` 'verbal phrase', `partykuła` 'particle', `przyimek` 'preposition', `wypowiedzenie` 'utterance', `zdanie` 'sentence', `znakkońca` 'ending punctuation'. The feature structure of the `fno` node dominating the terminal *język* 'tongue' is highlighted. The feature codes include: `przypadek` 'case', `rodzaj` 'gender', `liczba` 'number', `osoba` 'person', `rekcja` 'case government', and `neg` 'negation'. The values denote: `dop` 'genitive', `mnz` 'human inanimate', `poj` 'singular', and `nie` 'negated'.

annotations. Its morphosyntactic tagset is mostly equivalent to the one used in Walenty, although it uses Polish terms: `mian`=*mianownik* 'nominative', `dk`=*dokonany* 'perfective aspect', etc.

Fig. 1 shows the correct syntax tree from Składnica for example (1). Each non-terminal node includes a feature structure (FS). Here, the FS of the node `fno` (nominal phrase), above the terminal *język* 'tongue', is highlighted. It includes the feature `neg`=`nie` meaning that this node occurs within the scope of a negated verb. This makes it easy to validate constraints from Walenty entries, such as the structural genitive of direct objects.

A notable feature of Składnica is that dependents of the verbs are explicitly marked as either arguments (`fw`) or adjuncts (`fl`), i.e., valency is accounted for. Note, however, that the valency of head verbs in VMWEs can differ from the one of the same verbs occurring as simple predicates.

3 Projection

Since Składnica contains no explicit MWE annotations, we produced them automatically by projecting NCP-NE, SEJF and Walenty on the syntax trees. The projection for NCP-NE was straightforward and did not require manual validation, since Składnica is a subcorpus of the NCP, whose NE annotation and adjudication were performed manually. The projection for SEJF and Walenty, followed by a manual validation, consisted in searching for syntactic nodes satisfying all lexical constraints and part of syntactic constraints of a MWE entry. The required lexical nodes were to be contiguous for SEJF but not for Walenty.

Here, we give more details on the Walenty-to-Składnica projection, which was the most challenging one. It required defining correspondences at different levels. Explicit morphological values and phrase types could be translated rather straightforwardly due to largely compatible tagsets (`np`→`fno` 'nominal phrase', `mian`→`nom` 'nominative', etc.). Context-dependent values like `str` (structural case) were encoded in conditional statements taking combination of features into account. For instance, the argument specification `obj(np(str))` translated into a feature structure containing one of the following: [*category* = *fno*, *przypadek* = *bier*, *neg* = *tak*], [*category* = *fno*, *przypadek* = *dop*, *neg* = *nie*] (nominal object, either in the accusative in an affirmative sentence or in the genitive in a negative one).

Once these correspondences were defined, identifying a Walenty entry in Składnica consisted in checking if the current sentence contained a subtree in which: (i) the lexically constrained arguments and adjuncts (and their own, recursively embedded, lexically constrained dependents) were present, (ii) selected syntactic constraints (those concerning `np` and `prepnp` phrases) were fulfilled. For instance in Fig. 1, a head verb, a direct object with a lexicalized head and a lexicalized prepositional complement were searched for, but an ellipsis of the subject was allowed.

Query language The MWE projection task is handled by: (i) a query language, providing an interface between the MWE resources and the treebank, (ii) procedures for compiling lexicon entries into the queries, and (iii) an interpreter which runs a query over treebank subtrees to check whether the corresponding MWE entry occurs in them.

Formally, we defined our core query language using the following abstract syntax:

$$b \text{ (Booleans)} ::= \texttt{true} \mid \texttt{false}$$
$$n \text{ (node queries)} ::= b \mid n_1 \wedge n_2 \mid n_1 \vee n_2$$
$$\mid \texttt{mark} \mid \texttt{satisfy} \ (node \rightarrow b)$$
$$t \text{ (tree queries)} ::= b \mid t_1 \wedge t_2 \mid t_1 \vee t_2$$
$$\mid \texttt{root} \ n \mid \texttt{child} \ t \mid \ldots$$

Thus, the properties of a given syntactic node or tree can be verified via an appropriate node query (NQ) or tree query (TQ), respectively. Both kinds of queries are recursive and TQs can additionally build on NQs. For instance, from the query interpretation point of view, the TQ `root` n is satisfied for a given tree iff its root satisfies the NQ n. Also, the TQ `child` t is satisfied iff at least one of its root's children trees satisfies the TQ t. Finally, particular feature values (*category*, *przypadek*, etc.) can be verified using the NQ `satisfy` (*node* $\rightarrow b$), which takes an arbitrary node-level predicate (*node* $\rightarrow b$) and tells whether it is satisfied over the current syntactic *node*.

The particularity of this query language is the `mark` construction, which marks a syntactic node as a part of a MWE. When a TQ t containing `mark` has been executed over a tree T, t's result contains all nodes matched with `mark`, provided that T satisfies all the constraints encoded in t.

`Mark` does not check any constraints by itself, but it can be easily combined with other NQs via query conjunction (i.e., $n \wedge \texttt{mark}$).

Note that, based on our core language, more complex queries can be expressed, for instance:

$$\texttt{member} \ n \overset{\text{def}}{=} \texttt{root} \ n \vee \texttt{child} \ (\texttt{member} \ n) \quad (2)$$

The query interpreter is defined over the core language only and handles MWE-related marking. For instance, given a query of type $t_1 \vee t_2$, while evaluating t_1, some subtree nodes may be `marked` as potential MWE components. But if t_1 finally evaluates to `false`, all these markings are wiped out. This behavior is guaranteed by the implementation of the core disjunction ($\vee$) operator.

Compiling MWE entries Let us focus on the Walenty-to-query compilation and on the entry from Tab. 2 in particular. Its querified version checks that (i) the base form of the lexical head, reached via the head-annotated edges (marked in grayed in Fig. 1), corresponds to the main verb of the entry (i.e., *trzymać*), and (ii) each of the lexically-constrained elements of the frame (i.e., noun phrase *język* and prepositional phrase *za zębami*) is realized by one of the `child`-ren trees of the queried tree. Part (i) of the query is implemented by the version of the `member` query (see Eq. 2) restricted to head-annotated edges. Implementation of (ii) depends on the particular frame element. Tree queries corresponding to (i) and (ii) are then combined using the $\wedge$ operator.

The `obj{lex(np(str),sg,'język',natr)}` frame element is also translated to a $\wedge$-combined set of tree queries, which individually check that all the given restrictions are satisfied: the lexical head is *język*, the number is singular, etc. The node query which verifies that *język* is the lexical head is combined with `mark`, so that it is designated as a part of the resulting MWE annotation, provided that all the other entry-related constraints are also satisfied. Modifiers, if specified, are recursively compiled into tree queries which are then applied over `child`-ren trees. Here, `natr` specifies that no modifiers are allowed, constraint compiled into a query which checks that the corresponding tree

Source	TP	FP	CRead	All	CRate
NKJP	1,304	n/a	n/a	1,304	n/a
SEJF	368	18	23	409	0.94
Walenty	365	78	18	452	0.95
Total	2,037	96	41	2,165	0.95

Table 3: Projection results including true positives (TP), false positives (FP), compositional readings (CRead), compositionality rate (CRate).

is non-branching (i.e., has no other children apart from its head, constraint satisfied in Fig. 1 by the subtree rooted with `fno` placed over the leaf *język*).[3] The other element of the frame, which describes the prepositional argument *za zębami*, is compiled into a query in a similar way.

4 Results

Table 3 shows the projection results. Among the 2165 automatically identified candidate MWEs, those 1,304 stemming from NCP-NE were supposed correct (since resulting from manual double-annotation and adjudication). The 861 remaining candidates were manually validated. They contained 733 true positives, 96 false positives, and 41 candidates with a compositional reading, as in examples (3)-(4). Thus, the precision of the SEJF/Walenty projection was equal to 0.85. The idiomaticity rate (El Maarouf and Oakes, 2015), i.e., the ratio of occurrences with idiomatic reading to all correctly recognized occurrences, is about 0.95. We expect that if NEs were taken into account, this ratio would be even higher, since NEs seem to exhibit compositional readings relatively rarely. Note also that false positives are much more frequent for entries stemming from Walenty than for those from SEJF, which shows the higher complexity of verbal MWEs as compared to other, continuous, MWEs.

(3) . . . w **drugiej połowie** XIX wieku
'. . . in the **second half** of the 19th century'
MWE: (lit. *second half*) 'one's husband or wife'

(4) Odetchnęła głęboko i **przymknęła oczy**.
'(She) breathed profoundly and **closed** her **eyes**.'
MWE: *przymknąć oczy na coś* (lit. *to close one's eyes on sth*) 'to pretend not to see sth'

Notable errors in the projection procedure stem from allowing for the ellipsis of compulsory but non-lexicalized arguments. If all such arguments marked in Walenty were required in Składnica during the projection, correct MWEs occurrences with ellipted arguments would be missed, as in the case of the subject required in Tab. 2 but omitted in Fig. 1. Conversely, allowing for the ellipsis of such arguments results in some false positives, as in example (4), where the absence of the prepositional argument (headed by the preposition *na* 'on') excludes the idiomatic reading.

5 Summary and Perspectives

The automatic projection of MWEs resources on a treebank results in a manually validated resource containing over 2,000 VMWEs in about 9,000 constituency trees, and available under the GPL v3 license.[4] The results are represented in a simplified custom XML format, meant for an easy use, e.g., in automatic grammar extraction. This format refers to identifiers of sentences and tokens in the Składnica trees, which enables users to automatically project annotations on the original treebank.

We believe to have shown examples of fine-grained and high-quality MWE resources which might be promoted as standards for the international community. Adapting their formalisms to many languages should be possible with affordable efforts (already undertaken by us for French). In return, relatively reliable mapping procedures based on such resources may help bridge the gap towards large and comprehensive MWE-annotation in treebanks, which is currently a bottleneck in the MWE-oriented research.

Another interesting finding, worth confirming in other languages, is the high idiomaticity rate of MWEs. It is a hint that automated MWE identification based on purely syntactic methods and rich resources may achieve high accuracy, even in the absence of semantic non-compositionality models.

Future work includes repeating the experiments with the new version of Walenty released in 2016, as well as estimating the projection recall. We also wish to enhance the lexicon projection process, so as to account for more fine-grained constraints, and tune the degree of flexibility in constraint validation. Finally, an appropriate MWE annotation schema is needed in which each MWE occurrence would be linked to its corresponding entry in a MWE lexicon, and its required arguments, whether lexicalized or not, would be marked.

---

[3]The `non-branching` predicate is a part of the core language. We did not define it above for the sake of brevity.

[4]`http://zil.ipipan.waw.pl/Sk\%C5\%82adnicaMWE`

References

Anne Abeillé, Lionel Clément, and François Toussenel, 2003. *Building a treebank for French*, pages 165–187. Kluwer Academic Publishers.

Eduard Bejček, Pavel Straňák, and Daniel Zeman. 2011. Influence of Treebank Design on Representation of Multiword Expressions. In Alexander F. Gelbukh, editor, *Computational Linguistics and Intelligent Text Processing - 12th International Conference, CICLing 2011, Tokyo, Japan, February 20-26, 2011. Proceedings, Part I*, volume 6608 of *Lecture Notes in Computer Science*, pages 1–14. Springer.

António Branco, Francisco Costa, João Silva, Sara Silveira, Sérgio Castro, Mariana Avelãs, Clara Pinto, and João Graça. 2010. Developing a deep linguistic databank supporting a collection of treebanks: the cintil deepgrambank. In *Proceedings of the Seventh conference on International Language Resources and Evaluation (LREC'10)*. European Languages Resources Association (ELRA).

Marie Candito and Matthieu Constant. 2014. Strategies for Contiguous Multiword Expression Analysis and Dependency Parsing. In *Proceedings of the 52nd Annual Meeting of the Association for Computational Linguistics, ACL 2014, June 22-27, 2014, Baltimore, MD, USA, Volume 1: Long Papers*, pages 743–753.

Matthieu Constant and Joakim Nivre. 2016. A Transition-Based System for Joint Lexical and Syntactic Analysis. In *Proceedings of the 54th Annual Meeting of the Association for Computational Linguistics (Volume 1: Long Papers)*, pages 161–171, Berlin, Germany, August. Association for Computational Linguistics.

Monika Czerepowicka and Agata Savary. 2015. SEJF - a Grammatical Lexicon of Polish Multi-Word Expressions. In *Proceedings of Language and Technology Conference (LTC'15), Poznań, Poland*. Wydawnictwo Poznańskie.

Ismail El Maarouf and Michael Oakes. 2015. Statistical Measures for Characterising MWEs. In *IC1207 COST PARSEME 5th general meeting*.

Tomaž Erjavec, Darja Fišer, Simon Krek, and Nina Ledinek. 2010. The JOS Linguistically Tagged Corpus of Slovene. In *Proceedings of the Seventh conference on International Language Resources and Evaluation (LREC'10)*. European Languages Resources Association (ELRA).

Gulsen Eryigit, Kubra Adali, Dilara Torunoglu-Selamet, Umut Sulubacak, and Tugba Pamay. 2015. Annotation and Extraction of Multiword Expressions in Turkish Treebanks. In *Proceedings of NAACL-HLT 2015*, pages 70–76. Association for Computational Linguistics.

Jenny Rose Finkel and Christopher D. Manning. 2009. Joint Parsing and Named Entity Recognition. In *HLT-NAACL*, pages 326–334. The Association for Computational Linguistics.

Spence Green, Marie-Catherine de Marneffe, and Christopher D. Manning. 2013. Parsing Models for Identifying Multiword Expressions. *Computational Linguistics*, 39(1).

Joseph Le Roux, Antoine Rozenknop, and Matthieu Constant. 2014. Syntactic Parsing and Compound Recognition via Dual Decomposition: Application to French. In *Proceedings of COLING 2014, the 25th International Conference on Computational Linguistics: Technical Papers*, pages 1875–1885. Dublin City University and Association for Computational Linguistics.

Gyri Smørdal Losnegaard, Federico Sangati, Carla Parra Escartín, Agata Savary, Sascha Bargmann, and Johanna Monti. 2016. PARSEME Survey on MWE Resources. In Nicoletta Calzolari (Conference Chair), Khalid Choukri, Thierry Declerck, Marko Grobelnik, Bente Maegaard, Joseph Mariani, Asuncion Moreno, Jan Odijk, and Stelios Piperidis, editors, *Proceedings of the Tenth International Conference on Language Resources and Evaluation (LREC 2016)*, Paris, France, may. European Language Resources Association (ELRA).

Alexis Nasr, Carlos Ramisch, José Deulofeu, and André Valli. 2015. Joint Dependency Parsing and Multiword Expression Tokenization. In *Proceedings of the 53rd Annual Meeting of the Association for Computational Linguistics and the 7th International Joint Conference on Natural Language Processing (Volume 1: Long Papers)*, pages 1116–1126. Association for Computational Linguistics.

Agnieszka Patejuk. 2015. *Unlike coordination in Polish: an LFG account*. Ph.D. dissertation, Institute of Polish Language, Polish Academy of Sciences, Cracow.

Adam Przepiórkowski, Mirosław Bańko, Rafał L. Górski, and Barbara Lewandowska-Tomaszczyk, editors. 2012. *Narodowy Korpus Języka Polskiego [Eng.: National Corpus of Polish]*. Wydawnictwo Naukowe PWN, Warsaw.

Adam Przepiórkowski, Elżbieta Hajnicz, Agnieszka Patejuk, and Marcin Woliński. 2014. Extended phraseological information in a valence dictionary for NLP applications. In *Proceedings of the Workshop on Lexical and Grammatical Resources for Language Processing (LG-LP 2014)*, pages 83–91, Dublin, Ireland. Association for Computational Linguistics and Dublin City University.

Adam Przepiórkowski, Jan Hajič, Elżbieta Hajnicz, and Zdeňka Urešová. 2016. Phraseology in two Slavic valency dictionaries: Limitations and perspectives. *International Journal of Lexicography*, 29. Forthcoming.

Victoria Rosén, Gyri Smørdal Losnegaard, Koenraad De Smedt, Eduard Bejček, Agata Savary, Adam Przepiórkowski, Petya Osenova, and Verginica Barbu Mitetelu. 2015. A survey of multiword expressions in treebanks. In *Proceedings of the 14th International Workshop on Treebanks & Linguistic Theories conference*, Warsaw, Poland, December.

Agata Savary, Jakub Waszczuk, and Adam Przepiórkowski. 2010. Towards the Annotation of Named Entities in the National Corpus of Polish. In *Proceedings of the Seventh conference on International Language Resources and Evaluation (LREC'10)*. European Languages Resources Association (ELRA).

Agata Savary, Manfred Sailer, Yannick Parmentier, Michael Rosner, Victoria Rosén, Adam Przepiórkowski, Cvetana Krstev, Veronika Vincze, Beata Wójtowicz, Gyri Smørdal Losnegaard, Carla Parra Escartín, Jakub Waszczuk, Matthieu Constant, Petya Osenova, and Federico Sangati. 2015. PARSEME – PARSing and Multiword Expressions within a European multilingual network. In *7th Language & Technology Conference: Human Language Technologies as a Challenge for Computer Science and Linguistics (LTC 2015)*, Poznań, Poland, November.

Mojgan Seraji, Carina Jahani, Beáta Megyesi, and Joakim Nivre. 2014. A Persian Treebank with Stanford Typed Dependencies. In Nicoletta Calzolari (Conference Chair), Khalid Choukri, Thierry Declerck, Hrafn Loftsson, Bente Maegaard, Joseph Mariani, Asuncion Moreno, Jan Odijk, and Stelios Piperidis, editors, *Proceedings of the Ninth International Conference on Language Resources and Evaluation (LREC'14)*, Reykjavik, Iceland, may. European Language Resources Association (ELRA).

Zdeňka Urešová, Jan Štěpánek, Jan Hajič, Jarmila Panevova, and Marie Mikulová. 2014. PDT-vallex: Czech valency lexicon linked to treebanks. LINDAT/CLARIN digital library at Institute of Formal and Applied Linguistics, Charles University in Prague.

Veronika Vincze and János Csirik. 2010. Hungarian Corpus of Light Verb Constructions. In *Proceedings of the 23rd International Conference on Computational Linguistics (Coling 2010)*, pages 1110–1118. Coling 2010 Organizing Committee.

Jakub Waszczuk, Agata Savary, and Yannick Parmentier. 2016. Promoting multiword expressions in A* TAG parsing. In Nicoletta Calzolari, Yuji Matsumoto, and Rashmi Prasad, editors, *COLING 2016, 26th International Conference on Computational Linguistics, Proceedings of the Conference: Technical Papers, December 11-16, 2016, Osaka, Japan*, pages 429–439. ACL.

Eric Wehrli. 2014. The Relevance of Collocations for Parsing. In *Proceedings of the 10th Workshop on Multiword Expressions (MWE)*, pages 26–32, Gothenburg, Sweden, April. Association for Computational Linguistics.

Marek Świdziński and Marcin Woliński. 2010. Towards a bank of constituent parse trees for Polish. In Petr Sojka, Aleš Horák, Ivan Kopeček, and Karel Pala, editors, *Text, Speech and Dialogue: 13th International Conference, TSD 2010, Brno, Czech Republic*, volume 6231 of *Lecture Notes in Artificial Intelligence*, pages 197–204, Heidelberg. Springer-Verlag.

Lexicon Induction for Spoken Rusyn – Challenges and Results

Achim Rabus
Department of Slavonic Studies
University of Freiburg
Germany
achim.rabus@
slavistik.uni-freiburg.de

Yves Scherrer
Department of Linguistics
University of Geneva
Switzerland
yves.scherrer@unige.ch

Abstract

This paper reports on challenges and results in developing NLP resources for spoken Rusyn. Being a Slavic minority language, Rusyn does not have any resources to make use of. We propose to build a morphosyntactic dictionary for Rusyn, combining existing resources from the etymologically close Slavic languages Russian, Ukrainian, Slovak, and Polish. We adapt these resources to Rusyn by using vowel-sensitive Levenshtein distance, hand-written language-specific transformation rules, and combinations of the two. Compared to an exact match baseline, we increase the coverage of the resulting morphological dictionary by up to 77.4% relative (42.9% absolute), which results in a tagging recall increased by 11.6% relative (9.1% absolute). Our research confirms and expands the results of previous studies showing the efficiency of using NLP resources from neighboring languages for low-resourced languages.

1 Introduction

This paper deals with the development of a morphological dictionary for spoken varieties of the Slavic minority language Rusyn by leveraging the similarities between Rusyn and neighboring etymologically related languages. It is structured as follows: First, we give a brief introduction on the characteristics of the Rusyn minority language and the data our investigation is based upon. Afterwards, we describe our approach to lexicon induction using resources from several related Slavic languages and the steps we took to improve the matches from the dictionaries. Finally, we discuss the results and give an outlook on future work.

2 Rusyn and the Corpus of Spoken Rusyn

Rusyn belongs to the Slavic language family and is spoken predominantly in the Carpathian region, most notably in Transcarpathian Ukraine, Eastern Slovakia, and South Eastern Poland, where it is called Lemko.[1] Some scholars claim Rusyn to be a dialect of Ukrainian (Skrypnyk, 2013), others see it as an independent Slavic language (Pugh, 2009; Plishkova, 2009). While there is no denying the fact that Ukrainian is the standard language closest to the Rusyn varieties, certain distinct features at all linguistic levels can be detected. This makes the Rusyn varieties take an intermediary position between the East and West Slavic languages (for more details see, e.g., Teutsch (2001)). Nowadays, the speakers of Rusyn find themselves in a dynamic sociolinguistic environment and experience significant pressure by their respective roofing state languages Ukrainian, Slovak, or Polish. Thus, new divergences within the old Rusyn dialect continuum due to contact with the majority language, i.e., so-called border effects, are to be expected (Rabus, 2015; Woolhiser, 2005). In order to trace these divergences, and create an empirically sound basis for investigating current Rusyn speech, the Corpus of Spoken Rusyn (www.russinisch.uni-freiburg.de/corpus, Rabus and Šymon (2015)) has been created. It consists of several hours of transcribed speech as well as recordings.[2] Although the transcription in the corpus is not phonetic, but rather orthographic, both diatopic and individual varia-

---

[1] According to official data, there are 110 750 Rusyns, according to an "informed estimate" no less than 1 762 500, the majority of them living in the Carpathian region (Magocsi, 2015, p. 1).

[2] The corpus engine is CWB (Christ, 1994), the GUI functionality has been continuously expanded for several Slavic corpus projects (Waldenfels and Woźniak, 2017; Waldenfels and Rabus, 2015; Rabus and Šymon, 2015).

Proceedings of the 6th Workshop on Balto-Slavic Natural Language Processing, pages 27–32,
Valencia, Spain, 4 April 2017. ©2017 Association for Computational Linguistics

tion is reflected in the transcription. The reason for that is that exactly this variation is what we want to investigate using the corpus, i.e., more "Slovak" Rusyn varieties should be distinguished from more "Ukrainian" or "Polish" varieties. Besides, variation in transcription practices of different transcribers cannot be avoided.

At the moment, Rusyn does not have any existing NLP resources (annotated corpora or tools) to make use of. The aim of this paper is to investigate first steps towards (semi-)automatically annotating the transcribed speech data. It goes without saying that the different types of variation present in our data significantly complicate the task of developing NLP resources.

3   Lexicon Induction

We propose to build a morphosyntactic dictionary for Rusyn, using existing resources from etymologically related languages. The idea is that if we know that a Rusyn word X corresponds to the Ukrainian word Y, and that Y is linked to the morphosyntactic descriptions M_1, M_2, M_n, we can create an entry in the Rusyn dictionary consisting of X and M_1, M_2, M_n. The proposed approach is inspired by earlier work by Mann and Yarowsky (2001), who aim to detect cognate word pairs in order to induce a translation lexicon. They evaluate different measures of phonetic or graphemic distance on this task. While they show that distance measures adapted to the language pair by machine learning work best, we are not able to use them as we do not have the required bilingual training corpus at our disposal. Scherrer and Sagot (2014) use such distance measures as a first step of a pipeline for transferring morphosyntactic annotations from a resourced language (RL) towards an etymologically related non-resourced language (NRL).

Due to the high amount of variation and the heterogeneity of the Rusyn data (our NRL), we resolved to use resources from several neighboring RLs, namely from the East Slavic languages Ukrainian and Russian as well as from the West Slavic languages Polish and Slovak.[3] This makes sense, because the old Rusyn dialect continuum features both West Slavic and East Slavic linguistic traits, with more West Slavic features in the westernmost dialects and more East Slavic ones

---

[3] As a matter of fact, Russian is no neighboring language to Rusyn, but since for historical reasons there are numerous Russian borrowings in Rusyn and since NLP resources for Russian are developed quite well, we also include Russian.

Language	Source	Entries
Polish	MULTEXT-East	1.9M
Russian	MULTEXT-East	244k
Russian	TnT (RNC)	373k
Ukrainian	MULTEXT-East	300k
Ukrainian	UGtag	4.6M
Slovak	MULTEXT-East	1.9M

Table 1: Sizes of the morphosyntactic dictionaries used for induction.

in the easternmost dialects. Moreover, the respective umbrella languages – Ukrainian, Slovak, and Polish – exert considerable influence on the Rusyn vernacular. In fact, the overwhelming majority of Rusyn speakers are bilingual.

3.1   Data

Our RL data consist of morphosyntactic dictionaries (i.e., files associating word tokens with their lemmas and tags) from Ukrainian, Slovak, Polish, Russian. All of them were taken from the MULTEXT-East repository (Erjavec et al., 2010a; Erjavec et al., 2010b; Erjavec, 2012). As Rusyn is written in Cyrillic script, we converted the Slovak and Polish dictionaries into Cyrillic script first. During the conversion process, we made the tokens more similar to Rusyn by applying certain linguistic transformations (e.g., denasalization in the Polish case) and thus excluded some output tokens that could not possibly match any Rusyn tokens for obvious linguistic reasons.

As mentioned above, the standard language closest to the Rusyn varieties is Ukrainian. Several Ukrainian NLP resources exist, e.g., the Ukrainian National Corpus.[4] However, these resources cannot easily be used to train taggers or parsers. UGtag (Kotsyba et al., 2011) is a tagger specifically developed for Ukrainian; it is essentially a morphological dictionary with a simple disambiguation component. Its underlying dictionary is rather large and can be easily converted to text format, making it a good addition to the small MULTEXT-East Ukrainian dictionary. For Russian, we complemented the small MULTEXT-East dictionary with the TnT lexicon file based on data from the Russian National Corpus (Sharoff et al., 2008). We also harmonized the MSD tags (morphosyntactic descriptions) across all languages and data

---

[4] www.mova.info

sources. Table 1 sums up the used resources.

Our NRL data consist of 10 361 unique tokens extracted from the Corpus of Spoken Rusyn (which currently contains a total of 75 000 running words). In addition, we were able to obtain a small sample of morphosyntactically annotated Rusyn, amounting to 1 047 tokens; the induction methods are evaluated on this sample.

3.2 Exact Matches

As a baseline, we checked how many Rusyn word forms could be retrieved by exact match in the four RL lexicons. Despite Rusyn being closely related to the dictionary languages, the results are rather poor: merely 55.47% of all Rusyn tokens were found in at least one RL lexicon (see Table 2, first column).

We further show the relative contributions of the four RLs in Table 2. Ukrainian is by far the most successful language, both with respect to the overall matched words (i.e., words matched with Ukrainian and possibly other RLs) and to uniquely matched words (i.e., words matched with Ukrainian but not with any other RL). This is due to several factors: e.g., Ukrainian is the RL with the smallest linguistic distance to the Rusyn varieties, the Ukrainian dictionary is considerably larger than the other dictionaries, and the relative majority of tokens in the corpus belongs to "Ukrainian" varieties of Rusyn.

Table 2 also shows some ambiguity measures. On average, a Rusyn token is found in 1.66 resourced languages and associated with 3.28 tags. Trivially, a Rusyn word is matched with exactly one RL word, as both forms need to be identical for exact match.

We evaluated the correctness of the induced lexicon on the annotated Rusyn sample. More than 84% of the 1 047 words were covered, and the correct tag was among the induced ones for more than 78% of words. (We do not attempt to disambiguate the tags here, which is why we only report recall.) We also report noise, which is defined as the amount of covered but wrongly tagged words (i.e., coverage - recall). With a noise of only 6%, we can characterize exact match as a high-precision, low-recall method.

The poor coverage often results from orthographic mismatches by merely one or a few different letters between the Rusyn token and its RL counterpart. In order to improve the coverage, we propose different types of transformations, as described in the following sub-sections.

3.3 Daitch-Mokotoff Soundex Algorithm

Soundex is a family of phonetic algorithms for indexing words and, in particular, names by their pronunciation and regardless of their spelling (Hall and Dowling, 1980). The principle behind a Soundex algorithm is to group different graphemes into a small set of sound classes, where all vowels except the first of a word are discarded. The Daitch-Mokotoff Soundex is a variant of the original (English) Soundex that is adapted to Eastern European names (Mokotoff, 1997).

Matching soundex-transformed RL words with soundex-transformed NRL words allowed us to obtain a coverage of 97.16% (i.e., almost all NRL words were matched), but in fact, each matched NRL word was associated with as many as 630 RL words on average. Thus, this algorithm proved to be too radical as it identified a multitude of unrelated tokens. In particular, vowel removal neutralized nearly all inflectional suffixes. While Soundex algorithms have proved useful for matching names with different spellings, they are clearly not adapted to our task. Therefore, we had to resort to less radical transformation methods.

3.4 Hand-Written Transformation Rules

The Slavic RLs in question differ with respect to regular sound changes and morphological correspondences that are reflected in orthography. For instance, Rusyn dialects reflect Common Slavic *ě as i, while Russian yields e. Moreover, Rusyn verbs in the infinitive end in -ти, while Russian has -ть. About 40 such transformation rules were formulated for each language and implemented in *foma* (Hulden, 2009).

During the lexicon induction process, each RL word was transformed with the appropriate rules to resemble Rusyn. All rule applications were optional, yielding a multitude of candidates for each RL word. Whenever one of the candidates corresponded to an existing Rusyn word, this was counted as a match. As shown in Table 2, applying these transformation rules yielded a considerable increase of matched words (compared with exact match) to more than 76%. Ambiguity levels rise slightly, and the contributions of the different languages rise uniformly. The better coverage is confirmed on the test set, and tagging recall also in-

	Exact	Soundex	Rules	Leven.	R+L	L+R
Words matched with any RL	55.47%	97.16%	76.38%	98.09%	98.38%	98.09%
Words matched with PL	13.92%	87.24%	19.17%	25.80%	24.66%	22.89%
Words matched with RU	20.03%	92.57%	30.30%	37.26%	38.03%	34.41%
Words matched with SK	19.43%	93.45%	28.17%	39.62%	37.68%	35.63%
Words matched with UK	38.84%	96.06%	49.49%	70.09%	64.89%	63.69%
Words matched with PL only	3.91%	0.10%	5.16%	5.76%	6.34%	6.81%
Words matched with RU only	3.94%	0.12%	7.44%	6.15%	8.79%	8.82%
Words matched with SK only	4.14%	0.31%	6.69%	8.64%	9.33%	10.49%
Words matched with UK only	21.69%	1.27%	26.25%	33.46%	33.23%	36.12%
Average RL language ambiguity	1.66	3.80	1.66	1.76	1.68	1.60
Average RL word ambiguity	1.00	630.74	1.29	2.17	1.81	1.51
Average tag ambiguity	3.28	271.62	3.66	5.08	4.34	3.93
Coverage on test set	84.2%	—	90.4%	99.0%	99.6%	99.0%
Tagging recall on test set	78.2%	—	81.9%	87.3%	87.1%	86.4%
Noise on test set	6.0%	—	8.5%	11.7%	12.5%	12.6%

Table 2: Results of the different lexicon induction methods. Percentages show how many distinct Rusyn words were matched with any of the four RLs, with at least one of the RLs, and with exactly one RL. The last rows show the coverage, tagging recall and noise on the annotated Rusyn sample.

creases by more than 3%,[5] while the noise level increases by 2.5%.

3.5 Vowel-Sensitive Levenshtein Distance

As an alternative to hand-written rules, we also tested a vowel-sensitive variant of Levenshtein distance (Levenshtein, 1966), following Mann and Yarowsky (2001). In this variant, edit operations on vowels are assigned a weight of 0.5, whereas edit operations on consonants use the standard weight of 1. Using this variant was motivated by the fact that Rusyn vowels differ systematically and significantly from the vowels present in neighboring Slavic languages and also within different Rusyn varieties. We also normalize distances by the length of the longer word.

Initial experiments have shown that most NRL words lie within a small distance of an RL word, and that matches with high distance values are most often wrong. Because of that, we decided to discard all matches with distance values higher than 0.25. This considerably decreased word and tag ambiguity while losing merely 1.95% of matched tokens. Even with this threshold, the number of matched words as well as the tagging recall – but also the noise – is higher than with the

rules.[6] Future research will show whether the optimal threshold can be found automatically, e.g., by using a small annotated development corpus.

Despite the good coverage, we were concerned by the higher ambiguity values, which is why we decided to combine Levenshtein distance with the transformation rules.

3.6 Rules and Levenshtein

In this first combined approach, we complement the rules with Levenshtein results in order to increase coverage: Whenever the rules do not succeed in creating a match for a Rusyn word, we back off to the corresponding Levenshtein results. This combination outperforms both individual methods in terms of matches (98.38%, as compared to 76.38% and 98.09%). As expected, the resulting ambiguity levels lie between those of the rules and those of the Levenshtein method. The coverage on the test set also increases, but this is not followed by better tag recall.[7]

---

[5]This increase is statistically significant with $p < 0.05$: $\chi^2(1; N = 1047) = 4.32$.

[6]The tagging recall difference is statistically significant: $\chi^2(1; N = 1047) = 11.89; p < 0.001$.

[7]The tagging recall difference is not statistically significant: $\chi^2(1; N = 1047) = 0.02; p = 0.90$.

3.7 Levenshtein and Rules

In the second combined approach, we start with the Levenshtein results and filter them using the rules in order to further reduce ambiguity. The underlying idea is that in case of ambiguity, some of the Levenshtein-induced results will be correct and some will not. The correct ones will relate to the Rusyn words by known correspondences such as those implemented in the rules, while the incorrect ones will not. Hence, we took all Rusyn words matched (using Levenshtein) with more than one distinct RL word and transformed these RL words using the rules. We then checked whether the rules were able to "move" the RL words closer to Rusyn, i.e., whether the minimum Levenshtein distance of any transformed word was lower than the original Levenshtein distance. We only kept those RL words for which this check succeeded.

For example, the Levenshtein method matched the Rusyn word *береме* 'we take' with Polish *беремы*, Russian *берем*, *беремя*, Slovak *бериеме*, *берме*, and Ukrainian *берем*, *беремо*, all of which obtained a Levenshtein distance of 0.08$\overline{3}$ (one vowel substitution, insertion, or deletion in a word of length 6). The rule base contains rules which transform the Ukrainian ending -мо, the Russian ending -м, and the Polish ending -мы to Rusyn -ме. Hence, the Russian, Ukrainian and Polish forms are transformed to *береме*, reducing the distance to the Rusyn word to 0 (exact match). Therefore, we only keep *беремы* and *берем* as well as *беремо* and discard the other candidates. Since all three forms share the identical tag, the Rusyn word is morphologically disambiguated and only receives the correct reading as a verb in first person plural present tense.

This filtering approach resulted in an even further decrease of ambiguity while maintaining a high match rate: Average source word ambiguity dropped from 2.17 using the Levenshtein approach via 1.81 using rules and Levenshtein to 1.51 using Levenshtein and rules. This is close to the average source word ambiguity of 1.29 achieved when using exclusively the rules. However, a high amount of matched tokens could be maintained. While the combined Levenshtein and rules approach seems to be most successful in terms of matched words and ambiguity levels, the tagging recall actually suffers slightly.[8] This is to be expected, as reduc-

ing the ambiguity mainly increases the precision (sometimes at the expense of recall), which is not measured here.

4 Conclusion and Further Work

We have shown that a morphological dictionary for Rusyn can be created by leveraging existing resources of four etymologically closely related languages. Induction methods based on Levenshtein distance and hand-written philological rules significantly outperform exact match, both in terms of matched words and in terms of tagging recall. Also, the figures show that while there are significant differences in the individual contribution of each language, all languages contribute to the induction process.

Further work will be devoted to extending our work to lemmatization (which is available in the four RL dictionaries) and to making use of the newly created resources by statistical taggers (cf. Scherrer and Rabus (2017)).

Acknowledgments

We would like to thank Christine Grillborzer, Natalia Kotsyba, Bohdan Moskalevskyi, Andrianna Schimon, and Ruprecht von Waldenfels. The usual disclaimers apply.

Sources of external funding for our research include the German Research Foundation (DFG).

References

Oliver Christ. 1994. A modular and flexible architecture for an integrated corpus query system. In *Proceedings of COMPLEX'94: 3rd Conference on Computational Lexicography and Text Research*, pages 23–32.

Tomaž Erjavec, Ştefan Bruda, Ivan Derzhanski, Ludmila Dimitrova, Radovan Garabík, Peter Holozan, Nancy Ide, Heiki-Jaan Kaalep, Natalia Kotsyba, Csaba Oravecz, Vladimír Petkevič, Greg Priest-Dorman, Igor Shevchenko, Kiril Simov, Lydia Sinapova, Han Steenwijk, Laszlo Tihanyi, Dan Tufiş, and Jean Véronis. 2010a. MULTEXT-east free lexicons 4.0. Slovenian language resource repository CLARIN.SI.

Tomaž Erjavec, Ivan Derzhanski, Dagmar Divjak, Anna Feldman, Mikhail Kopotev, Natalia Kotsyba, Cvetana Krstev, Aleksandar Petrovski, Behrang QasemiZadeh, Adam Radziszewski, Serge Sharoff, Paul Sokolovsky, Duško Vitas, and Katerina Zdravkova. 2010b. MULTEXT-east

---

[8] The difference in tagging recall compared to Levenshtein is again not statistically significant: $\chi^2(1; N = 1\,047) = 0.34; p = 0.56$.

non-commercial lexicons 4.0. Slovenian language resource repository CLARIN.SI.

Tomaž Erjavec. 2012. MULTEXT-East: Morphosyntactic resources for Central and Eastern European languages. *Language Resources and Evaluation*, 1(46):131–142.

Patrick A. V. Hall and Geoff R. Dowling. 1980. Approximate string matching. *ACM Computing Surveys*, 12(4):381–402.

Mans Hulden. 2009. Foma: a finite-state compiler and library. In *Proceedings of the Demonstrations Session at EACL 2009*, pages 29–32, Athens, Greece, April. Association for Computational Linguistics.

Natalia Kotsyba, Andriy Mykulyak, and Ihor V. Shevchenko. 2011. UGTag: morphological analyzer and tagger for the Ukrainian language. In Stanisław Goźdź-Roszkowski, editor, *Explorations across Languages and Corpora*, pages 69–82, Frankfurt a. M.

V. I. Levenshtein. 1966. Binary Codes Capable of Correcting Deletions, Insertions and Reversals. *Soviet Physics Doklady*, 10:707–710, February.

Paul R. Magocsi. 2015. *With Their Backs to the Mountains: A History of Carpathian Rus' and Carpatho-Rusyns*. Central European University Press, Budapest.

Gideon S. Mann and David Yarowsky. 2001. Multipath translation lexicon induction via bridge languages. In *Proceedings of the Second Meeting of the North American Chapter of the Association for Computational Linguistics (NAACL 2001)*, pages 151–158, Pittsburgh, PA, USA.

Gary Mokotoff. 1997. Soundexing and genealogy. http://www.avotaynu.com/soundex.htm. Accessed: 2016-12-20.

Anna Plishkova. 2009. *Language and national identity: Rusyns south of Carpathians*, volume 14 of *Classics of Carpatho-Rusyn scholarship*. Columbia University Press and East European Monographs, New York.

Stefan M. Pugh. 2009. *The Rusyn language: A grammar of the literary standard of Slovakia with reference to Lemko and Subcarpathian Rusyn*, volume 476 of *Languages of the World/Materials*. Lincom Europa, München.

Achim Rabus and Andrianna Šymon. 2015. Na novŷch putjach isslidovanja rusyns'kŷch dialektu: Korpus rozhovornoho rusyns'koho jazŷka. In Kvetoslava Koporová, editor, *Rusyn'skŷj literaturnŷj jazŷk na Slovakiji: Zbornyk referativ z IV. Midžinarodnoho kongresu rusyn'skoho jazŷka*, pages 40–54. Prjašiv.

Achim Rabus. 2015. Current developments in Carpatho-Rusyn speech – preliminary observations. In Patricia A. Krafcik and Valerij Ivanovyč Padjak,

editors, *Juvilejnyj zbirnyk na čest' profesora Pavla-Roberta Magočija*, pages 489–496. Užhorod.

Yves Scherrer and Achim Rabus. 2017. Multi-source morphosyntactic tagging for spoken Rusyn. In *Proceedings of the Fourth Workshop on NLP for Similar Languages, Varieties and Dialects (VarDial 2017)*, Valencia, Spain.

Yves Scherrer and Benoît Sagot. 2014. A language-independent and fully unsupervised approach to lexicon induction and part-of-speech tagging for closely related languages. In *Proceedings of LREC 2014*, pages 502–8, Reykjavik, Iceland.

Serge Sharoff, Mikhail Kopotev, Tomaz Erjavec, Anna Feldman, and Dagmar Divjak. 2008. Designing and evaluating Russian tagsets. In *Proceedings of LREC 2008*, Marrakech, Morocco.

H. A. Skrypnyk, editor. 2013. *Ukrajinci-Rusyny: Etnolinhvistyčni ta etnokul'turni procesy v istoryčnomu rozvytku*. Instytut mystectvoznavstva, fol'klorystyky ta etnolohiji im. M.T. Ryl's'koho, Kyjiv.

Alexander Teutsch. 2001. *Das Rusinische der Ostslowakei im Kontext seiner Nachbarsprachen*, volume 12 of *Heidelberger Publikationen zur Slavistik. A, Linguistische Reihe*. Lang, Frankfurt am Main, Berlin, Bern.

Ruprecht von Waldenfels and Achim Rabus. 2015. Recycling the Metropolitan: building an electronic corpus on the basis of the edition of the Velikie Minei Čet'i. *Scripta & e-Scripta*, 14–15:27–38.

Ruprecht von Waldenfels and Michał Woźniak. 2017. SpoCo – a simple and adaptable web interface for dialect corpora. *Journal for Language Technology and Computational Linguistics*, 31(1).

Curt Woolhiser. 2005. Political borders and dialect divergence/convergence in Europe. In Peter Auer, Frans Hinskens, and Paul Kerswill, editors, *Dialect change*, pages 236–262. Cambridge Univ. Press, Cambridge.

The Universal Dependencies Treebank for Slovenian

Kaja Dobrovoljc[1], Tomaž Erjavec[2] and Simon Krek[3]

[1]Trojina, Institute for Applied Slovene Studies, Trg republike 3, 1000 Ljubljana, Slovenia
[2]Dept. of Knowledge Technologies, Jožef Stefan Institute, Jamova cesta 39, 1000 Ljubljana, Slovenia
[3]AI Laboratory, Jožef Stefan Institute, Jamova cesta 39, 1000 Ljubljana, Slovenia
`kaja.dobrovoljc@trojina.si`
`tomaz.erjavec@ijs.si`
`simon.krek@ijs.si`

Abstract

This paper introduces the Universal Dependencies Treebank for Slovenian. We overview the existing dependency treebanks for Slovenian and then detail the conversion of the ssj200k treebank to the framework of Universal Dependencies version 2. We explain the mapping of part-of-speech categories, morphosyntactic features, and the dependency relations, focusing on the more problematic language-specific issues. We conclude with a quantitative overview of the treebank and directions for further work.

1 Introduction

In syntactic parsing and the field of data-driven natural language processing in general, there has been a growing tendency to harmonize the numerous annotations schemes, developed for linguistic annotation of individual languages or specific language resources, that have prevented direct comparisons of annotated data and the performance of the resultant NLP tools. To overcome this heterogeneity inhibiting both theoretical and engineering advancements in the field, the Universal Dependencies[1] annotation scheme provides a universal inventory of morphological and syntactic categories and guidelines for their application, while also allowing for language-specific extensions, when necessary (Nivre, 2015).

The scheme is based on previous similar standardization projects (Marneffe et al., 2014; Petrov et al., 2012; Zeman, 2008), and has recently been substantially modified to its second version (UD v2), following five successive releases of treebanks pertaining to UD v1 (Nivre et al., 2016). In the v2.0 release[2], 72 treebanks for 47 different languages have been released, including the reference (written) Slovenian UD Treebank, set forward in the remainder of this paper.

2 Dependency Treebanks for Slovenian

The Slovenian UD Treebank represents the third generation of syntactically annotated corpora in Slovenian. The first was the Slovene Dependency Treebank (Džeroski et al., 2006), based on the Prague Dependency Treebank (PDT) annotation scheme (Hajičová et al., 1999) and consisting of approximately 30,000 tokens taken from the Slovenian component of the parallel MULTEXT-East corpus (Erjavec, 2012), i.e., the Slovenian translation of the novel "1984" by George Orwell.

As the PDT's scheme for analytical layer proved to be too complex given the financial and temporal constraints of subsequent projects, a new, simplified syntactic annotation scheme was developed within the JOS project (Erjavec et al., 2010). Within this scheme, the syntactic annotation layer consists of only 10 dependency relations, following the general assumption that specific syntactic constructions can be retrieved by combining these labels with the underlying word-level morphosyntactic descriptions (MSDs), wherein the JOS MSD tagset[3] is identical to the tagset defined in the MULTEXT-East Version 4 morphosyntactic specifications for Slovene (Erjavec, 2012).

The JOS annotation scheme was first applied to the jos100k corpus (Erjavec et al., 2010) consisting of approximately 100,000 tokens, sampled from the FidaPLUS reference corpus of written Slovene (Arhar and Gorjanc, 2007), and later extended to a larger sample of additional 400,000

---

[1]`http://universaldependencies.org/`

[2]While work on the individual treebanks for UD v2.0 has been finished, this version has, at the time of the writing of this paper, not yet been officially released.

[3]`http://nl.ijs.si/jos/msd/`

Proceedings of the 6th Workshop on Balto-Slavic Natural Language Processing, pages 33–38,
Valencia, Spain, 4 April 2017. ©2017 Association for Computational Linguistics

tokens in the Communication in Slovene (SSJ) project,[4] released as the ssj500k training corpus, with the latest version being v1.4 (Krek et al., 2015). The corpus is manually annotated with MSDs and lemmas but, due to financial constrains, only approximately one half (235,000) of the tokens were annotated on the syntactic layer. This subcorpus, known as the ssj200k treebank, currently represents the largest and the most representative collection of manually syntactically annotated data in Slovenian. It has been used in the development of several data-driven annotation tools (Grčar et al., 2012; Dobrovoljc et al., 2012; Ljubešić and Erjavec, 2016) and was chosen as the basis[5] for the construction of the Slovenian UD Treebank, using the conversion process described below.

3 Conversion from JOS to UD

To maintain a long-term compatibility between the two resources and maximize the level of consistency, the ssj200k conversion from JOS to UD annotation scheme was designed as a completely automatic procedure. Due to several discrepancies between the two annotation schemes, however, numerous conversion rules have been compiled on both morphological and syntactic level, whereas the tokenization, sentence segmentation and lemmatization principles of the original ssj200k treebank (currently) remain unchanged. In particular, we haven't used the option where tokens containing several (syntactic) words can be decomposed; this remains as future work.

3.1 Mapping of Morphosyntax

In terms of POS categorization, UD introduces a more fine-grained tagset of 17 POS categories in comparison with 12 POS categories in JOS, as it distinguishes between different types of (JOS-defined) verbs (AUX vs. VERB), conjunctions (CCONJ vs. SCONJ), characters (SYM vs. PUNCT), on the one hand, and subsumes the JOS Abbreviation POS as part of the X UD POS, on the other. A particularly challenging new category is the determiner (DET), reserved for nominal modifiers expressing the reference of the noun

phrase in context, not traditionally used in Slavic grammars. For its conversion, a lexicon-oriented approach was adopted, in which pronominal sub-categories in JOS were classified as either DET or PRON based on their typical syntactic behavior and their inflectional features, regardless of their context-specific syntactic role (Figure 1). Thus, predominantly pro-adjectival sub-categories (e.g. possessive or demonstrative pronouns) were converted to DET, while pro-nominal (e.g., personal pronouns) remained annotated as PRON, with lemmas in some sub-categories distributed between both POS categories (e.g., the JOS indefinite pronouns *nekdo*.PRON "somebody" vs. *mnog*.DET "many"). Similarly, a pre-determined list of indefinite quantifiers (e.g., *nekaj* "some", *več* "more", *veliko* "a-lot"), annotated as adverbs in JOS, has also been converted to DET.

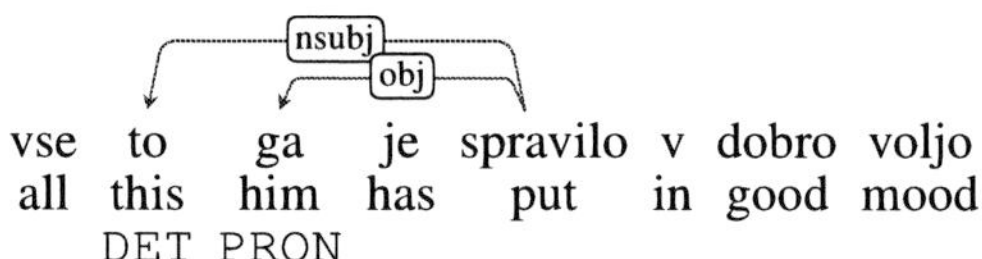

Figure 1: The annotation of JOS demonstrative (*to*) and personal (*ga*) pronouns in UD.

For the Slovenian UD Treebank 22 morphological features have been adopted, among which four are language- (Gender[psor], Number[psor], i.e., gender and number of the possessor with possessive adjectives) or treebank-specific (NumForm, Variant). In addition to the features not expressed morphologically in Slovenian (Evident), or not identifiable using automatic procedures (Polite), the Slovenian Treebank currently also lacks the universal Voice feature, as no morphological distinction has been made between predicative and attributive uses of participles in the JOS annotation scheme (e.g., *ukradena denarnica* "a stolen wallet" vs. *denarnica je bila ukradena* "the wallet was stolen").

The morphological layer conversion from JOS to UD is performed by a script which uses two semi-ordered tables (one for mapping the POS and the other for features). In total, the POS mapping contains 107 rules, of which 22 simply map a combination of the JOS POS and features to an UD POS, while 85 also specify the lemma of the token. There is only one rule that also takes into account the syntactic relation of the token, namely

---

[4] http://www.slovenscina.eu/

[5] It should be noted that several errata were discovered in ssj500k v1.4 in the process of conversion to UD v2.0. These were corrected and a new version of ssj500k will be released shortly. It is the new version that was used as the basis for the conversion to UD v2.0.

that for mapping an JOS auxiliary verb to the UD AUX or VERB. The feature mapping table contains 106 rules, of which 85 map a combination of the JOS POS and features, and possibly the already mapped UD POS to a UD feature, and 21 which are lemma-dependent.

3.2 Mapping of Syntax

Although both the JOS and the UD annotation scheme are based on the dependency grammar theory and adopt similar principles regarding the primacy of content words over function words, there are several significant differences between the two frameworks. Most notably, the UD annotation scheme introduces a much broader scope of syntactic analysis in comparison with JOS, where priority was given to parsing of predicates and their valency arguments, whereas semantically 'peripheral' sentence elements, such as sentence adverbs, discourse particles, interjections, vocatives, apposition, punctuation, clausal coordination, juxtaposition, etc. did not receive any syntactic analysis in JOS (as exemplified in Figure 2).

Secondly, the UD scheme also incorporates a much more detailed set of dependency relations (37 universal labels) than JOS (10 labels), as illustrated by the example given in Figure 3, in which the JOS *Atr* relation, intended for annotation of any head-modifier relation in a nominal phrase, converts to various types of nominal dependents in UD, such as different types of modifiers (amod, nmod, nummord, advmod, det, acl). In the same way, no distinction is made in JOS regarding the different syntactic structures of the dependents, whereas UD differentiates between nominal (nsubj, obj/iobj, obl) and clausal (csubj, ccomp, advcl) dependents performing the same syntactic role (see, for example, the two annotations of JOS *Obj* in Figure 2).

On the other hand, some semantic information is lost when converting data from JOS to UD, as JOS distinguishes between different types of arguments given their semantic role, such as between different types of adverbials or between semantically (non-)obligatory prepositional phrases, whereas UD only adopts the distinction between core arguments (i.e., subjects, objects, clausal complements) on the one hand, and oblique modifiers on the other, regardless of the degree of their obligatoriness in terms of valency and semantics.

In addition to categorization differences, the principles for determining the head-dependant direction mostly remain the same, with the exception of some specific constructions and the copula relation, in which the copula is dependent on the non-verbal predicate (see the cop relation in Figures 2 and 3).

In total, 32 different dependency relations have been used in the Slovenian UD treebank, including three extensions, i.e., cc:preconj for annotation of preconjuncts, flat:name for relations within personal names, and flat:foreign for relations within strings of foreign tokens. The eight missing universal relations in the treebank relate either to phenomena that do not occur in Slovenian (clf, compound), have not been found in the ssj200k treebank (dislocated, goeswith, reparandum) or do not enable reliable automatic identification (list, orphan, vocative).[6]

Among many syntactic particularities that have also be identified in other Slavic languages (Zeman, 2015), language-specific issues requiring additional consideration in the future include the treatment of (in)direct objects (with the iobj label currently only assigned in case of two competing objects), the inventory of TAMVE particles that could have been annotated as AUX/aux (such as *ne* "not", *lahko* "may" or *naj* "should"), and the treatment of the *se* reflexive pronoun (currently annotated as expl in Slovenian, regardless of its specific semantic role).

In total, the script for conversion of syntactic layer includes approximately 250 rules for dependency relation identification and/or head attachment, taking into account the lexical, morphological and syntactic features of individual tokens, their dependants or parents, as well as the features of tokens in the surrounding context. The conversion is performed in several iterations over tokens of a sentence, starting with the conversion of existing JOS-annotated constructions, and followed by different heuristics for annotation of previously un-annotated phenomena, including rules for root identification and punctuation attachment. In the last stage of the conversion, some mistakes and inconsistencies identified in the original ssj200k corpus are also corrected.

---

[6]Some of these relations, however, do occur in the manually annotated Spoken Slovenian UD Treebank (Dobrovoljc and Nivre, 2016).

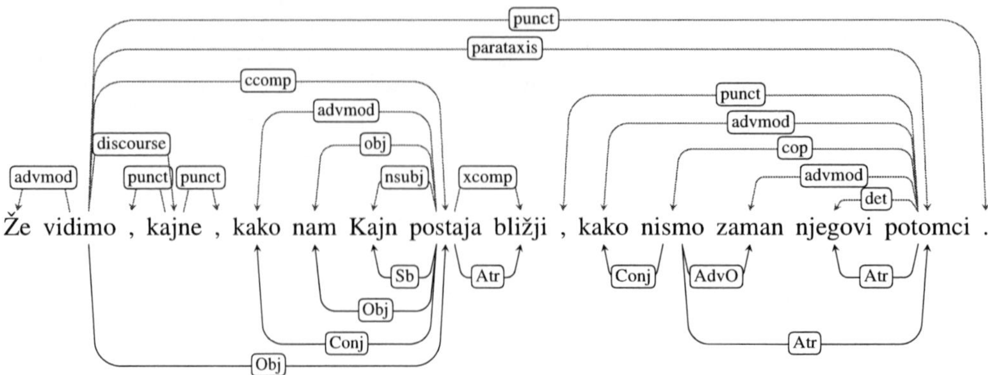

Figure 2: The comparison of UD (above) and JOS (below) annotation schemes in terms of complexity of dependency trees. All unanalysed tokens in JOS have been annotated as direct dependents of the root element.

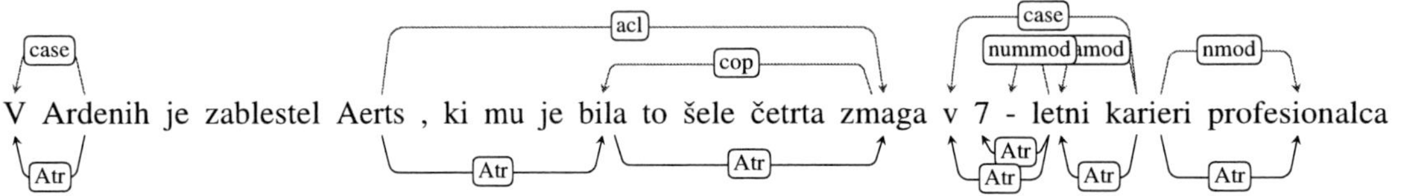

Figure 3: The comparison of UD (above) and JOS (below) annotation schemes in terms of complexity of dependency relation taxonomy.

4   The Slovenian UD Treebank

Many constructions in the ssj200k corpus could not be converted automatically, among which different types of clausal coordination, juxtaposition and predicate ellipsis prevail. Sentences with such constructions were therefore omitted from the conversion and the resulting Slovenian UD Treebank has about 40% less tokens than the original ssj200k treebank. Nevertheless, it remains comparable to UD treebanks available for other languages (Nivre and et al., 2016), both in terms of size and average sentence length (Table 1).

| | **sl-ud** | **ud-avg** | **ssj200k** |
	(UD 2.0)	(UD 1.4)	(v1.4)
tokens	140,670	191,697	235,865
sentences	8,000	10,560	11,411
tok./sent.	17.6	18.2	20.7

Table 1: The size of Slovenian UD Treebank (sl-ud) in comparison with the average UD Treebank (ud-avg) and the original ssj200k treebank.

This latest version of the Slovenian UD Treebank is planned to be released as part of UD version 2.0, scheduled for March 2017, under the CC BY-NC-SA 4.0 license. The treebank maintains full compatibility with the original ssj200k treebank, encoded according to the XML-based Text Encoding Initiative (TEI) Guidelines (TEI Consortium, 2012), by listing the original JOS morphosyntactic and syntactic annotations as part of the XPOSTAG and MISC CONLL-U[7] columns, respectively, and by keeping the original ssj200k/FidaPLUS sentence identifiers as part of the CONLL-U comment line.

5   Conclusions

This paper presented the latest Slovenian UD Treebank, obtained with automatic conversion from the ssj500k Treebank, which uses the JOS annotation scheme. This new language resource represents a valuable contribution to the Slovenian NLP landscape, where research on dependency parsing and syntactically annotated data is still scarce (Krek, 2012). In addition to further improvements of the treebank, both in terms of size and annotation quality, priority in future work

---

[7] http://universaldependencies.org/format.html

should be given to evaluation of impact of the new annotation scheme on tagging/parsing accuracy, and its potential transfer to other reference corpora for Slovenian.

Acknowledgments

The first author would like to than Joachim Nivre and Dan Zeman for their invaluable inspiration and help. The work presented here was supported by the IC1207 COST Action PARSEME (PARSing and Multi-word Expressions) and Slovenian research programme P2-0103 "Knowledge Technologies".

References

Špela Arhar and Vojko Gorjanc. 2007. Korpus FidaPLUS: Nova generacija slovenskega referenčnega korpusa (The FidaPLUS Corpus: A New Generation of the Slovene Reference Corpus). *Jezik in slovstvo*, 52(2):95–110.

Kaja Dobrovoljc and Joakim Nivre. 2016. The Universal Dependencies Treebank of Spoken Slovenian. In *Proceedings of the Tenth International Conference on Language Resources and Evaluation (LREC 2016)*, Paris, France, May. European Language Resources Association (ELRA).

Kaja Dobrovoljc, Simon Krek, and Jan Rupnik. 2012. Skladenjski razčlenjevalnik za slovenščino (Dependency Parser for Slovene). In *Zbornik Osme konference Jezikovne tehnologije*, Ljubljana, Slovenia.

Sašo Džeroski, Tomaž Erjavec, Nina Ledinek, Petr Pajas, Zdenek Žabokrtsky, and Andreja Žele. 2006. Towards a Slovene Dependency Treebank. In *Fifth International Conference on Language Resources and Evaluation, LREC'06*, Paris. ELRA.

Tomaž Erjavec, Darja Fišer, Simon Krek, and Nina Ledinek. 2010. The JOS Linguistically Tagged Corpus of Slovene. In *Proceedings of the Seventh conference on International Language Resources and Evaluation (LREC'10)*, Valletta, Malta, May. European Language Resources Association (ELRA).

Tomaž Erjavec. 2012. MULTEXT-East: morphosyntactic resources for Central and Eastern European languages. *Language Resources and Evaluation*, 46(1):131–142.

Miha Grčar, Simon Krek, and Kaja Dobrovoljc. 2012. Obeliks: statistični oblikoskladenjski označevalnik in lematizator za slovenski jezik (Obeliks: a statistical morphosyntactic tagger and lemmatiser for Slovene). In *Zbornik Osme konference Jezikovne tehnologije*, Ljubljana, Slovenia.

Eva Hajičová, Zdeněk Kirschner, and Petr Sgall. 1999. A Manual for Analytic Layer Annotation of the Prague Dependency Treebank (English translation). Technical report, ÚFAL MFF UK, Prague, Czech Republic.

Simon Krek, Kaja Dobrovoljc, Tomaž Erjavec, Sara Može, Nina Ledinek, and Nanika Holz. 2015. *Training corpus ssj500k 1.4*. Slovenian language resource repository CLARIN.SI.

Simon Krek. 2012. *Slovenski jezik v digitalni dobi – The Slovene Language in the Digital Age*. META-NET White Paper Series. Georg Rehm and Hans Uszkoreit (Series Editors). Springer. Available online at http://www.meta-net.eu/whitepapers.

Nikola Ljubešić and Tomaž Erjavec. 2016. Corpus vs. Lexicon Supervision in Morphosyntactic Tagging: the Case of Slovene. In *Proceedings of the Tenth International Conference on Language Resources and Evaluation (LREC 2016)*, Paris, France, may. European Language Resources Association (ELRA).

Marie-Catherine De Marneffe, Timothy Dozat, Natalia Silveira, Katri Haverinen, Filip Ginter, Joakim Nivre, and Christopher D. Manning. 2014. Universal Stanford Dependencies: a Cross-Linguistic Typology. In *Proceedings of the Ninth International Conference on Language Resources and Evaluation (LREC'14)*, Reykjavik, Iceland, May. European Language Resources Association (ELRA).

Joakim Nivre and et al. 2016. *Universal Dependencies 1.4*. LINDAT/CLARIN digital library at the Institute of Formal and Applied Linguistics, Charles University in Prague. http://hdl.handle.net/11234/1-1827.

Joakim Nivre, Marie-Catherine de Marneffe, Filip Ginter, Yoav Goldberg, Jan Hajic, Christopher D. Manning, Ryan McDonald, Slav Petrov, Sampo Pyysalo, Natalia Silveira, Reut Tsarfaty, and Daniel Zeman. 2016. Universal Dependencies v1: A Multilingual Treebank Collection. In *Proceedings of the Tenth International Conference on Language Resources and Evaluation (LREC 2016)*, Paris, France, May. European Language Resources Association (ELRA).

Joakim Nivre. 2015. Towards a Universal Grammar for Natural Language Processing. In Alexander Gelbukh, editor, *Computational Linguistics and Intelligent Text Processing*, volume 9041 of *Lecture Notes in Computer Science*, pages 3–16. Springer International Publishing.

Slav Petrov, Dipanjan Das, and Ryan McDonald. 2012. A Universal Part-of-Speech Tagset. In *Proceedings of the Eight International Conference on Language Resources and Evaluation (LREC'12)*, Istanbul, Turkey. European Language Resources Association (ELRA).

TEI Consortium, editor. 2012. *TEI P5: Guidelines for Electronic Text Encoding and Interchange*. TEI Consortium.

Daniel Zeman. 2008. Reusable Tagset Conversion Using Tagset Drivers. In *Proceedings of the 6th International Conference on Language Resources and Evaluation (LREC 2008)*, pages 213–218, Marrakech, Morocco. European Language Resources Association.

Daniel Zeman. 2015. Slavic Languages in Universal Dependencies. In *Proceedings of the conference "Natural Language Processing, Corpus Linguistics, E-learning"*, pages 151–163, Bratislava, Slovakia. RAM-Verlag.

Universal Dependencies for Serbian
in Comparison with Croatian and Other Slavic Languages

Tanja Samardžić
URPP Language and Space
University of Zürich
`tanja.samardzic@uzh.ch`

Mirjana Starović
Leksikom, Belgrade
`djelmas@eunet.rs`

Željko Agić
IT University of Copenhagen
`zeag@itu.dk`

Nikola Ljubešić
University of Zagreb
`nljubesi@ffzg.hr`

Abstract

The paper documents the procedure of building a new Universal Dependencies (UDv2) treebank for Serbian starting from an existing Croatian UDv1 treebank and taking into account the other Slavic UD annotation guidelines. We describe the automatic and manual annotation procedures, discuss the annotation of Slavic-specific categories (case governing quantifiers, reflexive pronouns, question particles) and propose an approach to handling deverbal nouns in Slavic languages.

1 Introduction

The notion Universal Dependencies (UD) refers to an international movement started with the goal to reduce to a minimum cross-linguistic variation in the formalisms used to label syntactic structure (McDonald et al., 2013; Nivre et al., 2016). This goal was defined following multilingual parsing campaigns (Buchholz and Marsi, 2006; Hajič et al., 2009) that revealed substantial cross-linguistic differences in the sets of labels and relations used in different treebanks, making it hard to compare parsers' performances across languages (McDonald and Nivre, 2007).

In this paper, we document the process of building a UD treebank for Serbian underlining the advantages of using the existing general framework, but also data and tools already available for other languages. The availability of shared resources is especially important for languages such as Serbian, which, more than 20 years after the publication of Penn Treebank (Marcus et al., 1994), still has no resource with annotated syntactic structure,

lagging behind its close relatives for which UD annotation is available.

Labeled as *automatic conversion with manual corrections* in the UD documentation,[1] our approach consists of four steps: 1) automatic porting of Croatian annotation to Serbian, 2) comparison and adaptation, 3) automatic conversion and correction, and 4) manual correction.

Despite the fact that Serbian can be parsed with the model already available for Croatian, as argued by Agić and Ljubešić (2015), building a Serbian treebank is useful for two reasons. First, it allows learning a more precise model for Serbian, taking into account important syntactic differences such as, for instance, the use of infinitive (Tiedemann and Ljubešić, 2012). Second, improvements and corrections in the Serbian treebank can be ported back and used for updating Croatian treebank. This does not only concern improvements in consistency resulting from detailed manual inspection, but also version updating. In particular, the currently available Croatian treebank follows the UD guidelines version 1 (UDv1), while Serbian follows the current version 2 (UDv2).

2 Applying Croatian Model to Serbian

To port the existing Croatian annotation to Serbian, we use the Croatian data and tools described by Agić and Ljubešić (2015).

The Serbian treebank consists of sentences that are aligned with Croatian sentences in the SETimes.HR corpus (Agić and Ljubešić, 2014) used to produce the first version of the Croatian UD treebank. As morphosyntactic annotation is needed as input for syntactic parsing, we

---

[1] `http://universaldependencies.org/`

Proceedings of the 6th Workshop on Balto-Slavic Natural Language Processing, pages 39–44,
Valencia, Spain, 4 April 2017. ©2017 Association for Computational Linguistics

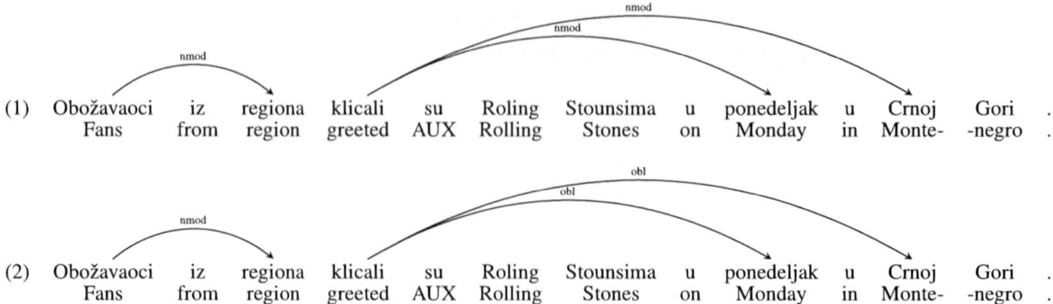

Figure 1: The difference between UDv1 (1) and UDv2 (2) in applying the label `nmod`.

In	Out	Context
auxpass	aux	ALL
csubjpass	csubj	ALL
dobj	obj	ALL
iobj	obl	ALL
nsubjpass	nsubj	ALL
mwe	fixed	ALL
remnant	orphan	ALL
dislocated	NA	ALL
name	flat	ALL
foreign	flat	ALL
nmod	obl	if the PoS of the head is V or A, or N if the lemma ends in *-nje*

Table 1: Automatic conversion from UD v1 to UD v2.

In	Out	Context
expl	NA	ALL
reparandum	NA	ALL
det	det:numgov	if the lemma is "koliko"
nummod	nummod:gov	if the word is a cardinal number and the head is in the genitive case
compound	amod	if the PoS is A
	nmod	if the PoS is N
	flat	otherwise if the lemma is not "sebe"
ALL	compound	if the lemma is "sebe"
ALL	det	if the word is a "possessive pronoun"
ALL	xcomp	if the head word is the modal "moći"

Table 2: Automatic version-independent updates.

add morphosyntactic definitions (MSD) following the modified Multext-East version 4 format (Erjavec, 2012) documented in the draft of version 5.[2] MSD annotation is first added automatically using the state-of-the-art Croatian tagger described by Ljubešić et al. (2016), and then corrected manually by two experts native in Serbian, resulting in gold MSD labels.

Once morphologically annotated, the Serbian side of SETimes.HR, coined SETimes.SR, was then parsed using the `mate-tools`, a graph-based dependency parser (Bohnet, 2010) trained on the Croatian UD v1.2 treebank data. The parser was trained with default parameters.

3   Category Comparison and Adaptation

In this step, we perform manual inspection of a sample of parsed sentences in order to decide what categories and relations to use for Serbian. We extract and evaluate a handful of examples of all annotated relations, comparing the annotation to the general guidelines and to the language-specific en-

[2]http://nl.ijs.si/ME/V5/msd/html/

tries for Croatian and other contemporary Slavic languages available in the current UD set: Bulgarian, Croatian, Czech, Polish, Russian, Slovak, Slovenian and Ukrainian.

We introduce two kinds of changes with respect to the initial set of categories implemented by the Croatian model. With the first set of changes, we convert general relations UDv1 to UDv2. With the second set of changes, we correct the existing annotation in order to resolve some of the issues raised on the UD web site and improve the descriptive adequacy of the annotation.

3.1   Version Updating

The most important conceptual novelty in the UDv2 guidelines, at least when it comes to Slavic syntax, is the treatment of core vs. oblique arguments of predicates. Based on well-established typological distinctions (Thompson, 1997; Andrews, 2007), UDv1 guidelines stated that a distinction should be made between core and oblique arguments, rather than between complements and adjuncts. Both `obj` and `iobj` were intended to be used for core arguments only, while other labels were intended for oblique arguments.

However, the Slavic treebanks that we consulted systematically use `iobj` to annotate oblique dependents. We believe that this is partly due to sometimes underspecified general guidelines and partly to the strong tradition of making the complement vs. adjunct distinction, which creates the need to distinguish between two kinds of oblique dependents (complements obligatory, adjuncts optional).

We adopt the distinction between core and oblique arguments by implementing the rows 3 and 4 in Table 1. We use `obj` only for direct objects (bare nominal dependents with accusative case) and the new label `obl` for all the other verb dependents, most of which are currently annotated with `iobj` in Croatian and all the other Slavic treebanks. Our new label `obl` includes Serbian counterparts of "dative subjects" indicated as a special construction in Russian documentation.

Another important change is narrowing the use of the relation `nmod` to the nominal domain, as illustrated in Figure 1. We implement this as shown in Table 1, row 11.

Three changes, (rows 1, 2, 5 in Table 1) are made following the UDv2 treatment of passive. We note that the change in the new version of the guidelines is convenient for describing Serbian, as well as other Slavic languages, because the distinction between passive and other intransitive constructions is considerably blurred in these languages.

Finally, we update the relations used for different kinds of conventionalised expressions (rows 6-10 in Table 1, NA as output means that the relation is removed from the list).

3.2 Version-independent Updates

A number of changes are made after inspecting Croatian counterparts of the constructions listed under "special constructions" in the UD language-specific documentations for Slavic languages (available only for Czech, Russian, and Bulgarian) with the goal to improve cross-linguistic parallelism. We make decisions on several issues discussed in this section.

The most prominent specific constructions, discussed in Czech and Russian documentations, are those involving **case governing quantifiers**, such as *koliko*, 'how much, how many', *nekoliko*

'some, several', *mnogo* 'much, many', *malo* 'little, few'. What is special in these constructions is that the case of the head nominal does not depend on the function of the nominal in a clause, but is determined by the quantifier (genitive case is required). To capture this phenomenon, general labels `nummod` and `det` are extended to `nummod:gov` and `det:numgov`, respectively. This specification is applied only in Czech and Russian, although it is relevant to the other Slavic languages too. In this case, we decide to follow Czech and Russian, as shown in Table 2, rows 3–4. We do not follow Czech in using `det:nummod` for those quantifiers that do not govern the case. Since this relation is syntactically equivalent to the simple `det` relation (quantifier agrees with the quantified noun in case), we leave the simple label.

The other constructions addressed in Czech documentation is "**reflexive pronoun**", whose short form can be assigned a whole range of functions. Czech documentation lists the following relations: `dobj`, `iobj`, `nmod`, `auxpass:reflex`, `expl`, and `discourse`. While annotation of this form is not explicitly addressed in the documentation of the other Slavic languages, it can have similar functions, which are likely to be annotated using different subsets of the relations listed above (for instance, the label `auxpass:reflex` is not used in any other Slavic language).

Croatian departs from all the other Slavic languages by using the relation `compound` for most of the instances of this form, rather than annotating fine-grained distinctions. This decision is based on the view of this form as a detachable morpheme belonging to the verb to which it is attached both in lexical and morphological sense. In this view, the "reflexive pronoun" becomes parallel with English or German verb particles, and the relation used for these particles can be applied to it. We note that this view is supported by substantial theoretical findings showing that the short reflexive form is not just a prosodic variant of the full reflexive pronoun and that, in fact, it is not a pronoun at all (Sells et al., 1987; Moskovljević, 1997). Furthermore, Reinhart and Siloni (2004) and Marelj (2004) argue that this form should be analysed in the same way in all its uses: as a free morpheme marking absence of one of the verb's core dependents. The functions listed above, and a whole range of other functions usually not mentioned in

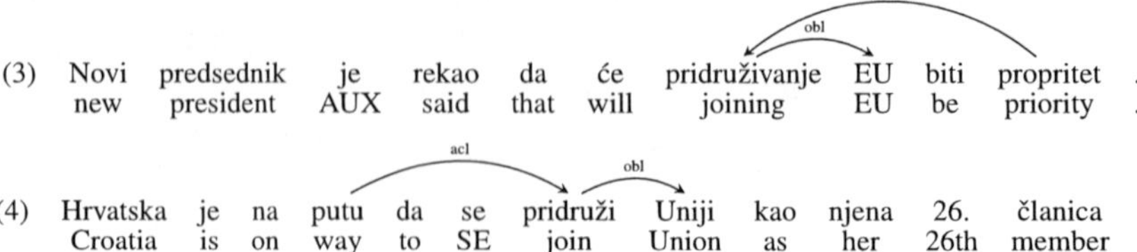

Figure 2: Parallelism between deverbal nouns (*pridruživanje*) and their source verbs (*pridružiti*).

grammars, are higher-level interpretations of the same syntactic form. Annotating these functions, in our opinion, should not be part of UD.

Based on these arguments, we follow Croatian in using the label `compound`, despite the fact that this is not in accordance with the other Slavic treebanks. We extend this relation to all instance of the short reflexive form and eliminate all the other labels (e.g., `dobj`), that are occasionally found in the initial annotation, as shown in the row 6 in Table 2. We also eliminate all the other uses of the relation `compound` (row 5 in Table 2).

The last specific construction, addressed in Bulgarian documentation, is the particle used to form **YES/NO questions**. This particle is assigned the relation `discourse` in Bulgarian, while the relation `mark` is used in Croatian. In this case too, we follow Croatian annotation as this particle does not link the sentence to a broader context, but rather marks the function of the sentence itself.

The revision of the relations resulted in removing two labels found not to be used in the annotation (rows 1-2 in Table 2).

In addition to the constructions listed in language-specific documentations, we note one more form whose annotation needs to be specifically documented: **deverbal nouns**. This category is not specific to Slavic languages, but its annotation might be due to a specific realisation of the distinction between result and process deverbal nominals (Grimshaw, 1990).

Deverbal nouns can have a different degree of nominal and verbal properties across languages and within a language. Those whose meaning is a result are closer to the nominal side of the scale, while those that describe a process are closer to the verbal side. While result nouns can be annotated as other abstract nouns, process deverbal nouns keep the initial verbal (non-finite) dependencies, which means that their dependents should be annotated in the same way as the dependents

Size in	Automatic		Manual		Start–End	
Tokens	N	%	N	%	N	%
26708	4499	17	3785	14	7423	28

Table 3: The amount of changed annotations in automatic conversion, manual correction, and in the resulting treebank compared with the initial annotation ported from Croatian (Start–End).

of the verbs from which they are derived (like infinitives and some participles). Some examples in general UD guidelines suggest that English *-ing* forms with nominal functions are treated as verbs in this respect.

Serbian (and Croatian) morphology allows drawing a relatively clear difference between result and process deverbal nouns: the suffix *-nje* is used to derive process nouns in a rather regular way, while a number of idiosyncratic suffixes are used to derive result nouns. We mark this distinction by annotating the dependents of deverbal nouns ending in *-nje* ((3) in Figure 2) in the same way as the dependents of the non-finite forms of their source verbs ((3) in Figure 2), while keeping their nominal function. We treat the other deverbal nouns (derived with other suffixes) as regular nominals.

As a result of this step, we did not manage to eliminate all the differences with other Slavic treebanks, but we believe that our analysis provides a good basis for future steps in this direction. Relatively frequent versioning planned within the UD work framework makes room for continuous improvements and adaptations. This can be expected to move the current annotation to a more synchronised state through active cross-linguistic exchange enabled by the common framework and based on sound arguments.

4 Automatic Conversion and Manual Correction

Here we describe the implementation of the described updates in 1200 sentences, out of the planned 3900.

Tables 1 and 2 show the full list of changes introduced automatically by means of a custom Python script that takes as input parsed sentences in the CoNLL-X format and outputs the same format with the changes. The tables contain all the changes discussed in the previous section, together with a number of changes performed to address issues concerning the current Croatian annotation that have been raised so far on the UD web site and that have not been addressed through the version updating (rows 5, 7, 8 in Table 2).

The processed files are then imported into DgAnnotator[3] and corrected by three experts, Croatian native speakers, coordinated and supervised by a Serbian expert. Manual correction included idiosyncratic or complex cases that could not be performed automatically. In addition to parser's errors, these corrections addressed shortcomings identified on the UD web site. In particular, we manually correct instances of relative pronouns, such as *što* 'what', *koji* 'which', that were annotated with `mark`. We assign such words a function that they have in the subordinate clause, mostly `nsubj` and `obj`.

Table 3 shows the amount of corrections made in each step. The counts refer to the number of tokens for which either the dependency link or relations are changed. We can see that a total of 28% tokens were changed between the initial ported annotation and the final Serbian treebank. Slightly more changes were made automatically than manually (17% vs. 14%). The fact that the sum of the changes is higher than the difference between initial and final annotation means that the annotators had to change back a number of annotations after the automatic conversion. This number is rather low (3% of tokens) but further inspections might show a way to improve automatic conversion. The percentage of manually corrected annotations is lower than it would be expected based on the parsing accuracy score of 79.6% reported by Agić and Ljubešić (2015). This is due to the fact that the Serbian side of the SETimes corpus is very similar to the Croatian side on which the

parser was trained.

5 Conclusion and Future Work

By describing the development of a new UD treebank for Serbian, we have demonstrated how the existing UD infrastructure can be used to improve cross-linguistic parallelism in syntactic annotation, but also to reduce costs of development of new treebanks. Such an infrastructure is especially useful for Slavic languages, whose syntax is similar enough to take advantage of cross-linguistic automatic parsing and common annotation guidelines.

The remaining 2700 sentences will be annotated and made available through the UD infrastructure by the end of April 2017, together with our language-specific guidelines and detailed statistics.

Acknowledgments

The annotation described in this paper is funded by the Swiss National Science Foundation grant No. 160501. We are thankful to our collaborators Daša Farkaš, Danijela Merkler and Matea Srebačić for their valuable contribution.

References

Željko Agić and Nikola Ljubešić. 2014. The SETimes.HR linguistically annotated corpus of Croatian. In *Proceedings of the Ninth International Conference on Language Resources and Evaluation (LREC'14)*, Reykjavik, Iceland. European Language Resources Association (ELRA).

Željko Agić and Nikola Ljubešić. 2015. Universal dependencies for Croatian (that work for Serbian, too). In *The 5th Workshop on Balto-Slavic Natural Language Processing*, pages 1–8, Hissar, Bulgaria, September. INCOMA Ltd. Shoumen, BULGARIA.

Avery D. Andrews. 2007. The major functions of the noun phrase. In Timothy Shopen, editor, *Language Typology and Syntactic Description Clause Structure*, pages 132–223, Cambridge, United Kingdom. Cambridge University Press.

Bernd Bohnet. 2010. Top accuracy and fast dependency parsing is not a contradiction. In *Proceedings of the 23rd International Conference on Computational Linguistics (Coling 2010)*, pages 89–97, Beijing, China, August. Coling 2010 Organizing Committee.

Sabine Buchholz and Erwin Marsi. 2006. CoNLL-X shared task on multilingual dependency parsing.

---

[3]`http://medialab.di.unipi.it/Project/ QA/Parser/DgAnnotator/`

In *Proceedings of the Tenth Conference on Computational Natural Language Learning (CoNLL-X)*, pages 149–164, New York City, June. Association for Computational Linguistics.

Tomaž Erjavec. 2012. MULTEXT-East: Morphosyntactic resources for central and eastern European languages. *Lang. Resour. Eval.*, 46(1):131–142, March.

Jane Grimshaw. 1990. *Argument Structure*. MIT Press, Cambridge, Mass.

Jan Hajič, Massimiliano Ciaramita, Richard Johansson, Daisuke Kawahara, Maria Antònia Martí, Lluís Màrquez, Adam Meyers, Joakim Nivre, Sebastian Padó, Jan Štěpánek, Pavel Straňák, Mihai Surdeanu, Nianwen Xue, and Yi Zhang. 2009. The conll-2009 shared task: Syntactic and semantic dependencies in multiple languages. In *Proceedings of the Thirteenth Conference on Computational Natural Language Learning (CoNLL 2009): Shared Task*, pages 1–18, Boulder, Colorado, June. Association for Computational Linguistics.

Nikola Ljubešić, Filip Klubička, Željko Agić, and Ivo-Pavao Jazbec. 2016. New inflectional lexicons and training corpora for improved morphosyntactic annotation of Croatian and Serbian. In Nicoletta Calzolari (Conference Chair), Khalid Choukri, Thierry Declerck, Sara Goggi, Marko Grobelnik, Bente Maegaard, Joseph Mariani, Helene Mazo, Asuncion Moreno, Jan Odijk, and Stelios Piperidis, editors, *Proceedings of the Tenth International Conference on Language Resources and Evaluation (LREC 2016)*, Paris, France, May. European Language Resources Association (ELRA).

Mitchell Marcus, Beatrice Santorini, and Mary Ann Marcinkiewicz. 1994. Building a large annotated corpus of english: the penn treebank. *Computational Linguistics*, 19(2):313–330.

Marijana Marelj. 2004. *Middles and argument structure across languages*. LOT, Utrecht.

Ryan McDonald and Joakim Nivre. 2007. Characterizing the errors of data-driven dependency parsing models. In *Proceedings of the 2007 Joint Conference on Empirical Methods in Natural Language Processing and Computational Natural Language Learning (EMNLP-CoNLL)*, pages 122–131, Prague, Czech Republic, June. Association for Computational Linguistics.

Ryan McDonald, Joakim Nivre, Yvonne Quirmbach-Brundage, Yoav Goldberg, Dipanjan Das, Kuzman Ganchev, Keith Hall, Slav Petrov, Hao Zhang, Oscar Täckström, Claudia Bedini, Núria Bertomeu Castelló, and Jungmee Lee. 2013. Universal dependency annotation for multilingual parsing. In *Proceedings of the 51st Annual Meeting of the Association for Computational Linguistics (Volume 2: Short Papers)*, pages 92–97, Sofia, Bulgaria, August. Association for Computational Linguistics.

Jasmina Moskovljević. 1997. Leksička detranzitivizacija i analiza pravih povratnih glagola u srpskom jeziku. *Južnoslovenski filolog*, LII:107–114.

Joakim Nivre, Marie-Catherine de Marneffe, Filip Ginter, Yoav Goldberg, Jan Hajič, Christopher D. Manning, Ryan McDonald, Slav Petrov, Sampo Pyysalo, Natalia Silveira, Reut Tsarfaty, and Daniel Zeman. 2016. Universal dependencies v1: A multilingual treebank collection. In Nicoletta Calzolari (Conference Chair), Khalid Choukri, Thierry Declerck, Sara Goggi, Marko Grobelnik, Bente Maegaard, Joseph Mariani, Helene Mazo, Asuncion Moreno, Jan Odijk, and Stelios Piperidis, editors, *Proceedings of the Tenth International Conference on Language Resources and Evaluation (LREC 2016)*, Paris, France, May. European Language Resources Association (ELRA).

Tanya Reinhart and Tal Siloni. 2004. Against the unaccusative analysis of reflexives. In Artemis Alexiadou, Elena Anagnostopoulou, and Martin Everaert, editors, *The Unaccusativity Puzzle: Studies on the syntax-lexicon interface*, pages 159–181. Oxford University Press.

Peter Sells, Annie Zaenen, and Draga Zec. 1987. Reflexivization variation: Relations between syntax, semantics, and lexical structure. In Masayo Iida and Draga Zec Stephen Wechsler, editors, *Working Papers in Grammatical Theory and Discourse Structure*, pages 169–238, Stanford, CA. CSLI.

Sandra A. Thompson. 1997. Discourse motivations for the core-oblique distinction as a language universal. In Akio Kamio, editor, *Directions in Functional Linguistics*, pages 59–82, Amsterdam, the Netherlands. Benjamins.

Jörg Tiedemann and Nikola Ljubešić. 2012. Efficient discrimination between closely related languages. In *Proceedings of COLING 2012*, pages 2619–2634, Mumbai, India, December. The COLING 2012 Organizing Committee.

Spelling Correction for Morphologically Rich Language:
a Case Study of Russian

Alexey Sorokin

Moscow State University / GSP-1, Leninskie Gory, 1
Faculty of Mathematics and Mechanics, 119991, Moscow, Russia
Moscow Institute of Physics and Technology / Institutskij per., 9,
Faculty of Innovations and High Technologies,
141701, Dolgoprudny, Russia
`alexey.sorokin@list.ru`

Abstract

We present an algorithm for automatic correction of spelling errors on the sentence level, which uses noisy channel model and feature-based reranking of hypotheses. Our system is designed for Russian and clearly outperforms the winner of SpellRuEval-2016 competition. We show that language model size has the greatest influence on spelling correction quality. We also experiment with different types of features and show that morphological and semantic information also improves the accuracy of spellchecking.

The task of automatic spelling correction has applications in different areas including correction of search queries, spellchecking in browsers and text editors etc. It attracted intensive attention in early era of modern NLP. Many researchers addressed both the problems of effective candidates generation (Kernighan et al., 1990; Brill and Moore, 2000) and their adequate ranking (Golding and Roth, 1999; Whitelaw et al., 2009). Recently, the focus has moved to close but separate areas of text normalization (Han et al., 2013) and grammar errors correction (Ng et al., 2014), though the task of spellchecking is far from being perfectly solved. Most of early works were conducted for English for which NLP tasks are usually easier than for other languages due to simplicity of its morphology and strict word order. Also there were studies for Arabic (papers of QALB-2014 Shared Task (Ng et al., 2014)) and Chinese (Wu et al., 2013), but for most languages the problem still is open. In context of Slavic languages, there were just a few works including Sorokin and Shavrina (2016) for Russian, Richter et al. (2012) for Czech and Hladek et al. (2013) for Slovak.

However, spelling correction becomes actual again due to intensive growth of social media. Indeed, corpora of Web texts including blogs, microblogs, forums etc. become the main sources for corpus studies. Most of these corpora are very large so they are collected and processed automatically with only limited manual correction. Hence, most texts in such corpora contain various types of spelling variation, from mere typos and orthographic errors to dialectal and sociolinguistic peculiarities. Moreover, orthographic errors are unavoidable since the more social media texts we have, the higher is the fraction of those, whose authors are not well-educated and therefore tend to make mistakes. That increases the percentage of out-of-vocabulary words in text, which affects the quality of any further NLP task from lemmatization to any kind of parsing or information extraction. Summarizing, it is desirable to detect and correct at least undoubtable misspellings in Web texts with high precision.

Unfortunately, there were very few studies dealing with spellchecking for real-world Web texts, e.g. LiveJournal or Facebook. Most authors investigated spelling correction in a rather restricted fashion. They focused on selecting a correct word from a small pre-defined confusion set (e.g., *adopt/adapt*), skipping a problem of detecting misprints or generating the set of possible corrections. Often researchers did not deal with real-world errors just randomly introducing typos in every word with some probability. Therefore, spelling correction has no "intelligent baseline" algorithm such as trigram HMM-models for morphological parsing or CBOW vectors for distributional similarity. One of the goals of our work is to propose such a baseline. The principal feature of our approach is that it works with entire sentences, not on the level of separate words.

A serious problem for research on spellcheck-

45

Proceedings of the 6th Workshop on Balto-Slavic Natural Language Processing, pages 45–53,
Valencia, Spain, 4 April 2017. ©2017 Association for Computational Linguistics

ing is the lack of publicly available datasets for spelling correction in different languages. Fortunately, recently such a corpus was created for Russian during SpellRuEval-2016 competition (Sorokin et al., 2016). Russian is rather complex for NLP tasks because of its developed nominal and verb morphology and free word order. Therefore it is well-suited for extensive testing of spelling correction algorithms, although our results are applicable to any other language having similar properties.

We propose a reranking algorithm for automatic spelling correction and evaluate it on SpellRuEval-2016 dataset. The paper is organized as follows: Section 1 summarizes previous work on automatic spelling correction focusing on context-sensitive approaches, Section 2 contains our algorithm, Section 3 describes test data, Section 4 analyzes the performance of our system depending on different settings and we conclude in Section 5.

1 Previous Work

Here we give a brief review of literature on spellchecking especially dealing with context-sensitive error correction.

- Edit distance model was introduced by Levenshtein (1966) and Damerau (1964), Kukich (1992) showed that about 80% of errors lie on distance of 1 edit.

- Weighted variants of error distances were considered in Kernighan et al. (1990) and Brill and Moore (2000).

- Toutanova and Moore (2002) added a pronunciation model for spelling correction, phonetic features were also exploited by Schaback and Li (2007).

- Noisy channel model of error correction based on ngrams appears in Mays et al. (1991) and Brill and Moore (2000). Other context-sensitive approaches include Golding and Roth (1999) and Hirst and Budanitsky (2005).

- Different sources of information were integrated by means of the final classifier in Flor (2012), who mainly uses semantic features, and Schaback and Li (2007), utilizing syntactic, phonetic and semantic information. Feature-based approach was also pursued by Xiong et al. (2014).

Since our method is also based on reranking, we compare it with the works of the last group. First, we work with sentences and consider each word as a potential typo while Schaback and Li (2007) and Flor (2012) try to correct isolated words using context features. To be applied to real-world texts their algorithm must be preceeded by a preliminary error detection stage which is not necessary in our approach. This makes the model more robust since error detection is a nontrivial task for social media texts due to high number of slang, proper names (including colloquial) etc. By its architecture our model more resembles Xiong et al. (2014), however, the set of features used differs significantly reflecting the difference between Chinese and Russian. As far as we know, our model is one of the first HMM-based systems used for spelling correction of a morphologically rich language.

There are also very few works dealing with spelling correction of Russian texts: Panina et al. (2013) uses feature-based approach to correct search queries. Works for other Slavic languages include Richter et al. (2012) for Czech, who used a feature-based method to correct errors in words given their context, and Hladek et al. (2013) who performed unsupervised error correction for Slovak. The present work is a part of ongoing research started by Sorokin and Shavrina (2016). The algorithm the latter is also based on reranking, however, they did not use morphological and semantic features. Actually, the effectiveness of these features was under question and one of the objectives of the work was to test their applicability in case of morphologically rich languages. We answer to this question positively.

2 Algoritm Description

Our system performs context-sensitive spelling error correction. The workcycle is divided into three main steps: candidate generation, n-best list extraction and feature-based ranking of hypotheses. Candidates are generated for every word in sentence since in real-world applications it is not known which words are mistyped. Pairs of consecutive words are also processed to deal with space insertion. There are four types of candidates:

1. Words from the dictionary on Levenstein distance of 1 from the observed word.

2. Words having the same phonetic code by the METAPHONE-style algorithm of Sorokin and Shavrina (2016).

3. Dictionary words or word pairs obtained by space/hyphen insertion/deletion. We also write several rules for candidate generation encoding frequent error patterns, for example the informal writing of *-*цца* instead of *-ться* or *-тся* in the infinitive suffix (**нравицца* ↦ *нравится*).

4. A manually written correction list including colloquial writings as **ваще* ↦ *вообще*, **оч* ↦ *очень*.

Not all candidate words have the same score. We calculate the frequencies of different errors on SpellRuEval development set and set the probabilities of different error types (Levenshtein correction, phonetic correction, space insertion/deletion etc.) proportional to their frequencies. This constitutes the basic error model $P(t|s)$ for transforming the hidden word s into observed word t.[1]

We construct hypotheses for the whole sentence choosing one word from each candidate set and extract n best candidate sentences using beam search. To score the sentences we used noisy channel model $p(\mathbf{s}|\mathbf{t}) = p(\mathbf{t}|\mathbf{s})p(\mathbf{s}) = \prod_i p(t_i|s_i)p(\mathbf{s})$, where $p(t_i|s_i)$ is the probability of transforming the i-th aligned group in the hidden correct sentence to i-th group in the observed sentence and $p(\mathbf{s})$ is a trigram language model probability. Actually, this is a hidden Markov model (HMM) with word bigrams being the states of HMM and candidate words being the output symbols.

Since our error model does not take into account weights of different edits and other helpful linguistic clues, we rerank the hypotheses using features. Our feature set includes the following features:

- Length of the sentence, scores of original error and language models.

- Weighted edit distance between source and correction. The model was learned on the development set of (Sorokin et al., 2016) using the algorithm of Brill and Moore (2000).

- The total number and the number of corrections for out-of-vocabulary, long, short and capitalized words.

- The number of words that can be transformed into two dictionary words by space insertion and actual number of such corrections.

- The number of possible word pairs that can form a single word by space deletion or hyphen insertion and actual number of such corrections (hyphen errors are very common in informal writing).

- Morphological and semantic features (see extensive description in Section 4).

We also tried to implement more fine-grained features for hyphen and space insertion/deletion. For example, we counted the occurrences of the word *no* in the sentence and the number of words having *no* as its prefix as well as the number of hyphen insertions in such words/word pairs to reflect the common error pattern *по-русски* "in Russian" ↦ *по русски* or *порусски*. However, most of such features appeared noisy in our experiments and were excluded from the final feature set. In total, our model includes 31 basic features, 9 morphological features, 6 semantic features and 1 morphosemantic feature – the unigram model score for the lemmatized sentence.

For every candidate sentence we obtain a feature vector with up to 47 dimensions. These vectors are ranked using a linear model returning the vector $\mathbf{u}_i$ with the highest scalar product $\langle \mathbf{w}, \mathbf{u}_i \rangle$. The weight vector $\mathbf{w}$ is learned using the method of Joachims (2006): in training phase we generate candidate sentences for each sentence of the training set; if $\mathbf{u}_0$ is the vector of the correct hypothesis and $\mathbf{u}_1, \ldots, \mathbf{u}_m$ of others, then the vectors $\mathbf{u}_0 - \mathbf{u}_1, \ldots, \mathbf{u}_0 - \mathbf{u}_m$ are assigned to the positive class and the opposite vectors to negative. Afterwards the weights can be learned by any linear classifier. We also experimented with the perceptron method of learning but the results were significantly worse.

3 Test Data

We used the development and test set of SpellRuEval contest (Sorokin et al., 2016). Development set consisted of 2001 and testing set of 2009 sentences respectively, taken from Livejournal segment of GICR corpus (Piperski et al., 2013). We refer the reader to the contest organizers paper for the full description of the dataset and just give a few examples:

---

[1] As usual in noisy channel models, the order of transformation is inversed in the error model.

1. Typos:

*Программа **преложила** посмотреть, что получилось*

Программа предложила посмотреть, что получилось

The program offered to see what happened

2. Colloquial writing:

а в результате в сумке кроме трусов и носков у меня больше **ниче не лежало*

а в результате в сумке кроме трусов и носков у меня больше ничего не лежало

As a result, there was nothing except underpants and socks in my bag

3. Space errors:

вот я и снова с вами к **сожелению не на долга*

вот я и снова с вами к сожалению ненадолго

I am again with you, but unfortunately, not for a long time

4. Hyphen errors:

фильм **помоему очень реальный про настоящие чувства*

фильм по-моему очень реальный про настоящие чувства

The film is very cool, I think, about real senses.

5. Real-word errors:

****пастель (pastel) очень уютная и мягкая но в то же время какая-то плотная***

постель очень уютная и мягкая но в то же время какая-то плотная

The bed is very soft and cosy but somehow dense

6. The combinations of different errors.

7. Correct sentences (799 of 2007).

Development set was used to train the reranker and to test hand-written rules of candidate generation. We built a trigram language model with Kneser-Ney smoothing using KenLM toolkit (Heafield, 2011). It was trained on the subset of GICR corpus containing 25mln words. The subset used for model training had no intersections with development and test sets. We also selected a 5mln word subset of this corpus to obtain cooccurrence counts and to investigate the dependence of performance quality from language model size.

The trigram model for morphological tags was trained on the subset of Golden Standard of GICR corpus,[2] the size of the training data was 10000 sentences. Instead of the full tags we used POS labels and selected grammemes: gender, number and case for nouns; gender, number, case, shortness and comparison degree for adjectives; mood for verbs and case for prepositions. Participles were considered as adjectives and pronouns as nouns or adjectives depending on their syntactic role. We used ABBYY Compreno dictionary containing about 3,7 mln word forms.[3]

We used logistic regression (though linear SVM showed almost the same results) for the final reranking, the implementation was taken from scikit-learn package (Pedregosa et al., 2011).

4 Results and Discussion

4.1 Comparison of Different Models

As our first experiment we compare 4 sets of features: WORD-LEVEL, including 31 features specified in Section 2; MORPHO, which also includes the morphological model score; SEM, extending WORD-LEVEL with semantic features and MORPHOSEM using both morphological and semantic information. For all 4 settings we run two experiments with different language models (trained on 5mln and on 25 mln words respectively). The morphological score is the negative log-probability of the sequence of morphological tags assigned to the words in proposed correction. We selected the most probable sequence considering all tags in the dictionary with equal probability. For the out-of-vocabulary words the tags and their probailities were guessed using simple suffix classifier.

Semantic scores were calculated from cooccurrence statistics. We calculated them as follows: first, all the lemmas of nouns, adjectives, verbs and adverbs appearing at least 100 times in our training data were selected. Then for every pair of such lemmas we calculated the number of times its members appear in the same sentence and kept all the pairs occurring at least 20 times. The set of pairs was pruned further: we kept w_2 as the potential pair of w_1 only if its probability to appear in the sentences containing w_1 is at least 3 times higher than its unconditional probability. From these statistics we extracted the following features

---

[2] http://www.webcorpora.ru/news/282
[3] http://www.abbyy.ru/isearch/compreno/, the dictionary itself is not open.

(w_2 is said to be a matching pair for w_1 if their pair is listed in the set of cooccurrence counts, lemma l_1 is frequent if it has at least one matching pair).

1. The number of words in the sentence whose lemma has a matching pair with some other word in the sentence.

2. Average number of matching lemmas for frequent lemmas in the sentence.

3. Maximal and average probabilities $p(l_2|l_1)$ for the lemma l_2 in the sentence to appear together with l_1 averaged over all l_1 in the sentence.

4. The number of frequent lemmas and whether the sentence contains at least one frequent lemma.

We compare our algorithm against the one of Sorokin and Shavrina (2016) – the top ranking system of SpellRuEval competition (BASELINE method). The results of our experiments are given in Table 1. Each row contains two subrows for smaller and larger language models. The following metrics are reported. They were calculated using the evaluation script of SpellRuEval-2016, for details refer to Sorokin et al. (2016).

1. Precision (the proportion of properly corrected tokens among all such tokens).

2. Recall (the fraction of misspelled tokens which were properly corrected).

3. F1-measure (the harmonic mean of precision and recall).

4. Accuracy (the percentage of correct output sentences).

5. The mean reciprocal rank (MRR) of correct output sentences and the number of times they appear in list of hypotheses (Coverage). Only the top 5 variants are taken into account.

Let T, F, W, M denote the number of exact corrections, the number of detected typos where the correction was wrong, the number of "false alarms", when a correctly spelled word was considered as typo and a number of missed typos, respectively. In this notation precision equals $\frac{T}{T+F+W}$ and recall is $\frac{T}{T+F+M}$. Therefore making an incorrect correction is worse than making

no correction since both these operations decrease recall, but the former also affects precision. Hence we think that the percentage of correctly predicted sentences is more adequate as performance measure. It is also the objective maximized by the learning algorithm.

We give a detailed analysis of results in the next section. The preliminary conclusions are the following:

1. The size of the language model is the most significant factor affecting the algorithm performance.

2. Using the score of morphological model leads to significant improvement, reducing error rate by 8% in terms of F1-measure (84.24% instead of 82.87)and by 5.9% in terms of sentence accuracy (78.34% instead of 76.99%).[4]

3. Using semantic features further improves performance.

4. The impact of complex features is more significant in case of smaller language model. It is expected: the less data you have, the more complex algorithm you need to achieve the same level of performance.

4.2 Further Results and Discussion

Our results are rather convincing in order to prove that morphological and semantic features are useful for better spelling correction. However, they are still far from being perfect, therefore we should ask about further improvements that can be achieved on this way. At first, let us illustrate how morphological model helps to select a correct hypothesis. Consider the sentence *к *сожаления, придётся постараться* which should be corrected to *к сожалению, придётся постараться* ("it's a pity, (I) have to make an effort"). Lexeme *сожаление* ("pity") is erroneously written in its Sg+Gen form *сожаления*, not Sg+Dat *сожалению*. However, the preposition *к* requires a dative after it. On the level of morphological tags we have an erroneous sequence Prep+Dat Noun+Neut+Sg+Gen and a correct sequence Prep+Dat Noun+Neut+Sg+Dat. Since a dative preposition never has a genitive immediately to the right, the former sequence has much lower probability and is penalized by the ranker.

---

[4]For the larger language model.

Model	Precision	Recall	F1	Accuracy	MRR	Cov
BASELINE	81.98	69.25	75.07	70.32	NA	NA
WORD-LEVEL	88.62	73.17	80.15	74.35	81.09	90.54
	89.89	76.86	82.87	76.99	83.95	93.23
MORPHO	89.10	74.73	81.29	75.85	82.23	91.09
	89.35	79.69	84.24	78.34	84.81	93.28
SEM	88.48	73.77	80.46	74.65	81.30	90.34
	89.94	77.21	83.09	77.14	84.09	93.28
MORPHOSEM	88.86	75.34	81.54	76.20	82.44	91.19
	89.89	79.54	84.40	78.44	84.88	93.33

Table 1: Comparison of different feature sets using Sorokin et al. (2016) dataset.

Certailnly, it has lower probability by language model already, but this is not sufficient to make a correction since it is a dictionary word which is corrected. Indeed, most of the dictionary words in the sentence are spelled correctly which means that the number of corrections in dictionary words should be a negative feature. Therefore additional evidence is required to overcome this negative gain. Also morphological model is less sparser than lexical therefore it leaves less probability to unseen events which means the cost of unlikely sequence is much higher.

However, not all incorrect sequences of morphological tags can be rejected by trigram model only, especially in case of restricted set of tags, like we have. For example, in Russian each preposition restricts possible cases of its dependent noun. Most prepositions select only one case, for example, *из* "from" allows only genitive after it; other prepositions like *за* "besides" can govern accusative and instrumental cases, but rules out other 4 main cases. Nouns and adjectives in noun groups agree in case, number and gender; a verb agrees with its subject (usually noun or pronoun) in number and in gender (in past tense). All these dependencies are unbounded which means that an arbitrary number of words can separate two elements of the same phrase. However, the emerging constraints may be used to determine that, for example, a verb in particular position cannot be finite and hence reject or penalize a corresponding hypothesis of the spellchecker. That observation seems promising since confusion of 3rd person and infinitive forms of a verb is a common orthographic mistake (*мне нравится кофе* "I like coffee" ↦ **мне нравиться кофе*, where *нравиться* is the infinitive form).

Therefore we added 4 groups of features, 2 features in each groups, which contain the following counts:

1. The total number of prepositions and the number of prepositions which do not have a noun to the right which agrees with them.

2. The total number of adjectives and the number of adjectives which do not have a noun to the right which agrees with them.

3. The total number of infinitives and the number of infinitives which do not have a head (a predicative or a transitive verb).

4. The total number of indicative verbs and the number of verbs that do not a have a subject which agrees with them.

We hoped that these features would be helpful to improve our system performance further, but this was not the case. Encoding additional information deteriorated the quality, possibly due to overfitting. However, we observed that careful encoding of these features is impossible due to high morphological complexity of Russian. For example, nouns usually follow their attributes, but may also precede them (*лицо, красное от мороза* "the face, red from frost"), subject is often only subsumed but omitted in the surface form or there is no subject at all like in impersonal sentences (*холодает* get_colder+Pres+Sing+3 "it is getting colder"). Adverbs are often homonymical to grammatically correct prepositional phrases (*вправду* "indeed" and *в* "in" *правду* "truth+Sg+Dat"), which forces the algorithm to oversegment them in order to increase the number of prepositions that agree with their nouns, etc. Summarizing, designing more complex morphological features requires additional research, probably in the framework of constraint grammars.

That is a nesessary step since among 559 sentences of the test set which were not properly corrected about 30 had an error in the verb form.

Even using only one morphological feature is not straightforward. Our reported results stand for the case when WORD-LEVEL model was trained first and the obtained score was used as a feature on the second step of the classification together with morphological model score. Otherwise error reduction is about twice less. The same happens with semantic features: trying to determine their weights together with word-level features, we obtain no gain at all. It implies that new features should be added hierarchically. In our best model semantics are added after learning the weight of morphology model.

During error analysis we have found that about one third of algorithm errors can be attributed as "semantical" which means that incorrect sentence cannot be rejected by morphological or statistical features since both variants are rare and belong to the same grammatical category. Often these are so-called "real-word errors", where the erroneous word is also in the dictionary. However, it is not trivial to extract a formal semantic score that favors one variant and refutes the other. Consider, for example, the mistyped sentence *География его выступлений *достегает Китая и Индии* "The geography of his performances *lashes China and India". Here the word **достегает* "(it) lashes" must be replaced by *достигает* "(it) reaches". A correction in the dictionary word is penalized, therefore there must be a valuable gain in language or semantic model score to compensate this penalty. But the verb *достигать* "to reach" does not cooccur frequently with other lexemes in the sentence like *география* "geography" and *выступление* "performance". The score of the language model is substantially higher for the correct variant, but it is not sufficient to compensate the correction in dictionary word. In this particular case additional preprocessing phase could be helpful since we might not have an exact phrase *"достигает Китая"* "reaches China" in our corpus, but certainly have other constructions of the form *"достигает Name_Of_Country"*. However, we do not have a ready implementation of this approach, but using class-based or factored language model together with some semantic classification seems a promising idea for further investigation.

Actually, morphological and semantic features are the instruments to remedy the weaknesses of n-gram language model, which is not powerful enough to discriminate between probable and unprobable sentences. Using more adequate language models might make fine-tuning of features unnesessary. A promising candidate to replace ngram models are neural language models (Mikolov et al., 2010) since they solve exactly the problem of choosing the optimal word in given context which is the main problem of spellchecking. We leave this question for future research.

4.3 Generalization of Results

Since lack of publicly available datasets is one of obstacles in spellchecking research, it is reasonable to ask to what extent our results depend on the size of the dataset and the source language. Table 2 shows the dependence between the size of development set used to tune the reranker weights and the quality of correction. We observed that even for the development set of 200 sentences (which is possible to collect and annotate manually) results are acceptable, though performance accuracy increases when we use more data. All results are averaged for 10 independent runs. Note that the gain from using more complex features increases with the size of development data which means that their weights are not tuned properly on smaller datasets.

Another question is whether our approach can be adapted to other languages. The architecture of the model is language-independent. Moreover, linguistically motivated features we design also are not specific to any language since they use only cooccurrence counts. Candidate search and some of word-level features encode language-specific information, but they reflect more the nature of Russian spelling errors in Russian, not the Russian word structure. Actually, a linguist can add any word-level feature; for example, instead of hyphen errors we may look for diacritic errors if the language uses diacritics, such as Czech. Our reranking model can also incorporate arbitrary sentence-level features reflecting morphological or lexical constraints. It makes our architecture perspective to design spellcheckers for other languages, not only for Russian.

Dev. set size	Model	Precision	Recall	F1	Accuracy
200	WORD-LEVEL	88.17	74.88	80.85	74.88
	MORPHO	88.19	76.06	81.66	75.70
	MORPHOSEM	87.30	76.35	81.44	75.44
500	WORD-LEVEL	89.15	75.49	81.73	75.65
	MORPHO	89.29	76.92	82.62	76.61
	MORPHOSEM	88.76	77.34	82.63	76.61
2008	WORD-LEVEL	89.89	76.86	82.87	76.99
	MORPHO	89.35	79.69	84.24	78.34
	MORPHOSEM	89.89	79.54	84.40	78.44

Table 2: Dependence of results on development set size.

5 Conclusions and Future Work

We develop a language-independent model for spelling correction and apply it to Russian language. Our algorithm outperforms the previous best system. Its another merit is flexibility that allows to incorporate arbitrary word-level and sentence-level features. Experimenting with features of different type, we observe that the main factor for spelling corrector performance is the quality of language model. However, morphological and semantic information is also helpful.

The direction of future work is three-fold: the first step is to augment traditional language models with neural ones and check whether this allows to deal better with long-distance dependencies which might be helpful in choosing the correct candidate. The second step is to apply our model to other languages with complex morphology and check whether the same features are beneficial as in case of Russian. The third one is to reimplement our model using finite-state tools since its main components (candidate search and their ranking) are actually finite-state operations.

Acknowledgements

The author is grateful to Andrey Sorokin and Ekaterina Yankovskaya for their careful help in preparing the paper. I also thank the anonymous BSNLP reviewers whose comments further improved the paper. The work was partially supported by the grant NSh-9091.2016.1 for leading scientific groups.

References

Eric Brill and Robert C. Moore. 2000. An improved error model for noisy channel spelling correction. In *Proceedings of the 38th Annual Meeting on Association for Computational Linguistics*, pages 286–293. Association for Computational Linguistics.

Fred J. Damerau. 1964. A technique for computer detection and correction of spelling errors. *Communications of the ACM*, 7(3):171–176.

Michael Flor. 2012. Four types of context for automatic spelling correction. *TAL*, 53(3):61–99.

Andrew R. Golding and Dan Roth. 1999. A winnow-based approach to context-sensitive spelling correction. *Machine learning*, 34(1-3):107–130.

Bo Han, Paul Cook, and Timothy Baldwin. 2013. Lexical normalization for social media text. *ACM Transactions on Intelligent Systems and Technology (TIST)*, 4(1):5.

Kenneth Heafield. 2011. Kenlm: Faster and smaller language model queries. In *Proceedings of the Sixth Workshop on Statistical Machine Translation*, pages 187–197. Association for Computational Linguistics.

Graeme Hirst and Alexander Budanitsky. 2005. Correcting real-word spelling errors by restoring lexical cohesion. *Natural Language Engineering*, 11(1):87–111.

Daniel Hladek, Jan Stas, and Jozef Juhar. 2013. Unsupervised spelling correction for slovak. *Advances in Electrical and Electronic Engineering*, 11(5):392.

Thorsten Joachims. 2006. Structured output prediction with support vector machines. In *Structural, Syntactic, and Statistical Pattern Recognition*, pages 1–7. Springer.

Mark D. Kernighan, Kenneth W. Church, and William A. Gale. 1990. A spelling correction program based on a noisy channel model. In *Proceedings of the 13th conference on Computational linguistics-Volume 2*, pages 205–210. Association for Computational Linguistics.

Karen Kukich. 1992. Techniques for automatically correcting words in text. *ACM Computing Surveys (CSUR)*, 24(4):377–439.

Vladimir I. Levenshtein. 1966. Binary codes capable of correcting deletions, insertions and reversals. In *Soviet physics doklady*, volume 10, page 707.

Eric Mays, Fred J. Damerau, and Robert L. Mercer. 1991. Context based spelling correction. *Information Processing & Management*, 27(5):517–522.

Tomas Mikolov, Martin Karafiát, Lukas Burget, Jan Cernockỳ, and Sanjeev Khudanpur. 2010. Recurrent neural network based language model. In *Interspeech*, volume 2, page 3.

Hwee Tou Ng, Siew Mei Wu, Ted Briscoe, Christian Hadiwinoto, Raymond Hendy Susanto, and Christopher Bryant. 2014. The CoNLL-2014 shared task on grammatical error correction. In *CoNLL Shared Task*, pages 1–14.

Marina Panina, Alexey Baitin, and Irina Galinskaya. 2013. Context-independent autocorrection of query spelling errors.[avtomaticheskoe ispravlenie opechatok v poiskovykh zaprosakh bez ucheta konteksta]. In *Computational Linguistics and Intellectual Technologies: Proceedings of the International Conference"Dialogue"*, number 12, pages 556–568.

F. Pedregosa, G. Varoquaux, A. Gramfort, V. Michel, B. Thirion, O. Grisel, M. Blondel, P. Prettenhofer, R. Weiss, V. Dubourg, J. Vanderplas, A. Passos, D. Cournapeau, M. Brucher, M. Perrot, and E. Duchesnay. 2011. Scikit-learn: Machine learning in Python. *Journal of Machine Learning Research*, 12:2825–2830.

Alexander Piperski, Vladimir Belikov, Nikolay Kopylov, Vladimir Selegey, and Serge Sharoff. 2013. Big and diverse is beautiful: a large corpus of russian to study linguistic variation. In *Proc. 8th Web as Corpus Workshop (WAC-8)*, pages 24–29.

Michal Richter, Pavel Straňák, and Alexandr Rosen. 2012. Korektor-a system for contextual spell-checking and diacritics completion. In *COLING (Posters)*, pages 1019–1028.

Johannes Schaback and Fang Li. 2007. Multi-level feature extraction for spelling correction. In *IJCAI-2007 Workshop on Analytics for Noisy Unstructured Text Data*, pages 79–86.

Alexey Sorokin and Tatiana Shavrina. 2016. Automatic spelling correction for russian social media texts. In *Proceedings of the Annual International Conference "Dialogue"*, number 15.

Alexey Sorokin, Alexey Baytin, Irina Galinskaya, and Tatiana Shavrina. 2016. Spellrueval: the first competition on automatic spelling correction for russian. In *Proceedings of the Annual International Conference "Dialogue"*, number 15.

Kristina Toutanova and Robert C. Moore. 2002. Pronunciation modeling for improved spelling correction. In *Proceedings of the 40th Annual Meeting on Association for Computational Linguistics*, pages 144–151. Association for Computational Linguistics.

Casey Whitelaw, Ben Hutchinson, Grace Y. Chung, and Gerard Ellis. 2009. Using the web for language independent spellchecking and autocorrection. In *Proceedings of the 2009 Conference on Empirical Methods in Natural Language Processing: Volume 2-Volume 2*, pages 890–899. Association for Computational Linguistics.

Shih-Hung Wu, Chao-Lin Liu, and Lung-Hao Lee. 2013. Chinese spelling check evaluation at sighan bake-off 2013. In *Proceedings of the 7th SIGHAN Workshop on Chinese Language Processing*, pages 35–42. Citeseer.

Jinhua Xiong, Qiao Zhao, Jianpeng Hou, Qianbo Wang, Yuanzhuo Wang, and Xueqi Cheng. 2014. Extended HMM and ranking models for chinese spelling correction. In *Proceedings of the Third CIPS-SIGHAN Joint Conference on Chinese Language Processing (CLP 2014)*, pages 133–138.

Debunking Sentiment Lexicons:
A Case of Domain-Specific Sentiment Classification for Croatian

Paula Gombar   Zoran Medić   Domagoj Alagić   Jan Šnajder

Text Analysis and Knowledge Engineering Lab

Faculty of Electrical Engineering and Computing, University of Zagreb

Unska 3, 10000 Zagreb, Croatia

`{paula.gombar,zoran.medic,domagoj.alagic,jan.snajder}@fer.hr`

Abstract

Sentiment lexicons are widely used as an intuitive and inexpensive way of tackling sentiment classification, often within a simple lexicon word-counting approach or as part of a supervised model. However, it is an open question whether these approaches can compete with supervised models that use only word-representation features. We address this question in the context of domain-specific sentiment classification for Croatian. We experiment with the graph-based acquisition of sentiment lexicons, analyze their quality, and investigate how effectively they can be used in sentiment classification. Our results indicate that, even with as few as 500 labeled instances, a supervised model substantially outperforms a word-counting model. We also observe that adding lexicon-based features does not significantly improve supervised sentiment classification.

1 Introduction

Sentiment analysis (Pang et al., 2008) aims to recognize both subjectivity and polarity of texts, information that can be beneficial in various applications, including social studies (O'Connor et al., 2010), marketing analyses (He et al., 2013), and stock price prediction (Devitt and Ahmad, 2007). In general, however, building a well-performing sentiment analysis model requires a fair amount of sentiment-labeled data, whose collection is often costly and time-consuming. A popular annotation-light alternative are sentiment polarity lexicons (Taboada et al., 2011): lists of positive and negative words that most likely induce the corresponding sentiment. The key selling points of senti-ment lexicons are that they are interpretable and quite easy to be compiled manually. If there is no sentiment-labeled data available, sentiment lexicons can be used directly for sentiment classification: the text is simply classified as positive if it contains more words from a positive than a negative lexicon, and classified as negative otherwise (we refer to this as *lexicon word-counting models*). On the other hand, if sentiment-labeled data is available, sentiment lexicons can be used as (additional) features for supervised sentiment classification models.

One challenge of sentiment analysis is that the task is highly domain dependent (Turney, 2002; Baccianella et al., 2010). This means that generic sentiment lexicons will often not be useful for a specific domain. A notorious example is the word *unpredictable*, which is typically positive in the domain of movie and book reviews, but generally negative in other domains.

The aim of this paper is to investigate how sentiment lexicons work for domain-specific sentiment classification for Croatian. Our main goal is to find out whether sentiment lexicons can be of use for sentiment classification, either as a part of a simple word-counting model or as an addition to a supervised model using word-representation features. To this end, we use a semi-supervised graph-based method to acquire sentiment lexicons from a corpus. We experiment with acquisition parameters, considering both generic and domain-specific seed sets and corpora. We compare all the acquired lexicons with the manually annotated ones. Moreover, we evaluate the lexicon-based models on the task of domain-specific sentiment classification and compare them against supervised models. Finally, we investigate whether a word-counting model can have an edge over a supervised model when the labeled data is lacking.

Proceedings of the 6th Workshop on Balto-Slavic Natural Language Processing, pages 54–59,
Valencia, Spain, 4 April 2017. ©2017 Association for Computational Linguistics

2 Related Work

There has been a lot of research on sentiment lexicon acquisition, covering both corpora- and resource-based approaches across many languages (Taboada et al., 2006; Kaji and Kitsuregawa, 2007; Lu et al., 2010; Rao and Ravichandran, 2009; Turney and Littman, 2003). A common approach includes bootstrapping, a method which constructs a sentiment lexicon starting from a small manually-labeled seed set (Hatzivassiloglou and McKeown, 1997; Turney and Littman, 2003). Moreover, a problem of lexicon domain dependence has also been addressed (Kanayama and Nasukawa, 2006).

Even though most research on sentiment lexicon acquisition and lexicon-based sentiment classification deals with English, there has been some work on Slavic languages as well, including Macedonian (Jovanoski et al., 2015), Croatian (Glavaš et al., 2012b), Slovene (Fišer et al., 2016), and Serbian (Mladenović et al., 2016). While we follow the work of Glavaš et al. (2012b), who focused on the task of semi-supervised lexicon acquisition, we turn our attention to evaluating the so-obtained lexicons on the task of sentiment classification.

3 Lexicon Acquisition

3.1 Dataset

For our experiments, we used a large sentiment-annotated dataset of user posts gathered from the Facebook pages of various Croatian internet and mobile service providers.[1] The dataset comprises 15,718 user posts categorized into three classes: positive (*POS*), negative (*NEG*), and neutral (*NEU*). The average post length is around 25 tokens. We randomly sampled 3,052 posts (245 positive, 1,638 negative, and 1,169 neutral), which we used for lexicon acquisition. The rest of the dataset (12,666 posts) was used for training and evaluation of supervised models.

3.2 Lexicon Construction

We acquired a domain-specific lexicon of unigrams, bigrams, and trigrams (henceforth: n-grams) using a semi-supervised graph-based method. We follow the previous work (Hatzivassiloglou and McKeown, 1997; Turney and Littman, 2003; Glavaš et al., 2012b) and employ

bootstrapping, which amounts to manually labeling a small set of seed words whose labels are then propagated across the graph. For this, we use a random walk algorithm.

Graph construction. We set all the corpus n-grams as nodes of a graph, which are connected if the words (nodes) co-occur within a same user post in the dataset. For edge weights, we experimented with two strategies: raw co-occurrence counts (co-oc) and pointwise mutual information (PMI). We also filtered out the n-grams that are made solely out of non-content words and that occur less than three times (unigrams) or two times (bigrams and trigrams).

Seed set. We expect that seed selection may affect label propagation in the graph. To investigate this, we experimented with different seed sets, each containing 3×15 n-grams (15 n-grams per class):

- Two generic, human-compiled seed sets (GH1, GH2) – Two Croatian native speakers compiled the generic seed sets following their intuition;

- Two domain-specific, human-compiled seed sets (DH1, DH2) – Two Croatian native speakers compiled the seed sets from frequency-sorted list of n-grams from the domain corpus following their intuition;

- One domain-specific, corpus-based seed set (DC1) – Starting from the 45 most frequent n-grams, we circularly assigned one n-gram to the positive, negative, and the neutral seed set, until all n-grams were exhausted (a *round-robin* approach). We used this seed set as a baseline.

An example of a domain-specific, human-compiled seed set is shown in Table 1.

Sentiment propagation. To propagate sentiment labels across graph nodes, we used the PageRank algorithm (Page et al., 1999). Since PageRank was originally designed to rank web pages by their relevance, we adapted it for sentiment propagation, following (Esuli and Sebastiani, 2007; Glavaš et al., 2012a). In each iteration, node scores were computed using the power iteration method:

$$\mathbf{a}^{(\mathbf{k})} = \alpha \mathbf{a}^{(\mathbf{k-1})} \mathbf{W} + (1 - \alpha)\mathbf{e}$$

where $\mathbf{W}$ is the weighted adjacency matrix of the graph, $\mathbf{a}$ is the computed vector of node scores, $\mathbf{e}$

---

[1] At this point, this dataset is not publicly available as it was constructed within a commercial project. The dataset may be open-sourced in the future.

	Croatian	Translation
Positive seeds	*hvala, zanimati, nov, dobar, brzina, super, lijepo, zadovoljan, besplatan, ostati, riješiti, biti zadovoljan, uredno, brzi, hvala vi*	*thanks, to interest, new, good, speed, super, nice, satisfied, free, to stay, to solve, to be satisfied, tidy, fast, thank you*
Negative seeds	*nemati, problem, ne moći, kvar, ne raditi, čekati, biti problem, prigovor, raskid, katastrofa, sramota, zlo, raskid ugovor, otići, smetnja*	*to not have, problem, to not be able, malfunction, to not work, to wait, to be a problem, objection, break-up, catastrophe, shame, evil, contract termination, to leave, nuisance*
Neutral seeds	*imati, dan, internet, broj, korisnik, mobitel, ugovor, tarifa, mjesec, poruka, nov, vip, reći, poziv, signal*	*to have, day, internet, number, user, cellphone, contract, rate, month, message, new, vip, to say, call, signal*

Table 1: Human-generated domain-specific seed set (lemmatized).

is a vector of normalized internal node scores, and α is the damping factor (we used a default value of 0.15). In the initialization phase, the adjacency matrix $\mathbf{W}$ was row-normalized and the nodes from the seed set were set to $\frac{1}{|SeedSet|}$, whereas the rest of the nodes were set to 0.

We then ran the algorithm twice, once with positive seeds and once with negative ones, obtaining ranked lists of positive and negative scores of all n-grams. To determine the final sentiment of an n-gram, we first calculated the difference between its ranks in the lists of positive and negative scores, and then compared it to a fixed threshold. If the difference between its ranks was below the threshold, the n-gram was classified as neutral. If not, it was classified as positive if its rank was higher in the list of positive scores and negative otherwise. We also tried using score difference, but rank difference worked better. Lastly, it is worth noting that, as the goal of our work is to determine the best possible performance of a lexicon-based sentiment classifier, we computed an oracle threshold by optimizing the threshold on the gold set, as described in the following section.

3.3 Lexicon Evaluation

Gold lexicon construction. We made use of our sentiment-labeled dataset to extract the most representative subset of n-grams for the annotation. More precisely, we ranked all the n-grams according to their χ^2 scores, which were calculated based on their co-occurrence with *POS*, *NEU*, and *NEG* user posts in the dataset. To obtain a final list of n-grams for the annotation, we selected 1,000 n-grams by uniformly sampling all these three lists from the top, making sure to avoid duplicates. Subsequently, five annotators labeled the dataset, and we obtained the final label as a majority vote (there were no ties).

Parameter	Optimal value
Weighting strategy	Raw co-occurrence counts
Seed set	DH2
Classification strategy	Rank difference
Classification threshold	77

Table 2: Parameters used for obtaining the best-performing domain-specific lexicon when evaluated against the gold lexicon.

	Generic		Domain-specific		
	GH1	GH2	DH1	DH2	DC1
Co-oc	37.9	40.0	43.8	**46.2**	38.3
PMI	36.7	38.1	39.9	45.0	35.8

Table 3: F1-scores of acquired lexicons evaluated against the gold lexicon.

Inter-annotator agreement. We measured the inter-annotator agreement (IAA) using both the Cohen's kappa (Cohen, 1960) and pairwise F1-score. We first calculated the agreement for all annotator pairs and averaged them to obtain the overall agreement. The averaged Cohen's kappa is 0.68, which is considered a substantial agreement, according to Landis and Koch (1977). The macro-averaged F1-score is 0.79.

Evaluating generated lexicons. We have acquired a total of 10 lexicons, combining two weighting strategies (raw co-occurrence count and PMI) with five different seed sets (cf. Section 3.2). We evaluated these against the human-annotated gold lexicon in terms of macro-averaged F1-score. Using optimal parameters from Table 2, we obtained the score of 0.46. The other lexicons' scores are reported in Table 3.

Seed-corpus type	P	R	F1
domain-domain	42.1	41.66	39.79
generic-domain	45.31	46.01	**44.77**
generic-generic	17.39	33.33	22.85

Table 4: Scores of word-counting models.

4 Sentiment Classification

After obtaining the optimal lexicon (in comparison to the gold lexicon), we test how well it performs on the task of sentiment classification of user posts. This task commonly incorporates sentiment lexicons in two ways: as a part of a simple word-counting approach, or as a source of lexicon-based features in a supervised model. We are interested in how simple word-counting approach fares against the more complex supervised one. The models are evaluated using a nested k-fold cross-validation (10×5 folds) on the subset of our sentiment-labeled dataset that was not used for lexicon acquisition.

4.1 Lexicon Word-Counting Classification

In this setup, a user post is classified as positive if it contains more positive than negative n-grams from the lexicon, and vice versa. In case of ties, the user post is predicted neutral. To investigate how different seed sets and corpora influence lexicon quality, we compare our best-performing lexicon (*domain-domain*;[2] Co-oc DH2) to two additional lexicons: a domain-specific lexicon built with generic seeds (*generic-domain*; Co-oc GH2) and a generic Croatian lexicon compiled by Glavaš et al. (2012b) (*generic-generic*).

We evaluated the models in terms of macro-averaged F1-scores, which we report in Table 4. Surprisingly, the *generic-domain* lexicon outperformed the one that seemed the best when compared against the gold lexicon (*domain-domain*).

4.2 Supervised Classification

For the supervised classification, we decided to use a simple logistic regression model with lexicon-based and word-representation features. Lexicon-based features capture how many words from the positive and negative lexicon appeared in a user post, as well as the average rank and score of words from the positive and negative lexicons. On the other hand, for word-representation fea-

Model	P	R	F1
domain-domain	63.82	43.01	**41.98**
generic-domain	39.19	41.11	39.08
SG	64.57	58.20	60.27
SG + generic-domain	65.60	59.39	61.42
SG + domain-domain	65.70	59.48	**61.53**
BoW	69.93	63.55	65.75
BoW + generic-domain	70.08	63.22	65.50
BoW + domain-domain	70.68	63.47	**65.90**

Table 5: Scores of supervised models with lexicon-based and word-representation features.

tures we use tf-idf-weighted bag-of-words vectors (BoW) and the popular skip-gram embeddings (SG) proposed by Mikolov et al. (2013). We build 300-dimensional vectors from hrWaC, a Croatian web corpus (Ljubešić and Erjavec, 2011), filtered by Šnajder et al. (2013) using the `word2vec` tool.[3] We set the negative sampling parameter to 5, minimum frequency threshold to 100, and we did not use hierarchical softmax. To construct user post skip-gram embeddings, we follow the common practice and average the embeddings of its content words.

For the evaluation, we decided to omit the *generic-generic* lexicon from our experiments due to its subpar performance in lexicon word-counting classification. To see how lexicon-based features affect the classification performance, we evaluate models that use them in conjunction with word-representation features and models that use them as the only features. The boost in the models' scores when using both types of features is not statistically significant (paired t-test with $p<0.001$). We report the scores in Table 5.

4.3 Discussion

Based on the results from Tables 4 and 5, we observe that any supervised model based on word-representation features (with or without lexicon-based features) greatly outperforms word-counting models and models based on lexicon-based features. This indicates that, in our case, it makes sense to use a simple word-counting model (F1-score of 44.77%) when annotating data is entirely infeasible, and a supervised model with word-representation features in all other cases (F1-score of 65.90%).

It is interesting to investigate whether the above

---

[2]Here, *domain-domain* refers to a lexicon built with a domain-specific seed set over a domain-specific corpus.

[3]`https://code.google.com/archive/p/word2vec/`

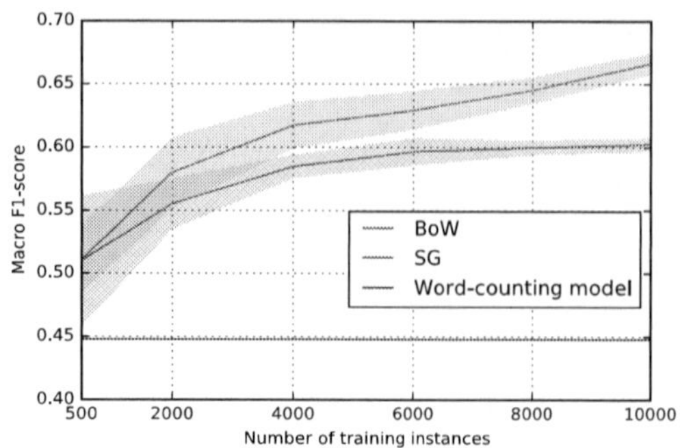

Figure 1: Learning curves of the supervised models (BoW and SG) and the word-counting model.

observation holds even when dealing with a relatively small amount of sentiment-labeled data. To that end, we inspect the learning curve of these models' performances (Figure 1). We observe that annotating as few as 500 instances already makes both supervised models outperform the lexicon word-counting model by a large margin.

5   Conclusion

We tackled the domain-specific sentiment lexicon acquisition and sentiment classification for Croatian. We used a semi-supervised graph-based model to acquire lexicons using both generic and domain-specific seed sets and corpora. Furthermore, we analyzed their quality against the human-annotated gold lexicons. Within the context of domain-specific sentiment classification, we used the obtained lexicons both as part of a lexicon word-counting model and as features for a supervised model, and showed that they do not yield any significant improvements. Finally, we reported that, even in the case of having as few as 500 labeled instances, simple word-counting models cannot compete with supervised models based on word-representation features. For future work, we plan to carry out a more extensive analysis across several different domains and languages.

Acknowledgments

The research has been carried out within the project "CATACX: Cog-Affective social media Text Analytics for Customer eXperience analysis (PoC6-1-147)", funded by the Croatian Agency for SMEs, Innovations and Investments (HAMAG-BICRO) from the Proof of Concept Program.

References

Stefano Baccianella, Andrea Esuli, and Fabrizio Sebastiani. 2010. SentiWordNet 3.0: An enhanced lexical resource for sentiment analysis and opinion mining. In *Proceedings of the 7th International Conference on Language Resources and Evaluation (LREC 2010)*, pages 2200–2204, Valletta, Malta.

Jacob Cohen. 1960. A coefficient of agreement for nominal scales. *Educational and psychological measurement*, 20(1):37–46.

Ann Devitt and Khurshid Ahmad. 2007. Sentiment polarity identification in financial news: A cohesion-based approach. In *Proceedings of the 45th Annual Meeting of the Association of Computational Linguistics (ACL 2007)*, pages 984–991, Prague, Czech Republic.

Andrea Esuli and Fabrizio Sebastiani. 2007. Pageranking wordnet synsets: An application to opinion mining. In *Proceedings of the 45th Annual Meeting of the Association for Computational Linguistics (ACL 2007)*, volume 7, pages 442–431, Prague, Czech Republic.

Darja Fišer, Jasmina Smailović, Tomaž Erjavec, Igor Mozetič, and Miha Grčar. 2016. Sentiment annotation of Slovene user-generated content. In *Proceedings of the 2016 Conference Language Technologies and Digital Humanities (JTDH 2016)*, pages 65–70, Ljubljana, Slovenia.

Goran Glavaš, Jan Šnajder, and Bojana Dalbelo Bašić. 2012a. Experiments on hybrid corpus-based sentiment lexicon acquisition. In *Proceedings of the Workshop on Innovative Hybrid Approaches to the Processing of Textual Data*, pages 1–9, Avignon, France.

Goran Glavaš, Jan Šnajder, and Bojana Dalbelo Bašić. 2012b. Semi-supervised acquisition of Croatian sentiment lexicon. In *International Conference on Text, Speech and Dialogue*, pages 166–173. Springer.

Vasileios Hatzivassiloglou and Kathleen R. McKeown. 1997. Predicting the semantic orientation of adjectives. In *Proceedings of the 8th Conference on European Chapter of the Association for Computational Linguistics (EACL 1997)*, pages 174–181, Madrid, Spain.

Wu He, Shenghua Zha, and Ling Li. 2013. Social media competitive analysis and text mining: A case study in the pizza industry. *International Journal of Information Management*, 33(3):464–472.

Dame Jovanoski, Veno Pachovski, and Preslav Nakov. 2015. Sentiment analysis in Twitter for Macedonian. In *Proceedings of the International Conference on Recent Advances in Natural Language Processing (RANLP 2015)*, pages 249–257, Hissar, Bulgaria.

Nobuhiro Kaji and Masaru Kitsuregawa. 2007. Building lexicon for sentiment analysis from massive collection of HTML documents. In *Proceedings of the 11th Conference on Computational Natural Language Learning (CoNLL 2007)*, pages 1075–1083, Prague, Czech Republic.

Hiroshi Kanayama and Tetsuya Nasukawa. 2006. Fully automatic lexicon expansion for domain-oriented sentiment analysis. In *Proceedings of the 2006 Conference on Empirical Methods in Natural Language Processing (EMNLP 2006)*, pages 355–363, Sydney, Australia.

J. Richard Landis and Gary G. Koch. 1977. The measurement of observer agreement for categorical data. *Biometrics*, 33:159–174.

Nikola Ljubešić and Tomaž Erjavec. 2011. hrWaC and slWac: Compiling web corpora for Croatian and Slovene. In *Proceedings of 14th International Conference on Text, Speech and Dialogue (TSD 2011)*, pages 395–402, Pilsen, Czech Republic.

Bin Lu, Yan Song, Xing Zhang, and Benjamin K Tsou. 2010. Learning Chinese polarity lexicons by integration of graph models and morphological features. In *Asia Information Retrieval Symposium*, pages 466–477. Springer.

Tomas Mikolov, Ilya Sutskever, Kai Chen, Greg S Corrado, and Jeff Dean. 2013. Distributed representations of words and phrases and their compositionality. In *Proceedings of the Neural Information Processing Systems Conference (NIPS 2013)*, pages 3111–3119, Lake Tahoe, USA.

Miljana Mladenović, Jelena Mitrović, Cvetana Krstev, and Duško Vitas. 2016. Hybrid sentiment analysis framework for a morphologically rich language. *Journal of Intelligent Information Systems*, 46(3):599–620.

Brendan O'Connor, Ramnath Balasubramanyan, Bryan R. Routledge, and Noah A. Smith. 2010. From tweets to polls: Linking text sentiment to public opinion time series. *ICWSM*, 11(122-129):1–2.

Lawrence Page, Sergey Brin, Rajeev Motwani, and Terry Winograd. 1999. The PageRank citation ranking: bringing order to the web.

Bo Pang, Lillian Lee, et al. 2008. Opinion mining and sentiment analysis. *Foundations and Trends in Information Retrieval*, 2(1–2):1–135.

Delip Rao and Deepak Ravichandran. 2009. Semi-supervised polarity lexicon induction. In *Proceedings of the 12th Conference of the European Chapter of the Association for Computational Linguistics (EACL 2009)*, pages 675–682, Athens, Greece.

Jan Šnajder, Sebastian Padó, and Željko Agić. 2013. Building and evaluating a distributional memory for Croatian. In *51st Annual Meeting of the Association for Computational Linguistics*, pages 784–789.

Maite Taboada, Caroline Anthony, and Kimberly Voll. 2006. Methods for creating semantic orientation dictionaries. In *Proceedings of the 5th Conference on Language Resources and Evaluation (LREC 2006)*, pages 427–432, Genoa, Italy.

Maite Taboada, Julian Brooke, Milan Tofiloski, Kimberly Voll, and Manfred Stede. 2011. Lexicon-based methods for sentiment analysis. *Computational linguistics*, 37(2):267–307.

Peter D. Turney and Michael L. Littman. 2003. Measuring praise and criticism: Inference of semantic orientation from association. *ACM Transactions on Information Systems (TOIS)*, 21(4):315–346.

Peter D. Turney. 2002. Thumbs up or thumbs down?: semantic orientation applied to unsupervised classification of reviews. In *Proceedings of the 40th Annual Meeting on Association for Computational Linguistics (ACL 2002)*, pages 417–424, Philadephia, Pennsylvania, USA.

Adapting a State-of-the-Art Tagger for
South Slavic Languages to Non-Standard Text

Nikola Ljubešić[1,2], Tomaž Erjavec[1], and Darja Fišer[3,1]

[1]Dept. of Knowledge Technologies, Jožef Stefan Institute
Jamova cesta 39, SI-1000 Ljubljana, Slovenia
[2]Dept. of Information and Communication Sciences, University of Zagreb
Ivana Lučića 3, HR-10000 Zagreb, Croatia
[3]Dept. of Translation, Faculty of Arts, University of Ljubljana
Aškerčeva cesta 2, SI-1000 Ljubljana, Slovenia
`{nikola.ljubesic,tomaz.erjavec}@ijs.si`
`darja.fiser@ff.uni-lj.si`

Abstract

In this paper we present the adaptations of a state-of-the-art tagger for South Slavic languages to non-standard texts on the example of the Slovene language. We investigate the impact of introducing in-domain training data as well as additional supervision through external resources or tools like word clusters and word normalization. We remove more than half of the error of the standard tagger when applied to non-standard texts by training it on a combination of standard and non-standard training data, while enriching the data representation with external resources removes additional 11 percent of the error. The final configuration achieves tagging accuracy of 87.41% on the full morphosyntactic description, which is, nevertheless, still quite far from the accuracy of 94.27% achieved on standard text.

1 Introduction

With the rise of social media, the potential from automatically processing the available textual content is substantial. However, there is a series of problems connected to processing Computer Mediated Communication (CMC) due to frequent deviation from the norm (Miličević and Ljubešić, 2016), such as omission of diacritics, non-standard word spellings and frequent use of colloquial expressions. For example, experiments on English part-of-speech tagging showed a drastic loss in accuracy when shifting from Wall Street Journal text (97%) to Twitter (85%) (Gimpel et al., 2011).

Part-of-speech (PoS) tagging is a crucial step in the text processing pipeline, as it gives invaluable information about the grammatical properties of words in context and thus enables, e.g., better information extractions from texts, high quality lemmatization, syntactic parsing, the use of factored models in machine translation etc.

This paper concentrates on adapting a state-of-the art tagger of standard Slovene (Ljubešić and Erjavec, 2016), Croatian and Serbian (Ljubešić et al., 2016) to CMC texts on the example of Slovene language by experimenting with in-domain training data and additional external resources and tools such as word clusters and word normalization.

The rest of the paper is structured as follows: Section 2 gives an overview of the related work on this problem, Section 3 introduces the dataset used, Section 4 describes the tagging experiments we performed, Section 5 reports on the error analysis of the results and Section 6 gives some conclusions and directions for further research.

2 Related Work

Early work on PoS tagging social media was, as usual, mostly focused on English (Gimpel et al., 2011; Owoputi et al., 2013). Recently there has been more work on other languages, primarily through the organization of shared tasks, such the EmpiriST on German (Beißwenger et al., 2016) and PoSTWITA on Italian.[1]

There are two main approaches to processing non-standard data: normalization and domain adaptation (Eisenstein, 2013). Most approaches nowadays follow the domain adaptation path al-

---

[1]`http://corpora.ficlit.unibo.it/`
`PoSTWITA/`

Proceedings of the 6th Workshop on Balto-Slavic Natural Language Processing, pages 60–68,
Valencia, Spain, 4 April 2017. ©2017 Association for Computational Linguistics

though the literature still lacks a detailed comparison of the two strategies on specific tasks.

In domain adaptation there are, again, two main strategies (Horsmann and Zesch, 2015): adding more labeled data (Daumé III, 2007; Hovy et al., 2015) and incorporating external knowledge (Owoputi et al., 2013). Horsmann and Zesch (2015) show that (1) adding manually annotated in-domain data is highly effective (but costly) and (2) adding out-of-domain training data or machine-tagged data is less effective than adding more external knowledge, especially word clustering information.

The contribution of our paper is the following: First, we perform the first experiments in annotating Slavic non-standard texts with part-of-speech and morphosyntactic information, therefore dealing with several hundreds of tags. Next, we investigate the impact of strategies that were proven to be most successful on English, German and Italian on a new language group and level of tag complexity. Last but not least, we release a split of a freely available dataset, as well as the tagger as a useful tool and a strong baseline for other researchers to improve on.

3 CMC Dataset

As the primary resource for training and evaluating our tagger of non-standard language we used the publicly available Janes-Tag v1.2 dataset (Erjavec et al., 2016c), which contains Slovene CMC texts, with the text types being tweets, forum posts, comments on blog posts and comments on news articles. The texts were sampled from the Janes corpus (Fišer et al., 2016), a large corpus (9 million texts with about 200 million tokens) of Slovene CMC. The texts in the Janes corpus are, inter alia, annotated with language standardness scores for each text. These scores were assigned automatically (Ljubešić et al., 2015) and classify texts into three levels of technical and linguistic standardness. Technical standardness (T1, quite standard – T3, very non-standard) relates to the use of spaces, punctuation, capitalization and similar, while linguistic standardness (L1 – L3) takes into account the level of adherence to the written norm and more or less conscious decisions to use non-standard language with respect to spelling, lexis, morphology, and word order. The texts for the Janes-Tag dataset were sampled so that they contain, for each text type, roughly the same number of T1L1, T1L3, T3L3, and T3L3 texts, except for tweets, where only T1L3 and T3L3 texts were included in order to maximize twitter-specific deviations from the norm.

The texts in Janes-Tag were first automatically annotated and then manually checked for the following levels of linguistic annotation: tokenization, sentence segmentation, normalization, part-of-speech tagging and lemmatization. Here normalization refers to giving the standard equivalent to non-standard word-forms, e.g., *jaz* (*I*) assigned to the source *jst*, *js*, *jest* etc., while tagging and lemmatization is then assigned to these normalized forms. It should be noted that two (or more) source word tokens can be normalized to one token or vice versa.

The tagset used is defined in the (draft) MULTEXT-East morphosyntactic specification Version 5[2] for Slovene, which are identical to the Version 4 specifications (Erjavec, 2012), except that four new tags have been added for CMC specific phenomena, such as hashtags and mentions. Version 5 tagset for Slovene defines all together 1900 different tags (morphosyntactic descriptions, MSDs), i.e., it is a fine-grained tagset covering all the inflectional properties of Slovene words.

The dataset is distributed in the canonical TEI encoding as well as in the derived vertical format used by concordancers such as CQP (Christ, 1994). Further details on the dataset can be found in (Erjavec et al., 2016a).

We split the dataset into training, development and testing subsets in a 80:10:10 fashion. We performed stratified sampling over texts with strata being text type and linguistic standardness in order for each subset to have the same distribution of texts given the two variables. This split is also available as part of (Erjavec et al., 2016c). Basic statistics of the dataset and subsets are given in Table 1.

Portion	Texts	Tokens
train	2,370	60,367
dev	294	7,425
test	294	7,484
Σ	2,958	75,276

Table 1: Janes-Tag dataset statistics.

It should be noted that in cases of $n : 1$ or $1 :$

---

[2]`http://nl.ijs.si/ME/V5/msd/`

n mappings between the original and normalized word token(s), we consider these in subsequent experiments as one token. The latter also means that one original token is assigned multiple PoS tags, e.g., *meuš* → *me boš* / Pp1-sa--y Va-f2s-n. These phenomena are, however, quite rare, occurring in our CMC dataset on only 0.4% of tokens.

4 Experiments

In this section we present experiments on introducing non-standard training data (4.1), adding word clustering information (4.2), measuring the impact of the standard inflectional lexicon (4.3), adding word normalization data (4.4) and combining standard and non-standard training data (4.5).

4.1 Impact of Non-Standard Data

In the first set of experiments we compare the state-of-the-art tagger for standard Slovene – the ReLDI tagger (Ljubešić and Erjavec, 2016) – with the same tagger implementation retrained on the training portion of the Janes-Tag dataset.

The ReLDI tagger is based on conditional random fields and uses the following features:

1. lowercased tokens at positions $\{-3, -2, ..., 3\}$;

2. focus token (token at position 0) suffixes of length $\{1, 2, 3, 4\}$;

3. tag hypotheses obtained from an inflectional lexicon for tokens at positions $\{-2, -1, ..., 2\}$;

4. focus token packed representation giving information about the case of the word and whether it occurs at the beginning of the sentence, e.g., u11-START starts with uppercase followed by at least two lowercase characters at the start of the sentence.

For obtaining tag hypotheses for Slovene, we use, just as in the standard setting, the Sloleks lexicon (Dobrovoljc et al., 2015).

We evaluate each of the our configurations on the development portion of Janes-Tag via accuracy on two levels:

1. the fine-grained tagset, which contains the complete morphosyntactic descriptions (MSDs): the MSD tagset comprises 960 different labels in the Janes-Tag dataset; and

2. the coarse-grained tagset, comprising only the first two letters of the MSD, i.e., covering the part-of-speech and, typically, its type (e.g., common vs. proper noun): we term this the PoS tagset, and it comprises 42 different labels in Janes-Tag.

The results of this experiment are presented in the first part of Table 2. The standard tagger (configuration reldi) shows very poor performance, especially given its results on standard data (94.27% MSD accuracy and 98.94% PoS accuracy). Simply training the tagger on the ∼60k tokens of in-domain training data (configuration reldi+janestag), as opposed to the 500k tokens of training data in the standard configuration, improves the tagger drastically, although its performance still does not come near the performance on standard data.

We also experimented with extending the feature set with features encoding whether the token is a hashtag, mention or URL similar to Gimpel et al. (2011), but did not obtain any improvements.

In the following experiments we refer to the reldi+janestag configuration for brevity as the janes configuration.

At this point our experiments could continue in two directions: (1) combining standard and non-standard training data or (2) enriching the process with external knowledge. Given the non-negligible size of our non-standard training subset, we decided to first focus on enriching the process with external knowledge and focus on combining the two types of training data at a later stage.

Configuration	MSD	PoS
reldi	68.67	73.13
reldi+janestag	84.15	89.85
janes+brown.web	85.17	91.12
janes+brown.cmc	85.51	91.31
janes+brown.all	85.70	91.52
janes-lex	81.14	87.62
janes+brown.all-lex	84.18	91.04
hunpos+janestag	83.78	89.70
hunpos+janestag-lex	80.65	87.66
janes+brown.all+normlex	86.03	91.65
janes+brown.all+normcsmt	86.28	91.72
janes+brown.all+normgold	87.97	93.19

Table 2: Results in accuracy on the first four sets of experiments.

4.2 Adding Word Clustering Information

In this set of experiments we investigate the improvements that can be obtained by introducing knowledge from word clusters calculated on large amounts of non-annotated texts. The word clustering technique that has recently shown best results for enriching various decision processes (Turian et al., 2010; Owoputi et al., 2013; Horsmann and Zesch, 2015) are Brown clusters (Brown et al., 1992). We calculate this hierarchical clustering representation of words given their context on three different sources: (1) the 1 billion token slWaC v2.0 web corpus of Slovene (Erjavec et al., 2015) (`brown.web`), (2) the 200 million token Janes v0.4 corpus (Fišer et al., 2016) of Slovene CMC (`brown.cmc`) and (3) a concatenation of the two corpora (`brown.all`). On each resource we build 2000 clusters from words occurring at least 50 times.

We additionally experiment with four different and common ways of including the binary hierarchical clustering information in our tagger: adding the feature corresponding to the focus tokens' (1) whole binary path, (2) each length of the binary path prefix, (3) even lengths of path prefixes (Owoputi et al., 2013) and (4) path prefixes of length 2^n, $n \in \{1, 2, 3, 4\}$ (Plank et al., 2014). Among the four approaches, the one including even path lengths only (3) proved to yield just slightly (up to half percent), but consistently better results than the remaining three approaches (1, 2, 4).

We report the results of using Brown binary paths of even lengths with different resources (`brown.web`, `brown.cmc`, `brown.all`) in the second part of Table 2. When comparing the bare configuration trained on non-standard data (`reldi+janestag`) with the configurations extended with various Brown clusters, we measure an improvement on MSD accuracy of 1.02% to 1.55% and an improvement on PoS accuracy of 1.27% to 1.67%. The results across our experiments consistently show that Brown clusters improve PoS accuracy more than MSD accuracy. This is to be expected as the large number of different MSD tags comes close to the overall number of clusters.

The differences in the results given the source used to calculate Brown clusters are minor but consistent with an increase in quality (`brown.cmc`) and quantity (`brown.web`) of the underlying data. While the Janes clusters perform better than the slWaC ones regardless of the significantly bigger size of the slWaC corpus, the best results are obtained with clusters calculated from a concatenation of the two resources.

4.3 Impact of the Inflectional Lexicon

In this set of experiments we measure the impact of the inflectional lexicon on the tagging process. As stated before, the ReLDI tagger, as well as the `janes` configuration, use the Sloleks inflectional lexicon (Dobrovoljc et al., 2015) containing 100 thousand lexemes (lemmas) with 2.7 million word-forms. We perform the following experiments as it is not infrequent that even though large inflectional lexicons do exist for Slavic languages, they are not (freely) available.

We investigate two scenarios: (1) training the ReLDI tagger on non-standard data without an inflectional lexicon (`janes-lex`) and (2) training the ReLDI tagger on non-standard data and previously best-performing Brown clusters without the inflectional lexicon (`janes+brown.all-lex`). With the second scenario we investigate to what extent the lack of an inflectional lexicon can be compensated with word clusters.

To obtain a comparison with a configuration not relying on the ReLDI tagger, in this set of experiments we additionally report the results obtained with the HunPos tagger (Halácsy et al., 2007), a tagger giving very good results on Slavic languages (Agić et al., 2013), trained on the Janes-Tag training subset with (configuration `hunpos+janestag`) and without the inflectional lexicon (configuration `hunpos+janestag-lex`).

The results in the third section of Table 2 show that the lack of an inflectional lexicon (`janes-lex`) deteriorates MSD accuracy by 3% and PoS accuracy by 2.2%. Adding Brown clusters into the configuration (`janes+brownall-lex`) generates MSD accuracy as high as when using an inflectional lexicon (`reldi+janestag`) and even improves PoS accuracy by 1.2%, which is in line with our previous observation on a greater impact of Brown clusters on PoS accuracy than MSD accuracy. However, this configuration still performs worse than the one using both the inflectional lexicon and Brown clusters, loosing 1.5% MSD accuracy and

0.5% PoS accuracy.

The results obtained with the HunPos tagger are very much in line with the results obtained with the ReLDI tagger. In both configurations, with (`hunpos+janestag` is to be compared to `reldi+janestag`) and without the inflectional lexicon (`hunpos+janestag-lex` is to be compared to `janes-lex`), the ReLDI tagger is half a percent better on MSD accuracy and just slightly better on PoS accuracy. A similar but stronger trend was measured on standard data (Ljubešić et al., 2016). The better performance of the ReLDI tagger is probably due to its stronger modeling technique, while the smaller difference in comparison with the comparative experiments on standard Slovene is most likely the result of the nine times smaller training dataset.

4.4 Adding Normalization Data

Another potentially useful resource for tagging non-standard Slovene texts is the Slovene dataset of normalized CMC texts, Janes-Norm 1.2 (Erjavec et al., 2016b) which is a superset of Janes-Tag. In each of the following experiments we use only the part of Janes-Norm which is not included in Janes-Tag. This portion of Janes-Norm is slightly above 100 thousand tokens in size.

The following experiments investigate whether additional improvements can be obtained by introducing normalization information to our classification process.

In the first experiment (configuration `janes+brown.all+normlex`) we use the available normalization data as a normalization lexicon consisting of original word forms and their normalized counterparts. We extend the tagger feature set with MSD hypotheses of all normalized forms. The MSD hypotheses are obtained from the Sloleks inflectional lexicon.

In the second experiment (configuration `janes+brown.all+normcsmt` we train the cSMTiser.[3] normalization tool which was already been used for normalizing Slovene user-generated and historical data (Ljubešić et al., 2016) as well as Swiss dialectal data (Scherrer and Ljubešić, 2016). The tool is based on character-level statistical machine translation and is in this case trained on pairs of tokens, not pairs of sentences, as the two approaches yield very similar results on Slovene CMC texts (Ljubešić et al., 2016).

Once the tool is trained, a lexicon similar to the one used in the first experiment is produced with the difference that (1) each token has just one normalization and (2) all tokens in the training and development set are covered in that lexicon. The feature set is extended as in the first experiment.

Given that we have the gold normalization available in our Janes-Tag dataset, we also calculated a ceiling for this tagger extension (configuration `janes+brown.all+normgold`) which uses the gold normalization for calculating the feature extension.

The results are presented in the final part of Table 2. Both automated approaches improve the previous best results (configuration `janes+brown.all`), the CSMT approach slightly outperforming the lexicon approach. However, the gold normalization approach shows that there is still room for improvement of 1.5% on both MSD and PoS levels. There are two possible reasons for this rather large gap: (1) in our two automated approaches we discard the context and (2) the same words that are hard to normalize are those that are hard to part-of-speech tag. The first issue could be partially resolved by training a sentence-level normalizer which is processing-wise much more costly, but does yield $\sim 10\%$ token error reduction as long as the texts are significantly non-standard (Ljubešić et al., 2016). The second issue could be only resolved with much more training data or better unsupervised techniques than Brown clustering.

4.5 Combining Standard and Non-Standard Training Data

In the final set of experiments we investigate the impact of combining existing standard training data with the newly developed non-standard data. We compare that impact on two configurations from our previous experiments: (1) the `reldi+janestag`, i.e., the `janes` configuration which is trained on Janes-Tag and does not use any external knowledge except the inflectional lexicon and (2) the `janes+brown.all+normdict` configuration which additionally uses Brown clusters and the normalization lexicon. We call the second configuration `janes+`.

We discard the configuration using cSMTiser (`janes+brownall+normcsmt`) since its improvement is minor and it makes the tagging pro-

---

[3]`https://github.com/clarinsi/csmtiser`

	janes		janes+	
nstd:std	MSD	PoS	MSD	PoS
-	84.15	89.85	86.03	91.65
1:10	86.05	90.51	87.38	91.77
1:5	85.98	90.49	87.70	91.97
1:3	86.32	90.77	**87.70**	**92.22**

Table 3: Results in accuracy on combining standard and non-standard training data.

cess dependent on one external tool.

We additionally investigate the impact of over-representing non-standard data by repeating the non-standard dataset once, twice and three times, yielding the ratio of non-standard and standard data of 1:10, 1:5 and 1:3. Further increases of the ratio of non-standard data did not generate any improvements, hence we do not report them.

The results of this set of experiments are given in Table 3. Adding standard training data has an overall positive impact, which is much greater on the basic configuration due to the lack of external resource supervision. However, the configuration using Brown clusters and the normalization lexicon always outperforms the basic configuration. Furthermore, over-representing non-standard data two or three times improves the results of the janes+ configuration while the results of the janes configuration are rather constant. This makes sense as more non-standard data enables the tagger to properly weigh the features using non-standard external knowledge.

In the 1:3 ratio of non-standard and standard data, the janes+ configuration outperforms the janes configuration by 1.4% for MSD accuracy and 1.5% for PoS accuracy. We tested whether these obtained differences are statistically significant with the McNemar's test for paired nominal data (McNemar, 1947). On the MSD level the obtained p-value was $2.57 * 10^{-9}$ while on the PoS level the p-value was $1.32 * 10^{-11}$.

Similarly, both the difference between the janes configuration not using and using standard data, as well as between the janes+ configuration not using and using standard data have proven to be statistically significant with $p < 0.001$ on the MSD level. On the PoS level the difference between using and not using standard data gave $p = 0.001$ for the janes configuration and $p = 0.02$ for the janes+ configuration.

5 Error Analysis

In order to gain more insight into the tagger behavior in various experimental settings, hence to better contextualize the results obtained in automatic evaluation as well as collect information useful for future improvements of the tagger, we performed manual evaluation of the erroneously tagged instances on the part-of-speech level.

Three types of the main sources of errors were observed: (1) non-standard lexis (e.g., *žvajzne* instead of the standard *udari*, Eng. *hit*), (2) non-standard word forms (e.g., *najsuperejši* instead of the standard *najbolj super*, Eng. *the greatest*), and (3) non-standard spelling (e.g., *uredu* instead of the standard *v redu*, Eng. *all right*).

In the manual error analysis, three experimental configurations were compared: (1) the original ReLDI tagger (`reldi`), (2) the ReLDI tagger trained on ssj500k and three times over-represented Janes-Tag (here referred to is `janes`) and (3) the ReLDI tagger trained on the same data as `janes` with the feature set extended with Brown clusters and the normalization lexicon (here referred to as `janes+`). The results of these three configurations on the test portion of the Janes-Tag dataset are presented in Table 4. We again check whether the difference between the `janes` and `janes+` configuration is statistically significant with the McNemar's test, obtaining a p-value of $1.53 * 10^{-10}$ on the MSD level and a p-value of $9.49 * 10^{-15}$ on the PoS level.

configuration	MSD	PoS
reldi	67.73	72.41
janes	85.85	90.22
janes+	87.41	91.98

Table 4: Results in accuracy of the three final configurations on the test portion of the dataset.

We first analysed the five most frequent errors in the `reldi` configuration, which represent 26% of all the errors of that configuration, and compared them with the `janes` and `janes+` configurations.

The most frequent error (which represented 7% of all the errors of that configuration) was the erroneous tagging of punctuation as abbreviations. An inspection of the erroneously tagged instances quickly revealed that this error was due to the non-standard multiplication of punctuation that was not observed in the training data of standard language.

The second most frequent error (which represented nearly 7% of all the errors) was the mistagging of mentions of user accounts in tweets as foreign words, which is hardly surprising as they too did not exist in the standard training data.

On third place (representing 5% of all the errors) are verbs erroneously tagged as foreign language elements, which were mostly due to non-standard spelling (e.g., *prlezla* instead of *prilezla*, Eng. *climbed*) and lexis (e.g., *šprehal* instead of *govoril*, Eng. *spoke*).

Coming fourth (comprising 4% of all the errors) are the verbs mistagged as common nouns, which too is mostly due to non-standard spelling (e.g., *morm* instead of *moram*, Eng. *must*) and lexis (e.g., *fura* instead of *vozi*, Eng. *drives*).

The fifth, and last type of errors with a substantial 3% share of all the errors are misattributions of adverbs as common nouns, again mostly due to non-standard spelling (e.g., *lohk* instead of *lahko*, Eng. *easily*).

Next, we checked how these five most common errors in the original `reldi` configuration fare in the `janes` and `janes+` configurations. The analysis shows that the first two types of errors (non-standard punctuation and mentions) disappear in both settings because the phenomena were now adequately represented in the training data. In a similar vein, the error in mistagged verbs as foreign words and general adverbs as common nouns decreases 10-fold in both configurations. The mistagging of verbs as common nouns drops 3 times in `janes` and 5 times in `janes+`, the difference between the two going back to more observed examples of the non-standard spelling instances in the additional resources, the Brown clusters and the normalization lexicon.

In the third part of the manual error analysis we examined the most frequent errors in the `janes` and `janes+` configurations. The most frequent type of errors (which represents roughly 4% of all the errors in both configurations) was the mistreatment of proper nouns as common ones due to non-standard capitalization and Twitter-specific abbreviations. In `janes`, the second most frequent error type (which represents 4% of all the errors) was the mistagging of verbs as common nouns for the same reasons as in the `reldi` configuration explained above. The third error type in `janes`

and second in `janes+` (comprising 3% of all the errors in both configurations) is the mistagging of adjectives as adverbs, which is a typical tagging error also for standard language. The fourth and fifth most frequent errors in `janes` are the erroneous tagging of foreign words as either proper or common nouns, which however sees a 25% decrease in `janes+` due to additional lexical supervision through Brown clusters.

6 Conclusions

The point of departure was the finding that applying a standard tagger to non-standard language results in a loss in accuracy almost comparable to results on English, more than doubling the amount of error. However, in the paper we have shown that retraining a standard tagger on 60 thousand tokens of non-standard data improves the results drastically.

Additional improvements can be made, primarily by (1) combining non-standard and standard training data (if a large amount of standard training data is available), (2) adding Brown clustering information and (3) adding any additional sort of relevant information, in our case word normalization information.

With a set of systematic experiments we have shown that Brown clusters improve coarse-grained tagging more than the fine-grained one, and that the tagging accuracy on PoS level improves more with Brown clusters than with adding 500k tokens of standard training data, while adding the given amount of standard training data achieves greater improvements on the MSD level. As future work, for enriching processes that have to distinguish between multiple hundreds of classes, a soft word clustering technique should be investigated.

We have observed a positive impact of both quality and quantity of the data used for calculating Brown clusters on the final tagging performance. While smaller amounts of in-domain data achieve better results than large amounts of out-of-domain data, merging these two yields the best results.

Using a large standard inflectional lexicon indirectly, through features, has a significant impact on the final tagging accuracy. A lack of such a resource can be compensated with Brown clusters, fully regarding MSD accuracy and even improving PoS accuracy. However, having both resources at ones' disposal generates the best results.

Finally, word normalization information can visibly improve the results by introducing MSD hypotheses of the normalized word forms in form of features.

While simply retraining the tagger on a combination of standard and non-standard training data removes more than half of the error of the standard tagger, adding additional features relying on external resources such as Brown clusters and word normalization removes additional 11% of the tagging error.

A practical contribution of the paper is that we make the data split[4] (Erjavec et al., 2016c) and the tagger[5] available. We expect the tagger to be used both as the currently best tagger for non-standard Slovene, as well as a strong baseline for future improvements on the problem.

We are currently finalizing datasets consisting of Croatian and Serbian tweets, prepared in a comparable fashion to Janes-Norm and Janes-Tag, and plan to add models for these two languages to the developed tagger in the near future.

Acknowledgments

The work described in this paper was funded by the Slovenian Research Agency national basic research project J6-6842 "Resources, Tools and Methods for the Research of Nonstandard Internet Slovene", the national research programme "Knowledge Technologies", by the Ministry of Education, Science and Sport within the "CLARIN.SI" research infrastructure and the Swiss National Science Foundation grant IZ74Z0 160501 (ReLDI).

References

Željko Agić, Nikola Ljubešić, and Danijela Merkler. 2013. Lemmatization and Morphosyntactic Tagging of Croatian and Serbian. In *Proceedings of the 4th Biennial International Workshop on Balto-Slavic Natural Language Processing*, pages 48–57, Sofia, Bulgaria, August. Association for Computational Linguistics.

Michael Beißwenger, Sabine Bartsch, Stefan Evert, and Akademie der Wissenschaften. 2016. EmpiriST 2015: A shared task on the automatic linguistic annotation of computer-mediated communication and web corpora. In *Proceedings of the 10th Web as Corpus Workshop (WAC-X) and the EmpiriST Shared Task. Berlin, Germany*, pages 44–56.

Peter F. Brown, Peter V. Desouza, Robert L. Mercer, Vincent J. Della Pietra, and Jenifer C. Lai. 1992. Class-based n-gram models of natural language. *Computational linguistics*, 18(4):467–479.

Oliver Christ. 1994. A modular and flexible architecture for an integrated corpus query system. In *Proceedings of COMPLEX 94: 3rd Conference on Computational Lexicography and Text Research*, pages 23–32.

Hal Daumé III. 2007. Frustratingly easy domain adaptation. In *Conference of the Association for Computational Linguistics*.

Kaja Dobrovoljc, Simon Krek, Peter Holozan, Tomaž Erjavec, and Miro Romih. 2015. Morphological lexicon Sloleks 1.2. `http://hdl.handle.net/11356/1039`.

Jacob Eisenstein. 2013. What to do about bad language on the internet. In *Proceedings of the Conference of the North American Chapter of the Association for Computational Linguistics*.

Tomaž Erjavec, Nikola Ljubešić, and Nataša Logar. 2015. The slWaC corpus of the Slovene Web. *Informatica*, 39(1):35.

Tomaž Erjavec, Jaka Čibej, Špela Arhar Holdt, Nikola Ljubešić, and Darja Fišer. 2016a. Gold-standard datasets for annotation of Slovene computer-mediated communication. In *Proceedings of RASLAN 2016: Recent Advances in Slavonic Natural Language Processing*, pages 29–40. Brno: Tribun EU.

Tomaž Erjavec, Darja Fišer, Jaka Čibej, and Špela Arhar Holdt. 2016b. CMC training corpus Janes-Norm 1.2. `http://hdl.handle.net/11356/1084`.

Tomaž Erjavec, Darja Fišer, Jaka Čibej, Špela Arhar Holdt, and Nikola Ljubešić. 2016c. CMC training corpus Janes-Tag 1.2. `http://hdl.handle.net/11356/1085`.

Tomaž Erjavec. 2012. MULTEXT-East: morphosyntactic resources for Central and Eastern European languages. *Language Resources and Evaluation*, 46(1):131–142. DOI: 10.1007/s10579-011-9174-8.

Darja Fišer, Tomaž Erjavec, and Nikola Ljubešić. 2016. JANES v0.4: Korpus slovenskih spletnih uporabniških vsebin (Janes v0.4: Corpus of Slovene User Generated Content). *Slovenščina 2.0: Empirical, Applied and Interdisciplinary Research*, 4(2):67–99.

Kevin Gimpel, Nathan Schneider, Brendan O'Connor, Dipanjan Das, Daniel Mills, Jacob Eisenstein, Michael Heilman, Dani Yogatama, Jeffrey Flanigan,

---

[4]`http://hdl.handle.net/11356/1085`
[5]`https://github.com/clarinsi/janes-tagger`

and Noah A. Smith. 2011. Part-of-speech tagging for Twitter: Annotation, features, and experiments. In *Proceedings of the 49th Annual Meeting of the Association for Computational Linguistics: Human Language Technologies: short papers-Volume 2*, pages 42–47. Association for Computational Linguistics.

Péter Halácsy, András Kornai, and Csaba Oravecz. 2007. HunPos: an open source trigram tagger. In *Proceedings of the 45th Annual Meeting of the ACL on Interactive Poster and Demonstration Sessions*, ACL '07, pages 209–212, Stroudsburg, PA, USA. Association for Computational Linguistics.

Tobias Horsmann and Torsten Zesch. 2015. Effectiveness of Domain Adaptation Approaches for Social Media PoS Tagging. *CLiC it*, page 166.

Dirk Hovy, Barbara Plank, Hector Martinez Alonso, and Anders Søgaard. 2015. Mining for unambiguous instances to adapt PoS taggers to new domains. In *Proceedings of NAACL*. Association for Computational Linguistics.

Nikola Ljubešić, Darja Fišer, Tomaž Erjavec, Jaka Čibej, Dafne Marko, Senja Pollak, and Iza Škrjanec. 2015. Predicting the Level of Text Standardness in User-Generated Content. In *Proceedings of Recent Advances in Natural Language Processing*.

Nikola Ljubešić, Katja Zupan, Darja Fišer, and Tomaž Erjavec. 2016. Normalising Slovene data: historical texts vs. user-generated content. In *Proceedings of KONVENS*.

Nikola Ljubešić and Tomaž Erjavec. 2016. Corpus vs. Lexicon Supervision in Morphosyntactic Tagging: the Case of Slovene. In *Proceedings of the Tenth International Conference on Language Resources and Evaluation (LREC 2016)*, Paris, France. European Language Resources Association (ELRA).

Nikola Ljubešić, Filip Klubička, Željko Agić, and Ivo-Pavao Jazbec. 2016. New Inflectional Lexicons and Training Corpora for Improved Morphosyntactic Annotation of Croatian and Serbian. In *Proceedings of the Tenth International Conference on Language Resources and Evaluation (LREC 2016)*, Paris, France. European Language Resources Association (ELRA).

Quinn McNemar. 1947. Note on the sampling error of the difference between correlated proportions or percentages. *Psychometrika*, 12(2):153–157.

Maja Miličević and Nikola Ljubešić. 2016. Tviterasi, tviteraši or twitteraši? Producing and analysing a normalised dataset of Croatian and Serbian tweets. *Slovenščina 2.0: empirical, applied and interdisciplinary research*, 4(2):156–188.

Olutobi Owoputi, Brendan O'Connor, Chris Dyer, Kevin Gimpel, Nathan Schneider, and Noah A. Smith. 2013. Improved part-of-speech tagging for online conversational text with word clusters. In *Proceedings of the Conference of the North American Chapter of the Association for Computational Linguistics*. Association for Computational Linguistics.

Barbara Plank, Dirk Hovy, Ryan T. McDonald, and Anders Søgaard. 2014. Adapting taggers to Twitter with not-so-distant supervision. In *COLING*, pages 1783–1792.

Yves Scherrer and Nikola Ljubešić. 2016. Automatic normalisation of the Swiss German ArchiMob corpus using character-level machine translation. In *Proceedings of Konferenz zur Verarbeitung natürlicher Sprache (KONVENS)*, Bochum, Germany.

Joseph Turian, Lev Ratinov, and Yoshua Bengio. 2010. Word representations: a simple and general method for semi-supervised learning. In *Proceedings of the 48th annual meeting of the association for computational linguistics*, pages 384–394. Association for Computational Linguistics.

Comparison of Short-Text Sentiment Analysis Methods for Croatian

Leon Rotim and **Jan Šnajder**
Text Analysis and Knowledge Engineering Lab
Faculty of Electrical Engineering and Computing, University of Zagreb
Unska 3, 10000 Zagreb, Croatia
`{leon.rotim, jan.snajder}@fer.hr`

Abstract

We focus on the task of supervised sentiment classification of short and informal
texts in Croatian, using two simple yet effective methods: word embeddings and
string kernels. We investigate whether
word embeddings offer any advantage over
corpus- and preprocessing-free string kernels, and how these compare to bag-of-
words baselines. We conduct a comparison on three different datasets, using different preprocessing methods and kernel
functions. Results show that, on two out
of three datasets, word embeddings outperform string kernels, which in turn outperform word and n-gram bag-of-words baselines.

1   Introduction

Sentiment analysis (Pang and Lee, 2008) – a task
of predicting whether the text expresses a positive, negative, or neutral opinion in general or with
respect to an entity – has attracted considerable
attention over the last two decades. Some of the
more popular applications include political popularity (O'Connor et al., 2010) and stock price prediction (Devitt and Ahmad, 2007). Social media texts,
including user reviews (Tang et al., 2009; Pontiki
et al., 2014) and microblogs (Nakov et al., 2016;
Kouloumpis et al., 2011), are particularly amenable
to sentiment analysis, with applications in social
studies (O'Connor et al., 2010; Wang et al., 2012)
and marketing analyses (He et al., 2013; Yu et al.,
2013). At the same time, social media poses a great
challenge for sentiment analysis, as such texts are
often short, informal, and noisy (Baldwin et al.,
2013), and make heavy use of figurative language
(Ghosh et al., 2015; Buschmeier et al., 2014).

Sentiment analysis is most often framed as a

supervised classification task. Many approaches
resort to rich, domain-specific features (Wilson et
al., 2009; Abbasi et al., 2008), including surface-
form, lexicon-based, and syntactic features. On
the other hand, there has been a growing trend
in using feature-light methods, including neural
word embeddings (Maas et al., 2011; Socher et
al., 2013) and kernel-based methods (Culotta and
Sorensen, 2004; Lodhi et al., 2002a; Srivastava et
al., 2013). In particular, two methods that stand out
in terms of both their simplicity and effectiveness
are word embeddings (Mikolov et al., 2013a) and
string kernels (Lodhi et al., 2002b).

In this paper we focus on sentiment classification
of short text in Croatian, a morphologically complex South Slavic language. We compare two simple yet effective methods – word embeddings and
string kernels – which are often used in text classification tasks. While both methods are easy to set
up, they differ in terms of preprocessing required:
word embeddings require a sizable, possibly lemmatized corpus, whereas string kernels require no
preprocessing at all. This motivates the main question of our research: do word embeddings offer
any advantage over corpus- and preprocessing-free
string kernels, and how do these methods compare to simpler bag-of-words methods? To the best
of our knowledge, this question has not explicitly
been addressed before, especially for a morphologically complex language like Croatian. We present
findings from the comparison on three different
short-text datasets in Croatian, manually labeled
for sentiment polarity, using different levels of morphological preprocessing. To spur further research,
we make one dataset publicly available.

2   Related Work

Sentiment classification for short and informal
texts has been the focus of considerable research,

Proceedings of the 6th Workshop on Balto-Slavic Natural Language Processing, pages 69–75,
Valencia, Spain, 4 April 2017. ©2017 Association for Computational Linguistics

e.g., (Thelwall et al., 2010; Kiritchenko et al., 2014), especially within the recent SemEval evaluation campaigns (Nakov et al., 2016; Rosenthal et al., 2015; Rosenthal et al., 2014). Recent research has focused on sentence-level sentiment classification using neural networks: Socher et al. (2012) and Socher et al. (2013) report impressive results using a matrix-vector recursive neural network (MV-RNN) and recursive neural tensor networks models over parse trees. Tree kernels present an alternative to neural-based approaches: Kim et al. (2015) and Srivastava et al. (2013) use tree kernels on sentence dependency trees and achieve competitive results. However, as noted by Le and Mikolov (2014), while syntax-based methods work well at the sentence level, it is not straightforward to extend them to fragments spanning multiple sentences. Another downside of these methods is that they rely on parsing, which often fails on informal texts.

Word embeddings (Mikolov et al., 2013a) and string kernels (Lodhi et al., 2002b) present an alternative to syntax-based methods. Tang et al. (2014) and Maas et al. (2011) learn sentiment-specific word embeddings, while Le and Mikolov (2014) reach state-of-the-art performance for both short and long sentiment classification of English texts. Zhang et al. (2008) report impressive performance on Chinese reviews using string kernels.

There has been limited research on sentiment analysis for Croatian. Biđin et al. (2014) applied MV-RNN to prediction of phrase sentiment, while Glavaš et al. (2013) addressed aspect-based sentiment analysis using a feature-rich model. More recently, Mozetič et al. (2016) presented a multilingual study of sentiment-labeled tweets and sentiment classification in different languages, including Croatian. However, they experiment only with classifiers using standard bag-of-words features.

3 Datasets

We conducted our comparison on three short-text datasets in Croatian.[1] The datasets differ in domain, genre, size, and the number of classes. Table 1 summarizes the datasets' statistics.

Game reviews (GR). This dataset originally consisted of longer reviews of computer games, in which annotators have labeled 1858 text spans that express positive or negative sentiment. We used the

	GR	TD	TG
# Positive	826	2091	2258
# Negative	1032	607	3883
# Neutral	–	269	1858
Total	1858	2967	7999
Avg. # words	7.97	11.12	22.04
Type-token ratio	0.35	0.18	0.21

Table 1: Datasets' statistics

text spans for our analysis. The spans were labeled by three annotators, and the final annotation was determined by the majority vote on a per-token basis. The spans need not contain full sentences nor need to be limited to a single sentence.

Domain-specific tweets (TD). This dataset contains tweets related to the television singing competition "The Voice of Croatia". The dataset contains 2967 tweets labeled as positive, neutral, or negative by three annotators. The inter-annotator agreement in terms of Fleiss' kappa is 0.721. The final label for each tweet was determined by the majority vote.

General-topic tweets (TG). This is a collection of 7999 general-topic tweets, labeled as positive, neutral, or negative by a single annotator.

The two Twitter datasets, TD and TG, mostly contain informal and often ungrammatical text, whereas the GR dataset is mostly edited, grammatical text. Furthermore, as can be seen from Table 1, Twitter datasets are fairly unbalanced across the three classes, whereas GR is more balanced across the two classes. The GR dataset exhibits the greatest lexical variance, as evidenced by the high type-token ratio. On the other hand, as indicated by the average number of words per text segment/tweet, the texts in TG are longer than the text in the other two datasets.

4 Models

We based all our experiments on the Support Vector Machine (SVM) classification algorithm. Besides being a high-performing algorithm, SVM offers the advantage of using various kernel functions, including string kernels. We used the LIBSVM implementation (Chang and Lin, 2011) for non-linear models and the LIBLINEAR implementation (Fan et al., 2008) for linear models.

Preprocessing. We applied the same preprocessing to all three datasets. For tokenization, we used the Google's SyntaxNet model for Croatian (An-

---

[1]The Game reviews dataset is available at `http://takelab.fer.hr/croSentCmp`. Due to Twitter terms of use, we do not make other two datasets publicly available.

	GR	TD	TG
# Words	1558	1915	9645
# Lemmas	1383	1484	8101
# Stems	1454	1516	7928
# N-grams	8357	9966	46474

Table 2: BoW baseline feature vector dimensions

dor et al., 2016).[2] Croatian is a highly inflectional language, which has been shown to negatively affect classification accuracy (Malenica et al., 2008). We therefore experimented with two morphological normalization techniques: lemmatization and stemming. For lemmatization, we used the CST lemmatizer for Croatian by Agić et al. (2013). The reported lemmatization accuracy is 97%. For stemming, which is a simple and less accurate alternative to lemmatization, we employed a simple rule-based stemmer by Ljubešić et al. (2007). The stemmer works by stripping the inflectional suffixes of nouns and adjectives. We performed no stopwords removal.

BoW baselines. We evaluated four bag-of-word (BoW) baselines. The baselines use words, stems, and lemmas as features. Additionally, we considered character n-grams, which have been proven useful for text classification of noisy texts (Cavnar et al., 1994). Character n-grams can be viewed as an alternative to morphological normalization, as well as a feature-based counterpart to string kernels. We experimented with 2-, 3-, 4-, and 5-grams, which we combined into a single feature set. From each dataset, we filtered out all words, lemmas, and stems occurring less than two times, and all n-grams occurring less than six times. Table 2 lists the vector feature dimensions after filtering. We used a linear kernel for all baseline models.

Word embeddings. Word embeddings (Mikolov et al., 2013a) belong to a class of predictive distributional semantics models (Turney and Pantel, 2010), which derive dense vector representations of word meanings from corpus co-occurrences. While it has been shown that word embeddings produce high-quality word representations, it has also been shown that they exhibit additive compositionality, i.e., they can be used to represent the compositional meaning of phrases and text fragments by means of simple vector averaging (Mikolov et al.,

2013b; Wieting et al., 2015). We trained 300-dimensional skip-gram word embeddings using the word2vec tool[3] on fhrWaC (Šnajder et al., 2013), a filtered version of the Croatian web corpus compiled by Ljubešić and Klubička (2014). We set the window size to 5, negative sampling parameter to 5, and used no hierarchical softmax. When averaging the vectors, we ignored the words, stems, or lemmas that are not covered in the corpus.

SVM's performance very much depends on the choice of the kernel function. For the word embeddings model, we experimented with three different kernels: the linear kernel, the radial basis function (RBF) kernel, and the cosine kernel (Kim et al., 2015). A linear kernel is tantamount to not using any kernel at all and effectively results in a linear model. In contrast, the RBF kernel yields a high-dimensional non-linear model. The cosine kernel is similar to a linear kernel, but additionally includes vector normalization (hence accounting for different-length vectors) and raising to a power:

$$CK(\boldsymbol{x}, \boldsymbol{y}) = \left[\frac{1}{2}\left(1 + \frac{\langle \boldsymbol{x}, \boldsymbol{y}\rangle}{\|\boldsymbol{x}\|\|\boldsymbol{y}\|}\right)\right]^{\alpha}$$

String kernels. A string kernel measures the similarity of two texts in terms of their string similarity, effectively mapping the instances to a high-dimensional feature space. This eliminates the need for features and morphological processing. We experimented with two widely used kernels: a subsequence kernel (SSK) (Lodhi et al., 2002a) and a spectrum kernel (SK) (Leslie et al., 2002). SSK maps each input string s to

$$\varphi_u(s) = \sum_{i:u=s[i]} \lambda^{l(i)}$$

where u is a subsequence searched for in s, i is a vector of indices at which u appears in s, l is a function measuring the length of a matched subsequence and $\lambda \leq 1$ is a weighting parameter giving lower weights to longer subsequences. The corresponding kernel is defined as:

$$K_n(s, t) = \sum_{u \in \Sigma^n} \langle \varphi_u(s), \varphi_u(t)\rangle$$

where n is maximum subsequence length for which we are calculating the kernel and Σ^n is a set of all finite strings of length n. The spectrum kernel can be viewed as a special case of SSK where vector of

---

[2] https://github.com/tensorflow/models/blob/master/syntaxnet/universal.md

[3] https://code.google.com/p/word2vec/

Model/Features	Kernel	GR	TD	TG
BoW baseline				
Words	Linear	0.712	0.673	0.485
N-grams	Linear	0.714	0.690	0.509
Stems	Linear	**0.765**	**0.716**	**0.517**
Lemmas	Linear	0.741	0.711	0.505
Word embeddings				
Words	Linear	0.801	0.653	0.550
Words	RBF	0.807	0.693	**0.565***
Words	Cosine	0.812	**0.715**	0.560
Lemmas	Linear	0.798	0.655	0.536
Lemmas	RBF	0.806	**0.715**	0.543
Lemmas	Cosine	**0.822***	0.711	0.546
String kernels				
–	SK	**0.781**	**0.722**	0.496
–	SSK	0.778	0.718	**0.506**

Table 3: F1-scores for the BoW, word embeddings, and string kernel models on the game reviews (GR), domain-specific (TD), and general-topic (TG) twitter datasets. The best-performing configuration for each model is indicated in bold. Statistically significant differences are marked with *.

indices i must yield contiguous subsequences and λ is set to 1. We compute the string kernels using the Harry string similarity tool.[4]

5   Experiments

Evaluation setup.   We evaluated all models using nested k-folded evaluation with hyperparameter grid search (C and γ for RBF, λ and n for SSK, n for SK, α for the cosine kernel). We used 10 folds in the outer and 5 folds in inner (model selection) loop. Following the established practice in evaluating sentiment classifiers (Nakov et al., 2013), we evaluated using the average of the F1-scores for the positive and the negative classes. We used a t-test (p<0.05, with Bonferroni correction for multiple comparisons where applicable) for testing the significance of differences between the F1-scores.

Results.   Table 3 shows the F1-scores on the three datasets for the baseline, word embeddings, and string kernel models, using different feature sets and kernel configurations. For BoW baselines, the best results are obtained using stemming on all three datasets, i.e., lemmatization does not outperform stemming on neither of the three datasets. For word embeddings, non-linear kernels, cosine kernel in particular, outperform the linear kernel. Lemmatization improves the performance only slightly on the GR dataset, and does not improve or even hurts

[4]http://www.mlsec.org/harry/index.html

the performance on the other two datasets. Finally, for string kernels, we obtain the best results with the spectrum kernel on GR and TD datasets, and subsequence kernel on the TG dataset.

Comparing the best results for the three models, we observe that both word embeddings and string kernels outperform the BoW baseline on the GR and TG datasets (statistically significant difference). Overall, word embeddings yield the best performance on these two datasets, while string kernels give the best performance on the TD dataset, though the difference is not statistically significant.

Comparing across the datasets, we notice that the performance on TD and TG datasets is worse than on the GR dataset. This can be traced back to the informality of TD and TG texts, and also the fact that these datasets have three sentiment classes, whereas the GR dataset has only two. The performance on the TG set is probably further impeded by the fact that it covers a variety of topics, and has been annotated by a single annotator.

Discussion.   We can make three main observations based on the results obtained. The first is that a word embedding model with a cosine kernel and with either words or lemmas as features significantly outperforms both the baseline and the string kernel model on two out of three datasets. This suggest that a word embedding model should be the model of choice for short-text sentiment analysis in Croatian. The second observation is that lemmatization was mostly not useful in our case: for BoW baseline, stems and n-grams offer better or comparable performance, while for word embeddings lemmatization improved performance on only one out of three datasets. While this could probably be traced back to the noisiness of the informal text (at least for TD and TG datasets), it suggests that lemmatization does not really pay off for this task, especially considering its complexity relative to stemming. Finally, we observe that, although string kernels did not significantly outperform the best baseline models, they do significantly outperform the BoW with words as features on two out of three datasets. Thus, in cases when both a stemmer and word embeddings are not available, string kernels may be the model of choice.

6   Conclusion

We addressed the task of short-text sentiment classification for Croatian using two simple yet effective methods: word embeddings and string kernels.

We trained a number of SVM models, using different preprocessing techniques and kernels, and compared them on three datasets exhibiting different characteristics. We find that word embeddings outperform the baseline bag-of-word-models and string kernels on two out of three datasets. Thus, word embeddings are a method of choice for short-text sentiment classification of Croatian. In cases when word embeddings are not an option, bag-of-words with simple stemming is the preferred method. Finally, if stemming is not available, string kernels should be used. We found lemmatization to be of limited use for this task.

References

Ahmed Abbasi, Hsinchun Chen, and Arab Salem. 2008. Sentiment analysis in multiple languages: Feature selection for opinion classification in web forums. *ACM Transactions on Information Systems (TOIS)*, 26(3):12.

Željko Agić, Nikola Ljubešić, and Danijela Merkler. 2013. Lemmatization and morphosyntactic tagging of Croatian and Serbian. In *Proceedings of the 4th Biennial International Workshop on Balto-Slavic Natural Language Processing (BSNLP 2013)*, Sofia, Bulgaria.

Daniel Andor, Chris Alberti, David Weiss, Aliaksei Severyn, Alessandro Presta, Kuzman Ganchev, Slav Petrov, and Michael Collins. 2016. Globally normalized transition-based neural networks. *arXiv preprint arXiv:1603.06042*.

Timothy Baldwin, Paul Cook, Marco Lui, Andrew MacKinlay, and Li Wang. 2013. How noisy social media text, how different social media sources? In *Proceedings of the 6th International Joint Conference on Natural Language Processing (IJCNLP)*, pages 356–364, Nagoya, Japan.

Siniša Biđin, Jan Šnajder, and Goran Glavaš. 2014. Predicting Croatian phrase sentiment using a deep matrix-vector model. In *Proceedings of the Ninth Language Technologies Conference, Information Society (IS-JT 2014)*, Ljubljana, Slovenija.

Konstantin Buschmeier, Philipp Cimiano, and Roman Klinger. 2014. An impact analysis of features in a classification approach to irony detection in product reviews. In *Proceedings of the 5th Workshop on Computational Approaches to Subjectivity, Sentiment and Social Media Analysis*, pages 42–49.

William B. Cavnar, John M. Trenkle, et al. 1994. N-gram-based text categorization. *Ann Arbor MI*, 48113(2):161–175.

Chih-Chung Chang and Chih-Jen Lin. 2011. LIB-SVM: A library for support vector machines. *ACM Transactions on Intelligent Systems and Technology*, 2:27:1–27:27.

Aron Culotta and Jeffrey Sorensen. 2004. Dependency tree kernels for relation extraction. In *Proceedings of the 42nd Annual Meeting on Association for Computational Linguistics*, page 423. Association for Computational Linguistics.

Ann Devitt and Khurshid Ahmad. 2007. Sentiment polarity identification in financial news: A cohesion-based approach. In *Proceedings of the 45th Annual Meeting of the Association of Computational Linguistics*, pages 984–991, Prague, Czech Republic. Association for Computational Linguistics.

Rong-En Fan, Kai-Wei Chang, Cho-Jui Hsieh, Xiang-Rui Wang, and Chih-Jen Lin. 2008. LIBLINEAR: A library for large linear classification. *Journal of machine learning research*, 9:1871–1874.

Aniruddha Ghosh, Guofu Li, Tony Veale, Paolo Rosso, Ekaterina Shutova, John Barnden, and Antonio Reyes. 2015. Semeval-2015 Task 11: Sentiment analysis of figurative language in Twitter. In *Proceedings of the 9th International Workshop on Semantic Evaluation (SemEval 2015)*, pages 470–478.

Goran Glavaš, Damir Korencic, and Jan Šnajder. 2013. Aspect-oriented opinion mining from user reviews in Croatian. In *Proceedings of the 4th Biennial International Workshop on Balto-Slavic Natural Language Processing (BSNLP)*, pages 18–23, Sofia, Bulgaria.

Wu He, Shenghua Zha, and Ling Li. 2013. Social media competitive analysis and text mining: A case study in the pizza industry. *International Journal of Information Management*, 33(3):464–472.

Jonghoon Kim, Francois Rousseau, and Michalis Vazirgiannis. 2015. Convolutional sentence kernel from word embeddings for short text categorization. In *Proceedings of the 2015 Conference on Empirical Methods in Natural Language Processing (EMNLP)*, pages 775–780, Lisbon, Portugal. Association for Computational Linguistics.

Svetlana Kiritchenko, Xiaodan Zhu, and Saif M. Mohammad. 2014. Sentiment analysis of short informal texts. *Journal of Artificial Intelligence Research*, 50:723–762.

Efthymios Kouloumpis, Theresa Wilson, and Johanna D. Moore. 2011. Twitter sentiment analysis: The good the bad and the omg! In *Proceedings of the Fifth International Conference on Weblogs and Social Media (ICWSM)*, pages 538–541, Barcelona, Spain.

Quoc V. Le and Tomas Mikolov. 2014. Distributed representations of sentences and documents. In *Proceedings of The 31st International Conference on Machine Learning (ICML)*, volume 14, pages 1188–1196.

Christina S. Leslie, Eleazar Eskin, and William Stafford Noble. 2002. The spectrum kernel: A string kernel for svm protein classification. In *Proceedings of the Pacific Symposium on Biocomputing*, volume 7, pages 566–575.

Nikola Ljubešić and Filip Klubička. 2014. {bs,hr,sr}WaC – web corpora of Bosnian, Croatian and Serbian. In *Proceedings of the 9th Web as Corpus Workshop (WaC-9)*, pages 29–35, Gothenburg, Sweden. Association for Computational Linguistics.

Nikola Ljubešić, Damir Boras, and Ozren Kubelka. 2007. Retrieving information in Croatian: Building a simple and efficient rule-based stemmer. *Digital information and heritage/Seljan, Sanja*, pages 313–320.

Huma Lodhi, Craig Saunders, John Shawe-Taylor, Nello Cristianini, and Chris Watkins. 2002a. Text classification using string kernels. *Journal of Machine Learning Research*, 2(Feb):419–444.

Huma Lodhi, Craig Saunders, John Shawe-Taylor, Nello Cristianini, and Chris Watkins. 2002b. Text classification using string kernels. *Journal of Machine Learning Research*, 2(Feb):419–444.

Andrew L. Maas, Raymond E. Daly, Peter T. Pham, Dan Huang, Andrew Y. Ng, and Christopher Potts. 2011. Learning word vectors for sentiment analysis. In *Proceedings of the 49th Annual Meeting of the Association for Computational Linguistics: Human Language Technologies-Volume 1*, pages 142–150, Stroudsburg, PA, USA. Association for Computational Linguistics.

Mislav Malenica, Tomislav Šmuc, Jan Šnajder, and B. Dalbelo Bašić. 2008. Language morphology offset: Text classification on a Croatian–English parallel corpus. *Information processing & management*, 44(1):325–339.

Tomas Mikolov, Kai Chen, Greg Corrado, and Jeffrey Dean. 2013a. Efficient estimation of word representations in vector space. *arXiv preprint arXiv:1301.3781*.

Tomas Mikolov, Ilya Sutskever, Kai Chen, Greg S. Corrado, and Jeff Dean. 2013b. Distributed representations of words and phrases and their compositionality. In *Proceedings of the Neural Information Processing Systems Conference (NIPS 2013)*, pages 3111–3119, Lake Tahoe, USA.

Igor Mozetič, Miha Grčar, and Jasmina Smailović. 2016. Multilingual Twitter sentiment classification: The role of human annotators. *PLOS ONE*, 11:1–26.

Preslav Nakov, Sara Rosenthal, Zornitsa Kozareva, Veselin Stoyanov, Alan Ritter, and Theresa Wilson. 2013. Semeval-2013 Task 2: Sentiment analysis in Twitter. In *Second Joint Conference on Lexical and Computational Semantics (*SEM), Volume 2: Seventh International Workshop on Semantic Evaluation (SemEval 2013)*, pages 312–320, Atlanta, Georgia.

Preslav Nakov, Alan Ritter, Sara Rosenthal, Fabrizio Sebastiani, and Veselin Stoyanov. 2016. Semeval-2016 Task 4: Sentiment analysis in Twitter. *Proceedings of SemEval*, pages 1–18.

Brendan O'Connor, Ramnath Balasubramanyan, Bryan R. Routledge, and Noah A. Smith. 2010. From tweets to polls: Linking text sentiment to public opinion time series. In *International Conference on Web and Social Media (ICWSM)*, pages 122–129, Washington, DC.

Bo Pang and Lillian Lee. 2008. Opinion mining and sentiment analysis. *Foundations and trends in information retrieval*, 2(1-2):1–135.

Maria Pontiki, Dimitris Galanis, John Pavlopoulos, Harris Papageorgiou, Ion Androutsopoulos, and Suresh Manandhar. 2014. Semeval-2014 task 4: Aspect based sentiment analysis. *Proceedings of SemEval*, pages 27–35.

Sara Rosenthal, Alan Ritter, Preslav Nakov, and Veselin Stoyanov. 2014. SemEval-2014 Task 9: Sentiment analysis in Twitter. In *Proceedings of the 8th international workshop on semantic evaluation (SemEval 2014)*, pages 73–80, Dublin, Ireland.

Sara Rosenthal, Preslav Nakov, Svetlana Kiritchenko, Saif M. Mohammad, Alan Ritter, and Veselin Stoyanov. 2015. SemEval-2015 Task 10: Sentiment analysis in Twitter. In *Proceedings of the 9th international workshop on semantic evaluation (SemEval 2015)*, pages 451–463.

Jan Šnajder, Sebastian Padó, and Željko Agić. 2013. Building and evaluating a distributional memory for Croatian. In *Proceedings of the 51st Annual Meeting of the Association for Computational Linguistics*, pages 784–789, Sofia, Bulgaria.

Richard Socher, Brody Huval, Christopher D. Manning, and Andrew Y. Ng. 2012. Semantic compositionality through recursive matrix-vector spaces. In *Proceedings of the conference on empirical methods in natural language processing (EMNLP)*, pages 1201–1211. Association for Computational Linguistics.

Richard Socher, Alex Perelygin, Jean Y. Wu, Jason Chuang, Christopher D. Manning, Andrew Y. Ng, and Christopher Potts. 2013. Recursive deep models for semantic compositionality over a sentiment treebank. In *Proceedings of the conference on empirical methods in natural language processing (EMNLP)*, volume 1631, page 1642.

Shashank Srivastava, Dirk Hovy, and Eduard H. Hovy. 2013. A walk-based semantically enriched tree kernel over distributed word representations. In *Proceedings of the Conference on Empirical Methods in Natural Language Processing (EMNLP)*, pages 1411–1416, Seattle, USA. Association for Computational Linguistics.

Huifeng Tang, Songbo Tan, and Xueqi Cheng. 2009. A survey on sentiment detection of reviews. *Expert Systems with Applications*, 36(7):10760–10773.

Duyu Tang, Furu Wei, Nan Yang, Ming Zhou, Ting Liu, and Bing Qin. 2014. Learning sentiment-specific word embedding for twitter sentiment classification. In *The 52nd Annual Meeting of the Association for Computational Linguistics (ACL)*, pages 1555–1565, Baltimore, MD, USA.

Mike Thelwall, Kevan Buckley, Georgios Paltoglou, Di Cai, and Arvid Kappas. 2010. Sentiment strength detection in short informal text. *Journal of the American Society for Information Science and Technology*, 61(12):2544–2558.

Peter D. Turney and Patrick Pantel. 2010. From frequency to meaning: Vector space models of semantics. *Journal of artificial intelligence research*, 37:141–188.

Hao Wang, Dogan Can, Abe Kazemzadeh, François Bar, and Shrikanth Narayanan. 2012. A system for real-time twitter sentiment analysis of 2012 us presidential election cycle. In *Proceedings of the ACL 2012 System Demonstrations*, pages 115–120. Association for Computational Linguistics.

John Wieting, Mohit Bansal, Kevin Gimpel, and Karen Livescu. 2015. Towards universal paraphrastic sentence embeddings. *arXiv preprint arXiv:1511.08198*.

Theresa Wilson, Janyce Wiebe, and Paul Hoffmann. 2009. Recognizing contextual polarity: An exploration of features for phrase-level sentiment analysis. *Computational linguistics*, 35(3):399–433.

Yang Yu, Wenjing Duan, and Qing Cao. 2013. The impact of social and conventional media on firm equity value: A sentiment analysis approach. *Decision Support Systems*, 55(4):919–926.

Changli Zhang, Wanli Zuo, Tao Peng, and Fengling He. 2008. Sentiment classification for Chinese reviews using machine learning methods based on string kernel. In *Proceedings of the 3rd International Conference on Convergence Information (ICCIT)*, volume 2, pages 909–914, Busan, Korea. IEEE.

The First Cross-Lingual Challenge on Recognition, Normalization and Matching of Named Entities in Slavic Languages

Jakub Piskorski[1], Lidia Pivovarova[2], Jan Šnajder[3], Josef Steinberger[4], Roman Yangarber[2]

[1]Joint Research Centre, Ispra, Italy, `first.last@jrc.ec.europa.eu`
[2]University of Helsinki, Finland, `first.last@cs.helsinki.fi`
[3]University of Zagreb, Croatia, `first.last@fer.hr`
[4]University of West Bohemia, Czech Republic, `jstein@kiv.zcu.cz`

Abstract

This paper describes the outcomes of the First Multilingual Named Entity Challenge in Slavic Languages. The Challenge targets recognizing mentions of named entities in web documents, their normalization/lemmatization, and cross-lingual matching. The Challenge was organized in the context of the 6th Balto-Slavic Natural Language Processing Workshop, co-located with the EACL-2017 conference. Eleven teams registered for the evaluation, two of which submitted results on schedule, due to the complexity of the tasks and short time available for elaborating a solution. The reported evaluation figures reflect the relatively higher level of complexity of named entity tasks in the context of Slavic languages. Since the Challenge extends beyond the date of the publication of this paper, updates to the results of the participating systems can be found on the official web page of the Challenge.

1 Introduction

Due to the rich inflection, derivation, free word order, and other morphological and syntactic phenomena exhibited by Slavic languages, analysis of named entities (NEs) in these languages poses a challenging task (Przepiórkowski, 2007; Piskorski et al., 2009). Fostering research and development on detection and lemmatization of NEs—and the closely related problem of entity linking—is of paramount importance for enabling effective multilingual and cross-lingual information access in these languages.

This paper describes the outcomes of the first shared task on multilingual named entity recognition (NER) that aims at recognizing mentions of named entities in web documents in Slavic languages, their normalization/lemmatization, and cross-lingual matching. The task initially covers seven languages and four types of NEs: person, location, organization, and miscellaneous, where the last category covers all other types of named entities, e.g., event or product. The input text collection consists of documents in seven Slavic languages collected from the web, each collection revolving around a certain "focus" entity. The main rationale of such a setup is to foster development of "all-rounder" NER and cross-lingual entity matching solutions that are not tailored to specific, narrow domains. The shared task was organized in the context of the 6th Balto-Slavic Natural Language Processing Workshop co-located with the EACL 2017 conference.

Similar shared tasks have been organized previously. The first *non-English* monolingual NER evaluations—covering Chinese, Japanese, Spanish, and Arabic—were carried out in the context of the Message Understanding Conferences (MUCs) (Chinchor, 1998) and the ACE Programme (Doddington et al., 2004). The first shared task focusing on *multilingual* named entity recognition, which covered some European languages, including Spanish, German, and Dutch, was organized in the context of CoNLL conferences (Tjong Kim Sang, 2002; Tjong Kim Sang and De Meulder, 2003). The NE types covered in these campaigns were similar to the NE types covered in our Challenge. Also related to our task is the Entity Discovery and Linking (EDL) track (Ji et al., 2014; Ji et al., 2015) of the NIST Text Analysis Conferences (TAC). EDL aimed to extract entity mentions from a collection of textual documents in multiple languages (English, Chinese, and Spanish), and to partition the entities into cross-document equivalence classes, by either linking mentions to a knowledge base or directly

Proceedings of the 6th Workshop on Balto-Slavic Natural Language Processing, pages 76–85,
Valencia, Spain, 4 April 2017. ©2017 Association for Computational Linguistics

clustering them. An important difference between EDL and our task is that we do not link entities to a knowledge base.

Related to cross-lingual NE recognition is NE transliteration, i.e., linking NEs across languages that use different scripts. A series of NE Transliteration Shared Tasks were organized as a part of NEWS—Named Entity Workshops—(Duan et al., 2016), focusing mostly on Indian and Asian languages. In 2010, the NEWS Workshop included a shared task on Transliteration Mining (Kumaran et al., 2010), i.e., mining of names from parallel corpora. This task included corpora in English, Chinese, Tamil, Russian, and Arabic.

Prior work targeting NEs specifically for Slavic languages includes tools for NE recognition for Croatian (Karan et al., 2013; Ljubešić et al., 2013), a tool tailored for NE recognition in Croatian tweets (Baksa et al., 2017), a manually annotated NE corpus for Croatian (Agić and Ljubešić, 2014), tools for NE recognition in Slovene (Štajner et al., 2013; Ljubešić et al., 2013), a Czech corpus of 11,000 manually annotated NEs (Ševčíková et al., 2007), NER tools for Czech (Konkol and Konopík, 2013), tools and resources for fine-grained annotation of NEs in the National Corpus of Polish (Waszczuk et al., 2010; Savary and Piskorski, 2011) and a recent shared task on NE Recognition in Russian (Alexeeva et al., 2016).

To the best of our knowledge, the shared task described in this paper is the first attempt at multilingual name recognition, normalization, and cross-lingual entity matching that covers a large number of Slavic languages.

This paper is organized as follows. Section 2 describes the task; Section 3 describes the annotation of the dataset. The evaluation methodology is introduced in Section 4. Participant systems are described in Section 5 and the results obtained by these systems are presented in Section 6. Finally, lessons learnt and conclusions are discussed in Section 7.

2 Task Description

The data for the shared task consists of text documents in seven Slavic languages: Croatian, Czech, Polish, Russian, Slovak, Slovene, and Ukrainian. The documents focus around a certain entity— e.g., a person or an organization. The documents were obtained from the web, by posing a query to a search engine and parsing the HTML of the re-

trieved documents.

The task is to recognize, classify, and "normalize" all named-entity mentions in each of the documents, and to link across languages all named mentions referring to the same real-world entity.

Formally, the Multilingual Named Entity Recognition task includes three sub-tasks:

- **Named Entity Mention Detection and Classification.** Recognizing all unique named mentions of entities of four types: persons (PER), organizations (ORG), locations (LOC), miscellaneous (MISC), the last covering mentions of all other types of named entities, e.g., products, events, etc.

- **Name Normalization.** Mapping each named mention of an entity to its corresponding *base form*. By "base form" we generally mean the lemma ("dictionary form") of the inflected word-form. In some cases normalization should go beyond inflection and transform a derived word into a base word's lemma, e.g., in case of personal possessives (see below). Multi-word names should be normalized to the *canonical* multi-word expression, rather than a sequence of lemmas of the words making up the multi-word expression.

- **Entity Matching.** Assigning an identifier (ID) to each detected named mention of an entity, in such a way that mentions of entities referring to the same real-world entity should be assigned the same ID (referred to as the cross-lingual ID).

The task does not require positional information of the name entity mentions. Consequently, for all occurrences of the same form of a NE mention (e.g., inflected variant, acronym, or abbreviation) within the same document no more than one annotation should be returned.[1] Furthermore, distinguishing case information is not necessary since the evaluation is case-insensitive. In particular, if the text includes lowercase, uppercase or mixed-case variants of the same entity, the system should produce only one annotation for all of these mentions. For instance, for "*ISIS*", "*isis*", and "*Isis*" (provided that they refer to the same NE type), only one annotation should be returned. Note that the recognition of nominal or pronominal mentions of entities is not part of the task.

---

[1]Unless the different occurrences have different entity types (different readings) assigned to them, which is rare.

2.1 Named Entity Classes

The task defines the following four NE classes.

Person names (PER). Names of real persons (and fictional characters). Person names should not include titles, honorifics, and functions/positions. For example, in the text fragment "*... CEO Dr. Jan Kowalski...*", only "*Jan Kowalski'"*" is recognized as a person name. Initials and pseudonyms are considered named mentions of persons and should be recognized. Similarly, named references to groups of people (that do not have a formal organization unifying them) should also be recognized, e.g., "*Ukrainians.*" In this context, mentions of a single member belonging to such groups, e.g., "*Ukrainian,*" should be assigned the same cross-lingual ID as plural mentions, i.e., "*Ukrainians*" and "*Ukrainian*" when referring to the nation should be assigned the same cross-lingual ID.

Personal possessives derived from a person name should be classified as a person, and the base form of the corresponding person name should be extracted. For instance, for "*Trumpov tweet*" (Croatian) it is expected to recognize "*Trumpov*" and classify it as PER, with the base form "*Trump.*"

Locations (LOC). All toponyms and geopolitical entities (cities, counties, provinces, countries, regions, bodies of water, land formations, etc.), including named mentions of *facilities* (e.g., stadiums, parks, museums, theaters, hotels, hospitals, transportation hubs, churches, railroads, bridges, and similar facilities).

In case named mentions of facilities may also refer to an organization, the LOC tag should be used. For example, from the text phrase "*The Schipol Airport has acquired new electronic gates*" the mention "*The Schipol Airport*" should be extracted and classified as LOC.

Organizations (ORG). All kinds of organizations: political parties, public institutions, international organizations, companies, religious organizations, sport organizations, educational and research institutions, etc.

Organization designators and potential mentions of the seat of the organization are considered to be part of the organization name.

For instance, from the text fragment "*Citi Handlowy w Poznaniu*" (a bank in Poznań), the full phrase "*Citi Handlowy w Poznaniu*" should be extracted.

When a company name is used to refer to a service (e.g., "*na Twiterze*" (Polish for "on Twitter"), the mention of "*Twitter*" is considered to refer to a service/product and should be tagged as MISC. However, when a company name is referring to a service which expresses the opinion of the company, e.g., "*Fox News*", it should be tagged as ORG.

Miscellaneous (MISC). All other named mentions of entities, e.g., product names—e.g., "*Motorola Moto X*"), events (conferences, concerts, natural disasters, holidays, e.g., "*Święta Bożego Narodzenia*" (Polish for "Christmas"), etc.

This category does not include temporal and numerical expressions, as well as identifiers such as email addresses, URLs, postal addresses, etc.

2.2 Complex and Ambiguous Entities

In case of complex named entities, consisting of nested named entities, only the *top-most* entity should be recognized. For example, from the text string "*George Washington University*" one should not extract "*George Washington*", but the entire string.

In case one word-form (e.g., "*Washington*") is used to refer to two different real-world entities in different contexts in the same document (e.g., a person and a location), the system should return two annotations, associated with different cross-lingual IDs.

2.3 System Input and Response

Input Document Format. Documents in the collection are represented in the following format. The first five lines contain meta-data; the core text to be processed begins from the 6th line and runs till the end of file.

```
<DOCUMENT-ID>
<LANGUAGE>
<CREATION-DATE>
<URL>
<TITLE>
<TEXT>
```

The `<URL>` field stores the origin from which the text document was retrieved. The values of the meta-data fields were computed automatically (see Section 3 for details). In particular, the values of <CREATION-DATE> and <TITLE> were not provided for all documents, either due to unavailability of such data or due to errors in web page parsing during the creation process.

System Response. For each input document, the systems should return one file as follows. The first line should contain only the <DOCUMENT-ID> field that corresponds to the input file. Each subsequent line should contain the following, tab-separated fields:

```
<MENTION> TAB <BASE> TAB <CAT> TAB <ID>
```

The value of the <MENTION> field should be the NE mention as it appears in text. The value of the <BASE> field should be the base form of the entity. The <CAT> and <ID> fields store information on the category of the entity (ORG, PER, LOC, or MISC) and cross-lingual identifier, respectively. The cross-lingual identifiers may consist of an arbitrary sequence of alphanumeric characters. An example of a system response (for a document in Polish) is given below.

```
16
Podlascy Czeczeni    Podlascy Czeczeni    PER    1
ISIS    ISIS    ORG    2
Rosji    Rosja    LOC    3
Rosja    Rosja    LOC    3
Polsce    Polska    LOC    4
Warszawie    Warszawa    LOC    5
Magazynu Kuriera Porannego    Magazyn Kuriera\
    Porannego    ORG    6
```

3 Data

3.1 Trial Datasets

The registered participants were provided two trial datasets: (1) a dataset related to *Beata Szydło*, the current prime minister of Poland, and (2) a dataset related to *ISIS*, the so-called "Islamic State of Iraq and Syria" terrorist group. These datasets consisted of 187 and 186 documents, respectively, with equal distribution of documents across the seven languages of interest.

3.2 Test Datasets

Two datasets were prepared for evaluation, each consisting of documents extracted from the web and related to a given entity. One dataset contains documents related to *Donald Trump*, the recently elected President of United States (henceforth referred to as TRUMP), and the second dataset contains documents related to the *European Commission* (henceforth referred to as ECOMMISSION).

The test datasets were created as follows. For each "focus" entity, we posed a separate search query to Google, in each of the seven target languages. The query returned links to documents only in the language of interest. We extracted the first 100 links[2] returned by the search engine, removed duplicate links, downloaded the corresponding HTML pages—mainly news articles or fragments thereof—and converted them into plain text, using a hybrid HTML parser. This process was done semi-automatically using the tool described in (Crawley and Wagner, 2010). In particular, some of the meta-data fields—i.e., creation date, title, URL—were automatically computed using this tool.

HTML parsing resulted in texts that included not only the core text of a web page, but also some additional pieces of text, e.g., a list of labels from a menu, user comments, etc., which may not constitute well-formed utterances in the target language. This occurred in a small fraction of texts processed. Some of these texts were included in the test dataset in order to maintain the flavour of "real-data." However, obvious HTML parser failure (e.g., extraction of JavaScript code, extraction of empty texts, etc.) were removed from the data sets. Some of the downloaded documents were additionally polished by removing erroneously extracted boilerplate content. The resulting set of partially "cleaned" documents were used to select *circa* 20–25 documents for each language and topic, for the preparation of the final test datasets. Annotations for Croatian, Czech, Polish, Russian, and Slovene were made by native speakers; annotations for Slovak were made by native speakers of Czech, capable of understanding Slovak. Annotations for Ukrainian were made partly by native speakers and partly by near-native speakers of Ukrainian. Cross-lingual alignment of the entity identifiers was performed by two annotators.

Table 1 provides more quantitative details about the annotated datasets. Table 2 gives the breakdown of entity classes. It is noteworthy that a high proportion of the annotated mentions have a base form that differs from the form appearing in text. For instance, for the TRUMP dataset this figure is between 37.5% (Slovak) and 57.5% (Croatian).

---

[2] Or fewer, in case the search engine did not return 100 links.

	TRUMP		ECOMMISSION	
Language	# docs	# ment	# docs	# ment
Croatian	25	525	25	436
Czech	25	479	25	417
Polish	25	692	24	466
Russian	26	331	24	385
Slovak	24	453	25	374
Slovene	24	474	26	434
Ukrainian	28	337	54	1078
Total	177	3291	203	3588

Table 1: Quantitative data about the test datasets. *#docs* and *#ment* refer to the number of documents and NE mention annotations, respectively.

Table 3 provides examples of genitive forms of the name *"European Commission"* that occurred in the ECOMMISSION corpus frequently.

While normalization of the inflected forms in Table 3 could be achieved by lemmatization of each of the constituents of the noun phrase separately and then concatenating the corresponding base forms together, many entity mentions in the test dataset are complex noun phrases, whose lemmatization requires detection of inner syntactic structure. For instance, the inflected form of the Polish proper name *Europejskiego Funduszu Rozwoju Regionalnego* (*European$_{GEN}$ Fund$_{GEN}$ Development$_{GEN}$ Regional$_{GEN}$*) consists of two basic genitive noun phrases, of which only the first one ("European Fund") needs to be normalized, whereas the second ("Regional Development") should remain unchanged. The corresponding base form is *"Europejski Fundusz Rozwoju Regionalnego"*. Since in some Slavic languages adjectives may precede or follow a noun in a noun phrase (like in the example above), detection of inner syntactic structure of complex proper names is not trivial (Radziszewski, 2013), and thus complicates the process of automated lemmatization. Complex person name declension paradigms (Piskorski et al., 2009) add another level of complexity.

It is worth mentioning that, for the sake of compliance with the NER guidelines in Section 2, documents that included hard-to-decide entity mention annotations were excluded from the test datasets for the present. A case in point is a document in Croatian that contained the phrase *"Zagrebačka, Sisačko-Moslavačka i Karlovačka županija"*—a contracted version of three named entities (*"Zagrebačka županija"*,

Entity type	TRUMP	ECOMMISSION
PER	48.4%	11.9%
LOC	26.9%	29.1%
ORG	18.3%	48.4%
MISC	6.4%	9.6%

Table 2: Breakdown of the annotations according to the entity type.

	Genitive	Nominative ("base")
hr	Europske komisije	Europska komisija
cz	Komisji Europejskiej	Komisja Europejska
pl	Evropskou komisí	Evropská komise
ru	Европейской комиссией	Европейская комиссия
sl	Evropske komisije	Evropska komisija
sk	Európskej komisie	Európska komisia
ua	Європейської Комісії	Європейська Комісія

Table 3: Inflected (genitive) forms of the name *"European Commission"* found in test data.

"Sisačko-Moslavačka županija", and *"Karlovačka županija"*) expressed using a head noun with three coordinate modifiers.

4 Evaluation Methodology

The NER task (exact case-insensitive matching) and Name Normalization task (also called "lemmatization") were evaluated in terms of precision, recall, and F1-scores. In particular, for NER, two types of evaluations were carried out:

- **Relaxed evaluation**: An entity mentioned in a given document is considered to be extracted correctly if the system response includes at least one annotation of a named mention of this entity (regardless whether the extracted mention is in base form);

- **Strict evaluation**: The system response should include exactly one annotation for *each* unique form of a named mention of an entity in a given document, i.e., capturing and listing all variants of an entity is required.

In relaxed evaluation mode we additionally distinguish between *exact* and *partial matching*, i.e., in the case of the latter an entity mentioned in a given document is considered to be extracted correctly if the system response includes at least one partial match of a named mention of this entity.

In the evaluation we consider various levels of granularity, i.e., the performance for: (a) all NE types and all languages, (b) each particular NE

TRUMP		cz	hr	pl	ru	sk	sl	ua
Phase	*Metric*			Language				
Recognition	Relaxed Partial	jhu 46.2	jhu 52.4	pw 66.6 / jhu 44.8	jhu 46.3	jhu 46.8	jhu 47.3	jhu 38.8
	Relaxed Exact	jhu 46.1	jhu 50.8	pw 66.1 / jhu 43.4	jhu 43.1	jhu 46.2	jhu 46.0	jhu 37.3
	Strict	jhu 46.1	jhu 50.4	pw 66.6 / jhu 41.0	jhu 41.8	jhu 47.0	jhu 46.2	jhu 33.2
Normalization				pw 60.5				
Entity matching	Document-level	jhu 5.4	jhu 7.3	jhu 6.3 / pw 10.8	jhu 11.2	jhu 10.1	jhu 9.5	jhu 0.0
	Single-language	jhu 19.3	jhu 17.6	jhu 18.2 / pw 4.9	jhu 18.9	jhu 22.6	jhu 28.7	jhu 10.7
	Cross-lingual	jhu 9.0						
ECOMMISSION		cz	hr	pl	ru	sk	sl	ua
Phase	*Metric*			Language				
Recognition	Relaxed Partial	jhu 47.6	jhu 45.9	pw 61.8 / jhu 47.3	jhu 46.0	jhu 49.1	jhu 47.9	jhu 18.4
	Relaxed Exact	jhu 44.4	jhu 43.1	pw 60.9 / jhu 42.4	jhu 44.1	jhu 46.4	jhu 43.9	jhu 14.7
	Strict	jhu 47.2	jhu 46.2	pw 61.1 / jhu 44.8	jhu 46.5	jhu 46.1	jhu 47.8	jhu 10.8
Normalization				pw 48.3				
Entity Matching	Document-level	jhu 25.0	jhu 16.0	jhu 13.7 / pw 13.4	jhu 13.7	jhu 13.1	jhu 36.8	jhu 0.6
	Single-language	jhu 27.3	jhu 22.1	jhu 17.5 / pw 4.6	jhu 24.9	jhu 30.6	jhu 32.2	jhu 4.8
	Cross-lingual	jhu 2.6						

Table 4: Evaluation results across all scenarios and languages.

type and all languages, (c) all NE types for each language, and (d) each particular NE type per language.

In the name normalization sub-task, only correctly recognized entity mentions in the system response and only those that were normalized (on both the annotation and system's sides) are taken into account. Formally, let $correct_N$ denote the number of all correctly recognized entity mentions for which the system returned a correct base form. Let key_N denote the number of all normalized entity mentions in the gold-standard answer key and $response_N$ denote the number of all normalized entity mentions in the system's response. We define precision and recall for the name normalization task as:

$$Recall_N = \frac{corrrect_N}{key_N}$$

$$Precision_N = \frac{corrrect_N}{response_N}$$

In evaluating the document-level, single-language and cross-lingual entity matching task we have adapted the Link-Based Entity-Aware metric (LEA) (Moosavi and Strube, 2016) which considers how important the entity is and how well it is resolved. LEA is defined as follows. Let $K = \{k_1, k_2, \ldots, k_{|K|}\}$ and $R = \{r_1, r_2, \ldots, r_{|R|}\}$ denote the key entity set and the response entity set, respectively, i.e., $k_i \in K$ ($r_i \in R$) stand for set of mentions of the same entity in the key entity set (response entity set). LEA recall and precision are then defined as follows:

$$Recall_{LEA} = \frac{\sum_{k_i \in K} (imp(k_i) \times res(k_i))}{\sum_{k_z \in K} imp(k_z)}$$

$$Precision_{LEA} = \frac{\sum_{r_i \in R}(imp(r_i) \times res(r_i))}{\sum_{r_z \in R} imp(r_z)}$$

where imp and res denote the measure of importance and the resolution score for an entity, respectively. In our setting, we define $imp(e) = \log_2 |e|$ for an entity e (in K or R), $|e|$ is the number of mentions of e—i.e., the more mentions an entity has the more important it is. To avoid biasing the importance of the more frequent entities log is used. The resolution score of key entity k_i is computed as the fraction of correctly resolved co-reference links of k_i:

$$res(k_i) = \sum_{r_j \in R} \frac{link(k_i \cap r_j)}{link(k_i)}$$

where $link(e) = (|e| \times (|e| - 1))/2$ is the number of unique co-reference links in e. For each k_i, LEA checks all response entities to check whether they are partial matches for k_i. Analogously, the resolution score of response entity r_i is computed as the fraction of co-reference links in r_i that are extracted correctly:

$$res(r_i) = \sum_{k_j \in K} \frac{link(r_i \cap k_j)}{link(r_i)}$$

Using LEA brings several benefits. For example, LEA considers resolved co-reference relations instead of resolved mentions and has more discriminative power than other metrics used for evaluation of co-reference resolution (Moosavi and Strube, 2016).

It is important to note at this stage that the evaluation was carried out in "case-insensitive" mode: all named mentions in system response and test corpora were lowercased.

5   Participant Systems

Eleven teams from seven countries—Czech Republic, Germany, India, Poland, Russia, Slovenia, and USA—registered for the evaluation task and received the trial datasets. Due to the complexity of the task and relatively short time available to create a working solution, only two teams submitted results within the deadline. A total of two unique runs were submitted.

JHU/APL team attempted the NER and Entity Matching sub-tasks. They employed a statistical tagger called SVMLattice (Mayfield et al., 2003),

with NER labels inferred by projecting English tags across bitext. The Illinois tagger (Ratinov and Roth, 2009) was used for English. A rule-based entity clusterer called "kripke" was used for Entity Matching (McNamee et al., 2013). The team (code "*jhu*") attempted all languages available in the Challenge. More details can be found in (Mayfield et al., 2017).

The G4.19 Research Group adapted Liner2 (Marcińczuk et al., 2013)—a generic framework which can be used to solve various tasks based on sequence labeling, which is equipped with a set of modules (based on statistical models, dictionaries, rules and heuristics) which recognize and annotate certain types of phrases. The details of tuning Liner2 to tackle the shared task are described in (Marcińczuk et al., 2017). The team (code "*pw*") attempted only the Polish-language Challenge.

The above systems met the deadline to participate in the first run of the Challenge—Phase I. Since the Challenge aroused significant interest in the research community, it was extended into Phase II, with a new deadline for submitting system responses, beyond the time of publication of this paper. Please refer to the Challenge web site[3] for information on the current status, systems tested, and their performance.

6   Evaluation Results

The results of the runs submitted for Phase I are presented in Table 4. The figures provided for the recognition are micro-averaged F1-scores.

For normalization, we report F1-scores, using the $Recall_N$ and $Precision_N$ definitions from Section 4, computed for entity mentions for which the annotation or system response contains a different base form compared to the surface form. This evaluation includes only correctly recognized entity mentions to suppress the influence of entity recognition performance.

Lastly, for entity matching, the micro-averaged F1-scores are provided, computed using LEA precision and recall values (see Section 4).

System *pw* performed substantially better on Polish than system *jhu*.

Considering the entity types, performance was overall better for LOC and PER, and substantially lower for ORG and MISC, which is not unexpected. Table 5 and 6 provide the overall aver-

---

[3]http://bsnlp.cs.helsinki.fi/shared_task.html

Metric	Precision	Recall	F1
PER	74.8	65.9	69.8
LOC	73.0	75.4	74.2
ORG	47.1	22.1	30.0
MISC	7.9	14.4	10.2

Table 5: Breakdown of the recognition performance according to the entity type for TRUMP dataset.

Metric	Precision	Recall	F1
PER	68.2	59.4	62.9
LOC	73.1	57.8	64.5
ORG	45.0	49.0	46.6
MISC	18.7	12.0	14.2

Table 6: Breakdown of the recognition performance according to the entity type for ECOMMIS-SION dataset.

age precision, recall, and F1 figures for the relaxed evaluation with partial matching for TRUMP and ECOMMISSION scenario respectively.

Considering the tested languages and scenarios, system *jhu* achieved best performance on TRUMP in Croatian, its poorest performance was on ECOMMISSION in Ukrainian. System *pw* performed better on the TRUMP scenario than on ECOMMISSION. Overall, the TRUMP scenario appears to be easier, due to the mix of named entities that predominate in the texts. The ECOMMISSION documents discuss organizations with complex geo-political inter-relationships and affiliations.

Furthermore, cross-lingual co-reference seems to be a difficult task.

7 Conclusions

This paper reports on the First multilingual named entity Challenge that aims at recognizing mentions of named entities in web documents in Slavic languages, their normalization/lemmatization, and cross-lingual matching. Although the Challenge aroused substantial interest in the field, only two teams submitted results on time, most likely due to the complexity of the tasks and the short time available to finalize a solution. While drawing substantial conclusions from the evaluation of two systems is not yet possible, we can observe though that the overall performance of the two systems on hidden test sets revolving around a specific entity is significantly lower than in the case of processing less-morphologically complex languages.

To support research on NER-related tasks for Slavic languages, including cross-lingual entity matching, the Challenge was extended into Phase II, going beyond the date of the publication of this paper. For the current list of systems that has been evaluated on the different tasks and their performance figures please refer to the shared task web page.

The test datasets, the corresponding annotations and various scripts used for the evaluation purposes are made available on the shared task web page as well.

We plan to extend the Challenge through provision of additional test datasets in the future, involving new entities, in order to further boost research on developing "all-rounder" NER solutions for processing real-world texts in Slavic languages and carrying out cross-lingual entity matching. Furthermore, we plan to extend the set of the languages covered, depending on the availability of annotators. Finally, some work will focus on the refining the NE annotation guidelines in order to properly deal with particular phenomena, e.g., co-ordinated NEs and contracted versions of multiple NEs, which were excluded from the first test datasets.

Acknowledgments

We thank Katja Zupan (Department of Knowledge Technologies, Jožef Stefan Institute, Slovenia), Anastasia Stepanova (State University of New York, Buffalo), Domagoj Alagić (TakeLab, University of Zagreb), and Olga Kanishcheva, Kateryna Klymenkova, Ekaterina Yurieva (the National Technical University, Kharkiv Polytechnic Institute), who contributed to the preparation of the Slovenian, Russian, Croatian, and Ukrainian test data. We are also grateful to Tomaž Erjavec from the Department of Knowledge Technologies, Jožef Stefan Institute in Slovenia, who contributed various ideas. Work on Czech and Slovak was supported by Project MediaGist, EU's FP7 People Programme (Marie Curie Action), no. 630786.

The effort of organizing the shared task was supported by the Europe Media Monitoring (EMM) Project carried out by the Text and Data Mining Unit of the Joint Research Centre of the European Commission.

References

Željko Agić and Nikola Ljubešić. 2014. The SE-Times.HR linguistically annotated corpus of Croatian. In *Ninth International Conference on Language Resources and Evaluation (LREC 2014)*, pages 1724–1727, Reykjavík, Iceland.

S. Alexeeva, S.Y. Toldova, A.S. Starostin, V.V. Bocharov, A.A. Bodrova, A.S. Chuchunkov, S.S. Dzhumaev, I.V. Efimenko, D.V. Granovsky, V.F. Khoroshevsky, et al. 2016. FactRuEval 2016: Evaluation of named entity recognition and fact extraction systems for Russian. In *Computational Linguistics and Intellectual Technologies. Proceedings of the Annual International Conference "Dialogue"*, pages 688–705.

Krešimir Baksa, Dino Golović, Goran Glavaš, and Jan Šnajder. 2017. Tagging named entities in Croatian tweets. *Slovenščina 2.0: empirical, applied and interdisciplinary research*, 4(1):20–41.

Nancy Chinchor. 1998. Overview of MUC-7/MET-2. In *Proceedings of Seventh Message Understanding Conference (MUC-7)*.

Jonathan B. Crawley and Gerhard Wagner. 2010. Desktop Text Mining for Law Enforcement. In *Proceedings of IEEE International Conference on Intelligence and Security Informatics (ISI 2010)*, pages 23–26, Vancouver, BC, Canada.

George R. Doddington, Alexis Mitchell, Mark A. Przybocki, Lance A. Ramshaw, Stephanie Strassel, and Ralph M. Weischedel. 2004. The Automatic Content Extraction (ACE) program—tasks, data, and evaluation. In *Fourth International Conference on Language Resources and Evaluation (LREC 2004)*, pages 837–840, Lisbon, Portugal.

Xiangyu Duan, Rafael E. Banchs, Min Zhang, Haizhou Li, and A. Kumaran. 2016. Report of NEWS 2016 Machine Transliteration Shared Task. In *Proceedings of The Sixth Named Entities Workshop*, pages 58–72, Berlin, Germany.

Heng Ji, Joel Nothman, and Ben Hachey. 2014. Overview of TAC-KBP2014 entity discovery and linking tasks. In *Proceedings of Text Analysis Conference (TAC2014)*, pages 1333–1339.

Heng Ji, Joel Nothman, and Ben Hachey. 2015. Overview of TAC-KBP2015 tri-lingual entity discovery and linking. In *Proceedings of Text Analysis Conference (TAC2015)*.

Mladen Karan, Goran Glavaš, Frane Šarić, Jan Šnajder, Jure Mijić, Artur Šilić, and Bojana Dalbelo Bašić. 2013. CroNER: Recognizing named entities in Croatian using conditional random fields. *Informatica*, 37(2):165.

Michal Konkol and Miloslav Konopík. 2013. CRF-based Czech named entity recognizer and consolidation of Czech NER research. In *Text, Speech and Dialogue*, volume 8082 of *Lecture Notes in Computer Science*, pages 153–160. Springer Berlin Heidelberg.

A Kumaran, Mitesh M. Khapra, and Haizhou Li. 2010. Report of NEWS 2010 transliteration mining shared task. In *Proceedings of the 2010 Named Entities Workshop*, pages 21–28, Uppsala, Sweden.

Nikola Ljubešić, Marija Stupar, Tereza Jurić, and Željko Agić. 2013. Combining available datasets for building named entity recognition models of Croatian and Slovene. *Slovenščina 2.0: empirical, applied and interdisciplinary research*, 1(2):35–57.

Michał Marcińczuk, Jan Kocoń, and Maciej Janicki. 2013. Liner2—a customizable framework for proper names recognition for Polish. In Robert Bembenik, Lukasz Skonieczny, Henryk Rybinski, Marzena Kryszkiewicz, and Marek Niezgodka, editors, *Intelligent Tools for Building a Scientific Information Platform*, volume 467 of *Studies in Computational Intelligence*, pages 231–253. Springer.

Michał Marcińczuk, Jan Kocoń, and Marcin Oleksy. 2017. Liner2—a generic framework for named entity recognition. In *Proceedings of the Sixth Workshop on Balto-Slavic Natural Language Processing (BSNLP 2017)*, Valencia, Spain.

James Mayfield, Paul McNamee, Christine Piatko, and Claudia Pearce. 2003. Lattice-based tagging using support vector machines. In *Proceedings of the Twelfth International Conference on Information and Knowledge Management*, CIKM '03, pages 303–308, New York, NY, USA. ACM.

James Mayfield, Paul McNamee, and Cash Costello. 2017. Language-independent named entity analysis using parallel projection and rule-based disambiguation. In *Proceedings of the Sixth Workshop on Balto-Slavic Natural Language Processing (BSNLP 2017)*, Valencia, Spain.

Paul McNamee, James Mayfield, Tim Finin, and Dawn Lawrie. 2013. HLTCOE participation at TAC 2013. In *Proceedings of the Sixth Text Analysis Conference, (TAC 2013)*, Gaithersburg, Maryland, USA.

Nafise Sadat Moosavi and Michael Strube. 2016. Which coreference evaluation metric do you trust? A proposal for a link-based entity aware metric. In *Proceedings of the 54th Annual Meeting of the Association for Computational Linguistics (ACL 2016)*, pages 632–642, Berlin, Germany.

Jakub Piskorski, Karol Wieloch, and Marcin Sydow. 2009. On knowledge-poor methods for person name matching and lemmatization for highly inflectional languages. *Information retrieval*, 12(3):275–299.

Adam Przepiórkowski. 2007. Slavonic information extraction and partial parsing. In *Proceedings of the Workshop on Balto-Slavonic Natural Language Processing: Information Extraction and Enabling Technologies*, ACL '07, pages 1–10, Stroudsburg, PA, USA. Association for Computational Linguistics.

Adam Radziszewski. 2013. Learning to lemmatise polish noun phrases. In *Proceedings of the 51st Annual Meeting of the Association for Computational Linguistics, ACL 2013, 4-9 August 2013, Sofia, Bulgaria, Volume 1: Long Papers*, pages 701–709.

Lev Ratinov and Dan Roth. 2009. Design challenges and misconceptions in named entity recognition. In *Proceedings of the Thirteenth Conference on Computational Natural Language Learning*, CoNLL '09, pages 147–155, Stroudsburg, PA, USA. Association for Computational Linguistics.

Agata Savary and Jakub Piskorski. 2011. Language Resources for Named Entity Annotation in the National Corpus of Polish. *Control and Cybernetics*, 40(2):361–391.

Magda Ševčíková, Zdeněk Žabokrtský, and Oldřich Kruza. 2007. Named entities in Czech: annotating data and developing NE tagger. In *International Conference on Text, Speech and Dialogue*, pages 188–195. Springer.

Tadej Štajner, Tomaž Erjavec, and Simon Krek. 2013. Razpoznavanje imenskih entitet v slovenskem besedilu. *Slovenščina 2.0: empirical, applied and interdisciplinary research*, 1(2):58–81.

Erik Tjong Kim Sang and Fien De Meulder. 2003. Introduction to the CoNLL-2003 shared task: Language-independent named entity recognition. In *Proceedings of the Seventh Conference on Natural Language Learning at HLT-NAACL 2003 - Volume 4*, CONLL '03, pages 142–147, Stroudsburg, PA, USA. Association for Computational Linguistics.

Erik Tjong Kim Sang. 2002. Introduction to the CoNLL-2002 shared task: Language-independent named entity recognition. In *Proceedings of the 6th Conference on Natural Language Learning - Volume 20*, COLING-02, pages 1–4, Stroudsburg, PA, USA. Association for Computational Linguistics.

Jakub Waszczuk, Katarzyna Głowińska, Agata Savary, and Adam Przepiórkowski. 2010. Tools and methodologies for annotating syntax and named entities in the National Corpus of Polish. In *Proceedings of the International Multiconference on Computer Science and Information Technology (IMCSIT 2010): Computational Linguistics – Applications (CLA'10)*, pages 531–539, Wisła, Poland. PTI.

Liner2 – a Generic Framework for Named Entity Recognition

Micha Marcińczuk and **Jan Kocoń** and **Marcin Oleksy**
Research Group G4.19
Wrocław University of Science and Technology
`michal.marcinczuk@pwr.edu.pl`
`jan.kocon@pwr.edu.pl, marcin.oleksy@pwr.edu.pl`

Abstract

In the paper we present an adaptation of Liner2 framework to solve the BSNLP 2017 shared task on multilingual named entity recognition. The tool is tuned to recognize and lemmatize named entities for Polish.

1 Introduction

Liner2 (Marcińczuk et al., 2013) is a generic framework which can be used to solve various tasks based on sequence labeling, i.e. recognition of named entities, temporal expressions, mentions of events. It provides a set of modules (based on statistical models, dictionaries, rules and heuristics) which recognize and annotate certain types of phrases. The framework was already used for recognition of named entities (different levels of granularity, including boundaries, coarse- and fine-grained categories) (Marcińczuk et al., 2012), temporal expressions (Kocoń and Marcińczuk, 2016b) and event mentions (Kocoń and Marcińczuk, 2016a) for Polish.

Task	P [%]	R [%]	F [%]
NER boundaries	86.04	83.02	84.50
NER top9	73.73	69.01	71.30
NER n82	67.65	58.83	62.93
TIMEX boundaries	86.68	81.01	83.75
TIMEX 4class	84.97	76.67	80.61
Event mentions	80.88	77.82	79.32

Figure 1: Precision (P), recall (R) and F-measure (F) for various task obtained with Liner2.

Table 1 contains results for various tasks obtained using Liner2. The results are for strict evaluation. NER refers to recognition of named entity mentions. *NER boundaries* is a model for recognition of named entity boundaries without categorization (Marcinczuk, 2015). The same configuration was used to train a coarse-grained (*NER top9*) and a fine-grained (*NER n82*) model on the KPWr corpus (Broda et al., 2012). The coarse-grained and fine-grained categories are described in Section 2.4.

TIMEX refers to recognition of temporal expression mentions. *TIMEX boundaries* is a model for recognition of temporal expression boundaries without categorization and *TIMEX 4class* is a model for recognition of four classes of temporal expressions: date, time, duration and set (Kocoń and Marcińczuk, 2016b).

The last model named *Event mentions* is for recognition of eight categories of event mentions: action, state, reporting, perception, aspectual, i_action, i_state and light_predicate (Kocoń and Marcińczuk, 2016a). The categorization is done according to the TimeML guideline (Saurí et al., 2006) adopted to Polish language.[1]

2 Solution Description

2.1 Overview

Liner2 processes texts which are tokenized and analyzed with a morphological tagger beforehand. The morphological analysis is optional but it might be useful in some tasks. In case of named entity recognition it has small impact on the results. According to our preliminary experiments on recognition of named entity boundaries the model without base forms and morphological information obtained the value of F-measure lower by only 0.5 percentage point.

After tokenization and morphological analysis the text is passed through a pipeline that consists of the following elements:

---

[1] `https://clarin-pl.eu/dspace/handle/11321/283`

Proceedings of the 6th Workshop on Balto-Slavic Natural Language Processing, pages 86–91,
Valencia, Spain, 4 April 2017. ©2017 Association for Computational Linguistics

1. A statistical model trained on a manually annotated corpus using a Conditional Random Fields modeling (Lafferty et al., 2001). The model uses a rich set of features which are described in Section 2.3.

2. A set of heuristics to merge, group and filter specific categories of named entities according to the BSNLP shared task guidelines.

3. A set of heuristics and dictionaries to lemmatize the named entities.

At this stage, the tool is tuned to recognize named entities for Polish according to the guidelines for the BSNLP 2017 shared task.

2.2 Pre-processing

The input text is tagged using the WCRFT tagger (Radziszewski, 2013) and a morphological dictionary called Morfeusz (Woliński, 2006).

2.3 Features

Liner2 uses the following set of token-level features to represent the input data:

1. **Orthographic features**

   - **orth** – a word itself, in the form in which it is used in the text,
   - n-**prefix** – n first characters of the encountered word form, where $n \in \{1, 2, 3, 4\}$. If the word is shorter than n, the missing characters are replaced with '_'.
   - n-**suffix** – n last characters of the encountered word, where $n \in \{1, 2, 3, 4\}$. If the word is shorter than n, the missing characters are replaced with '_'. We use prefixes to fill the gap of missing inflected forms of proper names in the gazetteers.
   - **pattern** – encode pattern of characters in the word:
     - ALL_UPPER – all characters are upper case letters, e.g. "NASA",
     - ALL_LOWER – all characters are lower case letters, e.g. "rabbit"
     - DIGITS – all character are digits, e.g. "102",
     - SYMBOLS – all characters are non alphanumeric, e.g. "-_-'",
     - UPPER_INIT – the first character is upper case letter, the other are lower case letters, e.g. "Andrzej",
     - UPPER_CAMEL_CASE – the first character is upper case letter, word contains letters only and has at least one more upper case letter, e.g. "CamelCase",
     - LOWER_CAMEL_CASE – the first character is lower case letter, word contains letters only and has at least one upper case letter, e.g. "pascalCase",
     - MIXED – a sequence of letters, digits and/or symbols, e.g. "H1M1".

   - **binary orthographic features**, the feature is 1 if the condition is met, 0 otherwise. The conditions are:
     - *(word) starts with an upper case letter,*
     - *starts with a lower case letter,*
     - *starts with a symbol,*
     - *starts with a digit,*
     - *contains upper case letter,*
     - *contains a lower case letter,*
     - *contains a symbol*
     - *contains digit.*

   The features are based on filtering rules described in (Marcińczuk and Piasecki, 2011), e.g., first names and surnames start from upper case and do not contain symbols. To some extent these features duplicate the *pattern* feature. However, the *binary features* encode information on the level of single characters (i.e., a presence of a single character with given criteria), while the aim of the *pattern* feature is to encode a repeatable sequence of characters.

2. **Morphological features** – are motivated by the NER grammars which utilise morphological information (Piskorski, 2004). The features are:

   - **base** – a morphological base form of a word,
   - **ctag** – morphological tag generated by tagger,
   - **part of speech, case, gender, number** – enumeration types according to

tagset described in (Przepiórkowski et al., 2009).

3. **Lexicon-based features** – one feature for every lexicon. If a sequence of words is found in a lexicon the first word in the sequence is set as B and the other as I. If word is not a part of any dictionary entry it is set to O.

4. **Wordnet-base features** – are used to generalise the text description and reduce the observation diversity. The are two types of these features:

   - **synonym** – word's synonym, first in the alphabetical order from all word synonyms in Polish Wordnet. The sense of the word is not disambiguated,
   - **hypernym n** – a hypernym of the word in the distance of n, where $n \in \{1, 2, 3\}$

2.4 Statistical Models

In the pipeline we used two models for named entity recognition: coarse-grained (*NER top9*) and fine-grained (*NER n82*). The coarse-grained model is used to recognize and categorize most of the named entity mentions. The fine-grained model, which has lower recall, is used to change the subcategorization of named entities to conform the BSNLP shared task guideline (see Section 2.5 for more details). Both statistical models were trained on the KPWr corpus (Broda et al., 2012).

The coarse-grained model recognizes the following set of named entity categories:

- event – names of events organized by humans,

- facility – names of buildings and stationary constructions (e.g. monuments) developed by humans,

- living – people names,

- location – names of geographical (e.g, mountains, rivers) and geopolitical entities (e.g., countries, cities),

- organization – names of organizations, institutions, organized groups of people,

- product – names of artifacts created or manufactured by humans (products of mass production, arts, books, newspapers, etc.),

- adjective – adjective forms of proper names,

- numerical – numerical identifiers which indicate entities,

- other – other names which do not fit into previous categories.

The fine-grained model defines more detailed categorization of named entities within the top nine categories. The complete list of named entity categories used in KPWr can be found in *KPWr annotation guidelines – named entities*.[2] The fine-grained model uses a subset of 82 categories and their list can be found in *Liner2.5 model NER*.[3]

2.5 Post-processing

During the post-processing step the following operations are performed:

1. A set of heuristics is used to join successive annotations. According to the guidelines for named entities used in the KPWr corpus nested names are annotated as a sequence of disjoint atomic names. In order to conform the shared task guidelines such names need to be merged into single names.

2. Coarse-grained categories used in the KPWr are mapped onto four categories defined in the shared task. There is a minor discrepancy between KPWr hierarchy of named entity categories and BSNLP categories – names of nations are subtype of organization in KPWr, while in BSNLP shared task they belong to PER category. To overcome this discrepancy we used the fine-grained model to recognize nation names and map them to PER category. Irrelevant for the shared task categories of named entities are discarded, i.e. *adjective*, *numerical* and *other*. The complete set of mapping rules is presented in Table 2.5.

3. Duplicated names, i.e. names with the same form and category, are removed from the set.

The set of heuristics and mapping between categories was defined using the training sets delivered by the organizers of the shared task.

ite

---

[2] `https://clarin-pl.eu/dspace/handle/11321/294`
[3] `https://clarin-pl.eu/dspace/handle/11321/263`

KPWr category	BSNLP category
nam_loc	LOC
nam_fac	LOC
nam_liv	PER
nam_org_nation	PER
nam_org	ORG
nam_eve	MISC
nam_pro	MISC
nam_adj	*ignored*
nam_num	*ignored*
nam_oth	*ignored*

Figure 2: Mapping from KPWr categories of named entities to BSNLP categories.

Task	P	R	F
Names matching			
Relaxed partial	66.24	63.27	64.72
Relaxed exact	65.40	62.78	64.07
Strict	71.10	58.81	66.61
Normalization	75.50	44.44	55.95
Coreference			
Document level	7.90	42.71	12.01
Language level	3.70	8.00	5.05
Cross-language level	n/a	n/a	n/a

Figure 3: Results obtained by our system in the Phase I of the BSNLP Challenge for Polish language.

2.6 Lemmatization

To lemmatize named entities we use the following resources:

NELexicon2[4] – a dictionary of more than 2.3 million proper names. Part of the lexicon consists of more than 110k name forms with their lemmas extracted from the Wikipiedia internal links. The links were extracted from a Wikipedia dump using a Pyhon script called *python-g419wikitools*.[5]

Morfeusz SGJP[6] – a morphological dictionary for Polish that contains near 7 millions of word forms. The dictionary was used to retain the plural form of nations names, i.e. „Polacy" (Eng. *Poles*) for „Polaków" (Eng. *Poles* in accusative). After tagging the base form for plural for is a singular form – „Polak" (Eng. *Pole* for „Polacy". According to the BSNLP shared task guidelines the number of the lemmatized form must be the same as in the text. We have extracted all upper case forms with a plural number from the Morfeusz dictionary. The list consists of near 1000 elements.

Algorithm 1 presents the lemmatization algorithm.

3 Evaluation and Summary

Table 3 contains the results obtained by our system in the Phase I of the BSNLP Challenge for Polish

language. *Names matching* refers to named entity recognition which was carried out in two ways:[7]

- *Relaxed evaluation: an entity mentioned in a given document is considered to be extracted correctly if the system response includes at least one annotation of a named mention of this entity (regardless whether the extracted mention is base form);*

- *Strict evaluation: the system response should include exactly one annotation for each unique form of a named mention of an entity that is referred to in a given document, i.e., capturing and listing all variants of an entity is required.*

Normalization refers to the named entity lemmatization task. *Coreference* refers to the document-level and cross-language entity matching.

Our system was tuned to recognize and lemmatize named entities only so we did not expect to obtain good results for the coreference resolution tasks. The performance for the strict named entity recognition in terms of precision is similar to our previous results (see *NER top9* in Table 1). However, the recall is significantly lower by more than 10 percentage points. This might indicate that our system does not recognize some of the subcategories of named entities.

At the time of this writing, this system has achieved the top score on the Polish language subtask of the first phase of this Challenge.

[5]https://clarin-pl.eu/dspace/handle/11321/336

[7]The description comes from the shared task description: http://bsnlp-2017.cs.helsinki.fi/shared_task.html.

Algorithm 1: Lemmatization algorithm.

Data: $Name$ – a named entity to lemmatize
$DictMorfPl$ – a dictionary of nominative plural forms with their nominative singular forms from the Morfeusz SGJP dictionary, e.x.: $Polak \rightarrow Polacy$
$DictPerson$ – a dictionary of people name forms and their nominative forms from NELexicon2. Parts of the names, i.e. first names and last names, are also included, e.x.:
$JanaNowaka \rightarrow JanNowak,\ Jana \rightarrow Jan,\ Nowaka \rightarrow Nowak$
$DictNelexicon$
Result: $Lemma$ – lemma for the NamedEntity

```
begin
    Lemma ⟵ NULL
    /* We use a set of heuristics devoted to PER category.          */
    if Name.type = PER then
        if Name.length = 1 & Name.number = pl & Name.base in DictMorfPl then
            | Lemma ⟵ DictMorfPl[Name.base]
        else if Name.text in DictPerson then
            | Lemma ⟵ DictPerson[Name.text]
        else if Name[0].case = nominative then
            | Lemma ⟵ Name.text
        else
            └ Lemma ⟵ concatenation of bases for each token in Name
    else if Name.base in DictNelexicon then
        | Lemma ⟵ DictNelexicon[Name.text]
    else if Name.length = 1 then
        | Lemma ⟵ Name.base
    else
        └ Lemma ⟵ Name.text
```

Acknowledgments

Work financed as part of the investment in the CLARIN-PL research infrastructure funded by the Polish Ministry of Science and Higher Education.

References

Bartosz Broda, Michał Marcinczuk, Marek Maziarz, Adam Radziszewski, and Adam Wardynski. 2012. Kpwr: Towards a free corpus of Polish. In *Proceedings of LREC*, volume 12.

Jan Kocoń and Michał Marcińczuk, 2016a. *Generating of Events Dictionaries from Polish WordNet for the Recognition of Events in Polish Documents*, pages 12–19. Springer International Publishing, Cham.

Jan Kocoń and Michał Marcińczuk. 2016b. Supervised approach to recognise Polish temporal expressions and rule-based interpretation of timexes. *Natural Language Engineering*, pages 1–34.

John D. Lafferty, Andrew McCallum, and Fernando C. N. Pereira. 2001. Conditional Random Fields: Probabilistic Models for Segmenting and Labeling Sequence Data. In *Proceedings of the Eighteenth International Conference on Machine Learning*, ICML '01, pages 282–289, San Francisco, CA, USA. Morgan Kaufmann Publishers Inc.

Michał Marcińczuk and Maciej Piasecki. 2011. Statistical proper name recognition in Polish economic texts. *Control and Cybernetics*, 40:393–418.

Michał Marcińczuk, Michał Stanek, Maciej Piasecki, and Adam Musiał. 2012. Rich set of features for proper name recognition in Polish texts. In *Security and Intelligent Information Systems*, pages 332–344. Springer Berlin Heidelberg.

Michał Marcińczuk, Jan Kocoń, and Maciej Janicki. 2013. Liner2 — A Customizable Framework for Proper Names Recognition for Polish. In Robert Bembenik, Łukasz Skonieczny, Henryk Rybiński, Marzena Kryszkiewicz, and Marek Niezgódka, editors, *Intelligent Tools for Building a Scientific Information Platform*, volume 467 of *Studies in Computational Intelligence*, pages 231–253. Springer.

Michal Marcinczuk. 2015. Automatic construction of complex features in conditional random fields for named entities recognition. In Galia Angelova, Kalina Bontcheva, and Ruslan Mitkov, editors, *Recent Advances in Natural Language Processing,*

RANLP 2015, 7-9 September, 2015, Hissar, Bulgaria, pages 413–419. RANLP 2015 Organising Committee / ACL.

Jakub Piskorski. 2004. Extraction of Polish named-entities. In *Proceedings of the Fourth International Conference on Language Resources and Evaluation, LREC 2004, May 26-28, 2004, Lisbon, Portugal*.

Adam Przepiórkowski, Rafał L. Górski, Barbara Lewandowska-Tomaszczyk, and Marek Łaziński. 2009. Narodowy korpus języka polskiego. *Biuletyn Polskiego Towarzystwa Językoznawczego*, 65:47–55.

Adam Radziszewski. 2013. A tiered CRF tagger for Polish. In R. Bembenik, Ł. Skonieczny, H. Rybiński, M. Kryszkiewicz, and M. Niezgódka, editors, *Intelligent Tools for Building a Scientific Information Platform: Advanced Architectures and Solutions*. Springer Verlag.

Roser Saurí, Jessica Littman, Robert Gaizauskas, Andrea Setzer, and James Pustejovsky. 2006. TimeML Annotation Guidelines, Version 1.2.1.

Marcin Woliński, 2006. *Morfeusz — a Practical Tool for the Morphological Analysis of Polish*, pages 511–520. Springer Berlin Heidelberg, Berlin, Heidelberg.

Language-Independent Named Entity Analysis Using Parallel Projection and Rule-Based Disambiguation

James Mayfield and **Paul McNamee** and **Cash Costello**
Johns Hopkins University Applied Physics Laboratory
{james.mayfield, paul.mcnamee, cash.costello}@jhuapl.edu

Abstract

The 2017 shared task at the Balto-Slavic NLP workshop requires identifying coarse-grained named entities in seven languages, identifying each entity's base form, and clustering name mentions across the multilingual set of documents. The fact that no training data is provided to systems for building supervised classifiers further adds to the complexity. To complete the task we first use publicly available parallel texts to project named entity recognition capability from English to each evaluation language. We ignore entirely the subtask of identifying non-inflected forms of names. Finally, we create cross-document entity identifiers by clustering named mentions using a procedure-based approach.

1 Introduction

The LITESABER project at Johns Hopkins University Applied Physics Laboratory is investigating techniques to perform analysis of named entities in low-resource languages. The tasks we are investigating include: named entity detection and coarse type classification, commonly referred to as named entity recognition (NER); linking of named entities to online databases such as Wikipedia; and clustering of entities across documents. We have applied some of our techniques to the BSNLP 2017 Shared Task. Specifically, we submitted results in two of the three categories: Named Entity Mention Detection and Classification (or NER), which asks systems to locate mentions of named entities in text and identify their types; and Entity Matching (also known as *cross-lingual identification*, or *cross-document coreference resolution*) which asks systems to determine when two entity mentions, either in the same document or in different documents, refer to the same real-world entity. We did not participate in the Name Normalization task, which asks systems to convert each entity mention to its lemmatized form. This paper describes our approach and results.

2 Approach to NER

Our approach to developing named entity recognizers for Balto-Slavic languages takes the following steps:

- Obtain parallel texts for the target language and English.
- Apply an English-language named entity recognizer to the English side of the corpus.
- Project the resulting annotations from English over to the target language by aligning tagged English words to their target language equivalents.
- Train a target language tagger off of the inferred named entity labels.

These steps are described further in the following subsections.

2.1 Parallel Collections

Exploitation of a parallel collection is at the heart of our method. English is a well-studied, high-resource language for which annotated NER corpora are available, therefore we used parallel collections with English on one side and the target Balto-Slavic language on the other.

Our parallel bitext comes from the OPUS archive[1] maintained by Tiedemann (2012). Over one million parallel sentences were available for six of the seven languages; Ukrainian was our least resourced language. Principal sources included Europarl (Koehn, 2005) and Open Subtitles. We

---

[1] http://opus.lingfil.uu.se

92

Proceedings of the 6th Workshop on Balto-Slavic Natural Language Processing, pages 92–96,
Valencia, Spain, 4 April 2017. ©2017 Association for Computational Linguistics

randomly sampled 250,000 sentences for each language, and after filtering for various quality issues we arrived at the data described in Table 1.

Language	Training # words	Test # words
Croatian	632,915	43,593
Czech	1,028,778	45,659
Polish	843,632	45,362
Russian	560,296	44,801
Slovak	1,081,397	45,611
Slovenian	966,431	45,444
Ukrainian	601,539	43,556

Table 1: Parallel collection sizes, in words.

2.2 English NER

Our first step was to identify the named entities on the English side of the parallel collections. There are many well-developed approaches to NER in English.[2] We chose to use the Illinois Named Entity Tagger from the Cognitive Computation Group at UIUC (Ratinov and Roth, 2009), which at the time of its publication had the highest reported NER score on the 2003 CoNLL English shared task (Tjong Kim Sang and De Meulder, 2003). It is a perceptron-based tagger that can take into consideration non-local features and external data sources.

2.3 Parallel Projection

Once we have tagged an English document we need to map those tags onto words in the corresponding target language document. Yarowsky *et al.* pioneered this style of parallel projection (2001), using it to induce part of speech taggers and noun phrase bracketers in addition to named entity recognizers. We use the Giza++ tool (Och and Ney, 2003) to align words in our parallel corpora. In most cases, a single English word will align with a single target language word. In these cases, the tag assigned to the English word is also assigned to the aligned target language word. In some cases, the alignment will be one-to-many, many-to-one, or many-to-many. For one-to-many alignments, the tag of the English word is applied to all of the aligned target language words. For many-to-one and many-to-many alignments, if any English word is tagged with an entity tag, then all aligned target language words are tagged

with the first such tag. Because Balto-Slavic languages are more heavily inflected than English, most alignments from English are one-to-one or many-to-one. In Czech, for example, our parallel collection produced 71M one-to-one and many-to-one alignments, but only 13M one-to-many alignments. We believe this favors the above heuristics for the BSNLP 2017 task, because one-to-many alignments are likely to be due to inflections in the Balto-Slavic language that encode English function words.

2.4 Supervised Tagging and Classification

Projection of named entity tags onto the Balto-Slavic side of the parallel collection gives us a training collection for a supervised NER system. Because we are training many recognizers, we prefer to rely on language-independent techniques. Features that work well for one language (*e.g.*, capitalization) will not necessarily work well for another. Thus, we prefer an NER system that can consider many different features, selecting those that work well for a particular language without overtraining. To this end, we use the *SVM-Lattice* named entity recognizer (Mayfield et al., 2003). *SVMLattice* uses support vector machines (SVMs) at its core. Like other discriminatively trained systems, support vector machines can handle large numbers of features without overtraining. *SVMLattice* trains a separate SVM for each possible transition from label to label. It then uses Viterbi decoding to identify the best path through the lattice of transitions for a given input sentence.

We did not include gazetteers as features, though their use has been shown to be beneficial in statistically trained NER systems. But we intend to investigate their use in future research.

3 Cross-Document Entity Coreference Resolution

We used the *Kripke* system (Mayfield et al., 2014) to identify co-referential mentions of the same named entity across the multilingual document collection. *Kripke* is an unsupervised agglomerative clusterer that produces equivalence sets of entities using a combination of procedural rules. We used the *uroman* transliterator[3] to convert Cyrillic names to the Roman alphabet to support cross-script clustering.

---

[2]See (Nadeau and Sekine, 2007) for a survey of approaches.

[3]`http://www.isi.edu/projects/nlg/software_1`

To avoid the customary quadratic-time complexity required for brute-force pairwise comparisons, *Kripke* maintains an inverted index of names used for each entity. Only entities matching by full name, or some shared words or character n-grams are considered as potentially coreferential. Related indexing techniques are variously known as blocking (Whang et al., 2009) or canopies (McCallum et al., 2000).

Approximate name matching is accomplished using techniques such as: Dice scores of padded character tri-grams, recursive longest common subsequence, and expanding abbreviations. Christen (2006) gives a nice survey of related methods.

Contextual matching is accomplished by comparing named entities that co-occur in the same document. Between candidate clusters, the intersection of names occurring in the clusters is computed. Names are weighted by normalized Inverse Document Frequency, so that rarer (*i.e.,* discriminating) names have greater weights. The top-k (*i.e.,* k=10) highest weighted names in common are examined, and if the sum of their weights exceeds a cutoff, then the contextual similarity is deemed adequate.

A series of five clustering passes was performed. In early iterations matching criteria are strict, and merges have both good name string and context matching. This builds high-precision clusters in the beginning, using relaxed conditions in successive rounds to elevate entity recall.

For the BSNLP shared task the documents in the evaluation corpora are based on a focal entity. As a result the same name string found in different documents almost surely refers to the same entity. *Kripke* was designed for more diverse corpora, where this is less often the case.

4   NER Experiments

We had no collections with ground truth for six of the seven BSNLP languages. To gauge performance, we divided the induced label collection (*i.e.,* the Balto-Slavic side of the parallel collection) into training and test sets (Table 1). We then built an *SVMLattice* tagger using the training set, and applied it to the test set, assuming that the projected tags were entirely accurate. The results are shown in Table 2.

Digging slightly deeper into these results (Table 3), we see that in general, performance is highest on locations, and lowest for the miscellaneous

	Precision	Recall	F_1
Croatian	70.75	53.44	60.89
Czech	74.89	61.43	67.49
Polish	75.68	60.07	66.98
Russian	68.19	36.94	47.92
Slovak	76.97	63.30	69.47
Slovenian	78.44	61.03	68.65
Ukrainian	73.98	40.80	52.59

Table 2: NER results using projected labels.

class. The organization class is inconsistent, being high in some languages and low in others.

	PER	ORG	LOC	MISC
Croatian	65.82	39.10	63.45	53.87
Czech	51.11	70.26	71.57	56.74
Polish	48.30	72.28	71.57	48.48
Russian	50.39	35.99	54.93	35.38
Slovak	61.19	70.53	75.27	58.96
Slovenian	57.50	73.00	71.75	54.26
Ukrainian	63.94	17.63	50.74	32.53

Table 3: F_1 Scores for the Four Entity Categories.

The one language for which we have some curated ground truth is Russian. The LDC collection LDC2016E95 (LORELEI Russian Representative Language Pack) contains, among other things, named entity annotations for 239 Russian documents.[4] We built a named entity recognizer for Russian using the methodology described above, and applied it to 10% of these LDC data. We used the CoNLL evaluation script to score the run. The results are shown in Table 4. Note that the label set for the LDC data is slightly different than the BSNLP label set; in particular, there is no MISC category (although the overall scores count all MISC labels as incorrect).

	Precision	Recall	F_1
Overall	52.13	22.69	31.61
PER	40.43	33.33	36.54
ORG	16.00	3.45	5.67
LOC	77.02	26.11	38.99

Table 4: Results on annotated Russian text.

We note from these results that the tagger is doing much more poorly on ORGs than is suggested by the experiments on projected labels. Thus, we

---

[4]We did not include the 765 annotated Tweets in our tests.

must view the results on ORGs for the other languages with a degree of skepticism. Possible reasons include wider variation in organization names than the other categories, the use of acronyms and abbreviations, or greater difficulty in aligning organization names.

5 Phase I Shared Task Results

Table 5 reports NER precision, recall, and F_1 scores for the seven languages.[5] Examining gross trends in the data, wee see that higher scores are obtained on the trump corpus. Performance is relatively consistent across language. However, recall is lower-than average in Polish and Russian, and dramatically lower for Ukrainian, particularly on the ec test set.

	trump			ec		
---	P	R	F_1	P	R	F_1
ces	51.6	41.7	46.1	48.8	45.7	47.2
hrv	52.0	49.0	50.4	48.1	44.4	46.2
pol	66.8	29.7	41.1	58.1	36.6	44.9
rus	56.2	33.3	41.8	51.3	42.7	46.6
slk	56.6	40.2	47.0	47.9	44.6	46.2
slv	54.1	40.4	46.3	49.3	46.5	47.8
ukr	47.7	25.5	33.3	27.4	6.80	10.9
all	55.0	37.4	44.5	47.7	32.2	38.4

Table 5: NER results for the strict matching condition, by language.

Looking at performance by entity type (Table 6), we see best results for the PER and LOC classes, similar to our findings in Table 3 above. The ORG and MISC classes are substantially worse; scores for MISC are approximately zero.

	PER	ORG	LOC	MISC
ces	53.30	21.77	68.12	0.00
hrv	60.10	29.36	63.19	3.39
pol	35.29	13.19	68.73	0.00
rus	41.77	14.55	65.03	0.00
slk	57.52	18.67	63.20	2.94
slv	55.92	18.18	65.63	0.00
ukr	29.56	6.45	56.83	0.00
all	49.26	18.16	64.80	1.08

Table 6: F_1 scores by type and language for the trump test set with strict matching.

[5]Note, the task only permits reporting unique mentions in a document, unlike the CoNLL evaluations were every mention must be identified.

We have not had sufficient time to perform an in-depth analysis of the data. One reason for low performance on ORG and MISC classes may be that these entity mentions contain more words on average than PER and LOC entities, and our projected alignments may be less reliable for longer spanning entities. Additionally, our trained English model is based on the CoNLL dataset, and those tagging guidelines may be inconsistent with the BSNLP 2017 shared task guidelines. For example, demonyms and nationalities were tagged as MISC in CoNLL,[6] but PER in BSNLP 2017.

	trump			ec		
---	P	R	F_1	P	R	F_1
ces	56.4	11.7	19.4	45.8	19.5	27.3
hrv	46.8	10.9	17.7	43.7	14.8	22.1
pol	62.4	10.7	18.2	43.9	11.0	17.5
rus	50.3	11.6	18.9	51.4	16.5	25.0
slk	58.0	14.0	22.6	46.2	22.9	30.6
slv	58.8	19.1	28.8	48.4	24.2	32.2
ukr	48.7	6.0	10.7	36.0	2.6	4.9
all	54.8	12.1	19.8	45.7	14.0	21.4

Table 7: Per-language entity coreference.

Within-language entity coreference resolution was similar across the two test sets (see Table 7). Precision was higher than recall, as we expected. Performance merging across the seven languages was lower than for single-language clustering.

6 Conclusions

Using a parallel collection to project named entity tags, and training a named entity recognizer on the resulting collection, is a feasible approach to developing named entity recognition in a variety of languages. Performance of such NER systems is clearly below that achievable with ground truth labels for training data. However, for a variety of downstream tasks, performance such as we see for the Balto-Slavic languages is acceptable.

Acknowledgment

This material is based upon work supported by the Defense Advanced Research Projects Agency (DARPA) under Contract No. HR0011-16-C-0102.

[6]http://www.cnts.ua.ac.be/conll2003/ner/annotation.txt

References

Peter Christen. 2006. A comparison of personal name matching: Techniques and practical issues. Technical Report TR-CS-06-02, Australian National University.

Philipp Koehn. 2005. Europarl: A Parallel Corpus for Statistical Machine Translation. In *Conference Proceedings: the tenth Machine Translation Summit*, pages 79–86, Phuket, Thailand. AAMT, AAMT.

James Mayfield, Paul McNamee, Christine Piatko, and Claudia Pearce. 2003. Lattice-based tagging using support vector machines. In *Proceedings of the Twelfth International Conference on Information and Knowledge Management*, CIKM '03, pages 303–308, New York, NY, USA. ACM.

James Mayfield, Paul McNamee, Craig Harmon, Tim Finin, and Dawn Lawrie. 2014. KELVIN: Extracting Knowledge from Large Text Collections. In *AAAI Fall Symposium on Natural Language Access to Big Data*. AAAI Press, November.

Andrew McCallum, Kamal Nigam, and Lyle Ungar. 2000. Efficient clustering of high-dimensional data sets with application to reference matching. In *Knowledge Discovery and Data Mining (KDD)*.

David Nadeau and Satoshi Sekine. 2007. A survey of named entity recognition and classification. *Linguisticae Investigationes*, 30(1):3–26, January. Publisher: John Benjamins Publishing Company.

Franz Josef Och and Hermann Ney. 2003. A systematic comparison of various statistical alignment models. *Computational Linguistics*, 29(1):19–51.

Lev Ratinov and Dan Roth. 2009. Design challenges and misconceptions in named entity recognition. In *Proceedings of the Thirteenth Conference on Computational Natural Language Learning*, CoNLL '09, pages 147–155, Stroudsburg, PA, USA. Association for Computational Linguistics.

Jörg Tiedemann. 2012. Parallel data, tools and interfaces in opus. In Nicoletta Calzolari, Khalid Choukri, Thierry Declerck, Mehmet Uğur Doğan, Bente Maegaard, Joseph Mariani, Jan Odijk, and Stelios Piperidis, editors, *Proceedings of the Eighth International Conference on Language Resources and Evaluation (LREC-2012)*, pages 2214–2218, Istanbul, Turkey, May. European Language Resources Association (ELRA). ACL Anthology Identifier: L12-1246.

Erik F. Tjong Kim Sang and Fien De Meulder. 2003. Introduction to the CoNLL-2003 shared task: Language-independent named entity recognition. In *Proceedings of the Seventh Conference on Natural Language Learning at HLT-NAACL 2003 - Volume 4*, CoNLL '03, pages 142–147, Stroudsburg, PA, USA. Association for Computational Linguistics.

Steven Euijong Whang, David Menestrina, Georgia Koutrika, Martin Theobald, and Hector Garcia-Molina. 2009. Entity resolution with iterative blocking. In *SIGMOD 2009*, pages 219–232. ACM.

David Yarowsky, Grace Ngai, and Richard Wicentowski. 2001. Inducing multilingual text analysis tools via robust projection across aligned corpora. In *Proceedings of the First International Conference on Human Language Technology Research*, HLT '01, pages 1–8, Stroudsburg, PA, USA. Association for Computational Linguistics.

Comparison of String Similarity Measures for Obscenity Filtering

Ekaterina Chernyak
National Research University
Higher School of Economics
Moscow, Russia
`echernyak@hse.ru`

Abstract

In this paper we address the problem of filtering obscene lexis in Russian texts. We use string similarity measures to find words similar or identical to words from a stop list and establish both a test collection and a baseline for the task. Our experiments show that a novel string similarity measure based on the notion of an annotated suffix tree outperforms some of the other well known measures.

1 Introduction

String similarity measures are widely used in the majority of Natural Language Processing tasks (Gomaa and Fahmy, 2013), such as spelling correction (Angell et al., 1983), information retrieval (Schütze, 2008), text preprocessing for further classification or clustering (Islam and Inkpen, 2008), duplicate detection (Elmagarmid et al., 2007), etc. The performance and suitability of different string similarity measures has already been demonstrated in an extensive amount of previous work. Here, we study the suitability of different similarity measures as a tool to detect and filter obscene lexis in Russian texts. The goal is to compare the performance of different string similarity measures in finding obscene words and their derivatives. Since the Russian obscene language follows the whole language tendencies, such as highly inflectional morphology, the amount of obscene words and their derivatives is enormous. The words, generated by social network and social media users, may contain not only explicitly obscene words and/or their derivatives, but also their combinations and paronyms. This makes out task specially challenging.

Although the problem is quite different from a single word query retrieval, because there is no need to introduce neither document nor user relevance, we nevertheless exploit IR metrics to evaluate the quality of results.

In this publication, we want to address the following research questions:

- the suitability of using string similarity measures for obscenity filtering in Russian texts, and, if so,

- the choice of the string similarity measure for the task.

2 Related Work

Obscenity and profanity filtering can be seen as a part of developing content filters (such as parental controls (Weir and Duta, 2012)), cyberbullying detectors (Dadvar et al., 2013) and spam filters (Yoon et al., 2010). Another application of obscenity filtering is found in sentiment analysis, where obscene words are treated as indicators of negative (Ji et al., 2013) or sarcastic reviews (Bamman and Smith, 2015). A more complex application of obscenity filtering is identifying implicitly abusive content (Weir and Duta, 2012). In this case not only the usage of obscene language but also the intentions of the author are crucial.

Unlike the current trends in Natural Language Processing obscenity and profanity filtering does not exploit machine learning, but is usually done using rule-based approach. In almost all application a stop list of words, that are considered obscene is required. The task is than to find occurrence of stop word or their derivations.

3 Data and Annotation

The input data set is twofold. First, we used the extensive list of the words, prohibited for url naming in Cyrillic ."рф" domain zone, further referred as the stop list. This stop list was released by

Proceedings of the 6th Workshop on Balto-Slavic Natural Language Processing, pages 97–101,
Valencia, Spain, 4 April 2017. ©2017 Association for Computational Linguistics

Russian Federal Service for Supervision of Consumer Rights Protection and Human Welfare, responsible for naming in the ."рф" domain zone. The stop list consists of slightly more than 4000 items, all of them being obscene words and their derivatives. Second, we manually created the collection of texts, rich in obscene lexis. To maintain style diversity, we collected texts from various sources, starting from scientific works on Russian obscenity etymology, poems of classical Russian poets (Pushkin, Esenin, Mayakovsky) and postmodern prose (Yu. Aleshkovsky, I. Guberman, V. Sorokin) up to underground music lyrics (by bands Leningrad, Krasnaya Plesen') and social media sources (Lurkmore, LJ, vk.com, etc).

Next, to minimize the amount of data to be annotated, we tokenized all the the text and removed numbers and punctuation signs and created one frequency dictionary for further annotation. We annotated all unique words in a binary way: a word is either an obscene word (1) or a normal word (0). In total, there were 294916 tokens and 60868 unique words, of them 1261 were annotated as obscene. As we were quite limited in human recourses, the frequency dictionary was split in several annotation tasks in an non-overlapping way, so that one word was considered only by a single annotator.[1] Hence no agreement measures can be computed, although it might be an interesting direction for future work, which will allow to study whether there are any differences in the perception of obscenity.

4 String Similarity Measures

Formally speaking, for every word t from the input frequency dictionary we have to decide whether it is obscene or not. To make this decision we look for the most similar stop word s from the stop list, i.e for $s^* = \mathrm{argmax}_{s \in \mathrm{stop\ list}} sim(s, t)$. If $sim(s^*, t)$ is higher than a predefined threshold, we consider t obscene.

4.1 Coincidence

For each word in the frequency dictionary, we check whether the word itself or the lemma of the word of the stem of the word are present in the stop list. To lemmatize words we used two of the available Russian lemmatizers, mystem (Segalovich, 2003), developed by Yandex, and pymoprhy2 (Ko-

robov, 2015), which is an open source project. We also stemmed all the words and the stop words using Porter stemmer (Porter, 2001) and repeated the same procedure for stems: for each word in the frequency dictionary we checked, whether its stem coincides with one of the stop word stems.

4.2 Jaccard Coefficient

Jaccard coefficient is a well-known set-theoretical similarity measure. Given to sets, A and B, their similarity sim is measured as $\frac{|A \cap B|}{|A \cup B|}$. To apply Jaccard coefficient to the measure similarity between two strings, we need to split these string in character n-grams, i.e., sequences of n consequent letters. For example, the Jaccard coefficient for the string "mining" and "dining" based on 3-grams is equal to $\frac{3}{5}$ and based on 4-grams – to $\frac{2}{3}$. In our study we experiment with different values of n from 3 to 6.

4.3 Annotated Suffix Tree

Annotated suffix tree (AST) is a data structure, used to calculate and store all frequencies of all fragments of an input string collection. First introduced for spam filtering (Pampapathi et al., 2006), it was effectively used in a variety of NLP tasks, such as text summarization (Yakovlev and Chernyak, 2016), fuzzy full text search (Frolov, 2016), etc. The AST is an extended version of the suffix tree, which is used for a variety of NLP tasks too (Ravichandran and Hovy, 2002; Zamir and Etzioni, 1998).

To construct an AST for a single string, we need first to split this string in suffixes $s_i = s[i :]$. Next we take the first suffix s_1 and create a chain of nodes in an empty AST with frequencies equal to unity. For all next suffixes we do the following: we check, if there is a path in the AST, which coincides with the beginning of the current suffix, i.e., so-called *match*. If there is such a match for the current suffix in the AST, we increase the frequencies of the matched nodes by unity and add the not matched characters to end of the match, if any. Same way can construct a generalized AST for the collection of input strings. Fig. 1 shows and example of a generalized AST for string "mining" and "dining".

We adopt a scoring procedure from (Pampapathi et al., 2006) and use it as a similarity measure. Briefly, the scoring procedure computes average frequency of the input string in the AST. Given again a string s, we split it in the suffixes s_i. The

---

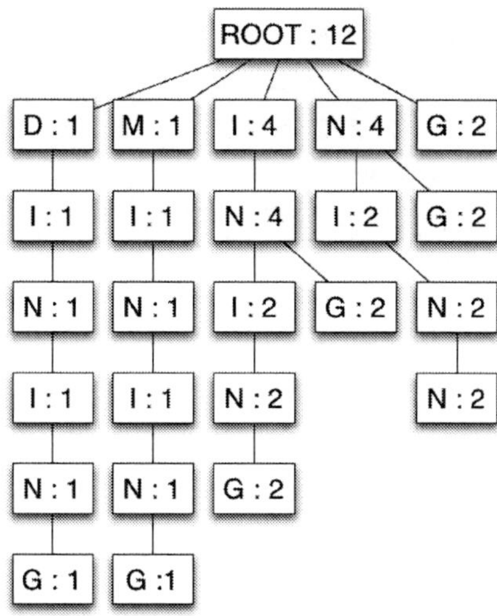

Figure 1: The generalized AST for string "mining" and "dining".

first step of scoring is to match and score each suffix individually:

$$score(match(s_i, AST)) = \frac{\sum_{n \in match} \frac{f(n)}{f(p(n))}}{|match|}$$

where $f(n)$ is the frequency of the node n and $f(p(n))$ is its parent frequency. Next, we sum up the individual scores and weight them by the length of the string:

$$SC(s, AST) = \frac{\sum_{s_i}(score(match(s_i, AST)))}{|s|}.$$

The final SC function may serve as string similarity function.

For our task we construct one generalised AST from the stop list and match and score each word to this AST. Based on the achieved values we decide, is the word obscene or not.

4.4 Edit Distance

Edit distance, also known as Levenshtein distance, stands for the number operations needed to transform a string s_1 into a string s_2, given that they are generated from the common alphabet Σ. Usually the possible operations are limited to insertion, deletion and substitution. For example, the edit distance between strings "mining" and "dining" is equal to 1, since only one substitution operation is required to transform one string into another.

5 Evaluation

Note, that for different similarity measures both the range and the threshold differ. For example,

	time complexity
word, lemma or stem coincidence	$O(n * m)$ to check symbol-wise coincidence with each stop word
AST-based similarity measure	$O(m^2)$ to check suffix-wise coincidence with an AST build for the stop list
Jaccard similarity measure	$O(n^2 * m)$ to check all possible pairs of a word a and stop word
edit distance	$O(n^2 * m)$ to check all possible pairs of a word a and stop word

Table 1: Time complexity of exploiting different similarity measures.

the word, lemma or stem coincidence coincidence results only in two values, namely, 0 and 1. Jaccard and AST-based similarity measures range between $[0, 1]$, while the edit distance has no upper bound. Hence, the thresholds are defined in in various ways: the lemma or stem coincidence should be equal to unity to consider the word obscene. We tested Jaccard similarity measure with the threshold equal to 0.8, the edit distance with threshold equal to 5 and 8. For the AST-based similarity measure the value of 0.2 has proven to be a more or less meaningful threshold, since it is around 1/3 of the maximal observed similarity value (Pampapathi et al., 2006; Frolov, 2016; Yakovlev and Chernyak, 2016).

After we get a set of candidate obscene words using one of the similarity measures, we can evaluate it by such standard measures, as recall, precision, F-measure and accuracy.

Of these four measures we would consider recall the most important one, since a good filter should have as few false negatives as possible and the number of false positives is not that crucial in our task.

The last but not least feature for comparison of string similarity measure in task of obscenity filtering is the time complexity of computing similarity values. Since the obscenity filtering is likely to be done online, the method used should be as fast as possible. Let us list the time complexity of exploiting different similarity measures using the following O – notation and the following notations: let n be the number of stop words, m – the maximal length of a stop word, $m \ll n$, see Table 1.

6 Results and Discussion

Final results are presented in Table 2 below. If we take precision into account, obviously the best results are achieved by using word coincidence, followed by lemma and stem coincidence. Although there is no drastic difference between using pymorphy2 or mystem lemmatizers, the latter gives better results than the former. Stemming works slightly worse, than lemmatisation. The precision of using Jaccard coefficient is almost comparable to the one, achieved by word coincidence, with recall being slightly higher. The precision of AST-based similarity measure and edit distance is significantly lower than everything else.

If we consider recall now, the best results are achieved by using edit distance, although the precision of this method is almost close, which does make the results unreliable. The edit distance is followed by AST-based similarity, which overcomes the stem coincidence by almost 20%.

To evaluate the over-all performance we may use accuracy or F-measure. From this point of view, the highest results are achieved by using stem or lemma coincidence, followed by AST-based similarity and Jaccard coefficient.

Let us analyze errors (i.e. false positive and false negative words). During our experiments we noticed the following possible errors:

1. very short words, such as "уг" [abbreviation for "depressing shit"] or "ссы" ["to piss"] result usually in false negatives for the AST-based similarity;

2. long or event compound words, such as "говнофотограф" ["bad photographer"], "скопипиздить" ["to copy paste illegally"] are tough for all measures and result in false negatives. The only measure that is capable to discover such words is the AST-based similarity measure due to it suffix nature;

3. the AST-based similarity measure usually considers verbs as obscene words, which increases the number of false positives. For example, all verbs, that end with "ать" [verbal ending "at$'$"] tend to be considered as obscene;

4. the Jaccard coefficient suffers from paronyms, such as "эксперименты" ["experiments"] – "экскременты" ["excrement"], which increase the number of false positives;

5. the pure results of edit distance are caused by the substitution of wrong symbols. For ex-

	Pr	R	acc	F_2
word coincidence	**0.7288**	0.1363	0.9810	0.2297
lemma coincidence				
pymorphy2	0.6492	0.2466	0.9815	0.3574
mystem3	0.6807	0.3195	**0.9827**	0.4349
stem coincidence	0.6113	0.4028	0.9822	**0.4856**
AST	0.1578	**0.6201**	0.9233	0.2516
Jaccard similarity measure, 0.8				
3-grams	0.6799	0.1633	0.9810	0.2634
4-grams	0.7126	0.1475	0.9810	0.2430
5-grams	0.7168	0.1284	0.9808	0.2179
6-grams	0.6989	0.0975	0.9803	0.1711
edit distance				
$d < 8$	0.0234	**0.9127**	0.8086	0.0456
$d < 5$	0.0209	**0.9825**	0.9629	0.0409

Table 2: Comparison of results.

ample, the word "манере" ["manner"] has edit distance equal to 3 to the word "засере" ["young punk"], although it is not obscene by now means.

To cope with some of the errors, we might exploit additional POS filtering and preprocessing as well as some compound splitting algorithms. Anyway it remains an open question whether the edit distance is applicable for the task at all.

7 Conclusions

In this project we establish both a text collection and a baseline for both obscene filtering. We have so far achieved quite moderate results, which nevertheless allow us to make some preliminary conclusions and think of the future directions for improvement.

1. Straightforward similarity measures such as word, lemma or stem coincidence do not cope well with the problem of obscene filtering, no matter what lemmatisation tool or stemming algorithm is used;

2. If we consider recall as the main quality measure, the best results are achieved either AST-based similarity measure or Jaccard coefficient on character n-grams;

3. The edit distance is of too general nature to be applicable for the problem;

4. If the filtering should be conducted online, the AST similarity measure is the best one in terms of time complexity of calculations.

Our main future directions are, first of all, improvements based on conducted error analysis, and, secondly, developing a filter for obscene multiword expressions, such as послать на хуй" ["to fuck off"] and euphemisms, such as послать на три буквы" ["to fuck off"]. The filtering of obscene multiword expressions might be seen as a problem analogous to semantic role labelling, where the obscene word is the main one and the rest are its arguments. The filtering of euphemisms looks much more complicated to us and may require using compositional semantics tools.

Acknowledgements

This work was supported by RFBR grants #16-01-00583 and #16-29-12982 and was prepared within the framework of the Basic Research Program at the National Research University Higher School of Economics (HSE) and supported within the framework of a subsidy by the Russian Academic Excellence Project "5-100".

References

Richard C. Angell, George E. Freund, and Peter Willett. 1983. Automatic spelling correction using a trigram similarity measure. *Information Processing & Management*, 19(4):255–261.

David Bamman and Noah A. Smith. 2015. Contextualized sarcasm detection on Twitter. In *Ninth International AAAI Conference on Web and Social Media*.

Maral Dadvar, Dolf Trieschnigg, Roeland Ordelman, and Franciska de Jong. 2013. Improving cyberbullying detection with user context. In *European Conference on Information Retrieval*, pages 693–696. Springer.

Ahmed K. Elmagarmid, Panagiotis G. Ipeirotis, and Vassilios S. Verykios. 2007. Duplicate record detection: A survey. *IEEE Transactions on knowledge and data engineering*, 19(1).

Dmitry Frolov. 2016. Using annotated suffix trees for fuzzy full text search. In *Communications in Computer and Information Science, Information Retrieval, 10th Russian Summer School, RuSSIR*. Springer.

Wael H. Gomaa and Aly A. Fahmy. 2013. A survey of text similarity approaches. *International Journal of Computer Applications*, 68(13).

Aminul Islam and Diana Inkpen. 2008. Semantic text similarity using corpus-based word similarity and string similarity. *ACM Transactions on Knowledge Discovery from Data (TKDD)*, 2(2):10.

Xiang Ji, Soon Ae Chun, and James Geller. 2013. Monitoring public health concerns using twitter sentiment classifications. In *Healthcare Informatics (ICHI), 2013 IEEE International Conference on*, pages 335–344. IEEE.

Mikhail Korobov. 2015. Morphological analyzer and generator for Russian and Ukrainian languages. In *International Conference on Analysis of Images, Social Networks and Texts*, pages 320–332. Springer.

Rajesh Pampapathi, Boris Mirkin, and Mark Levene. 2006. A suffix tree approach to anti-spam email filtering. *Machine Learning*, 65(1):309–338.

Martin F. Porter. 2001. Snowball: A language for stemming algorithms.

Deepak Ravichandran and Eduard Hovy. 2002. Learning surface text patterns for a question answering system. In *Proceedings of the 40th annual meeting on association for computational linguistics*, pages 41–47. Association for Computational Linguistics.

Hinrich Schütze. 2008. Introduction to information retrieval. In *Proceedings of the international communication of association for computing machinery conference*.

Ilya Segalovich. 2003. A fast morphological algorithm with unknown word guessing induced by a dictionary for a web search engine. In *MLMTA*, pages 273–280. Citeseer.

George R.S. Weir and Ana-Maria Duta. 2012. Strategies for neutralising sexually explicit language. In *Cybercrime and Trustworthy Computing Workshop (CTC), 2012 Third*, pages 66–74. IEEE.

Maxim Yakovlev and Ekaterina Chernyak. 2016. Using annotated suffix tree suffix tree similarity similarity measure for text summarisation. In *Analysis of Large and Complex Data*, pages 103–112. Springer.

Taijin Yoon, Sun-Young Park, and Hwan-Gue Cho. 2010. A smart filtering system for newly coined profanities by using approximate string alignment. In *Computer and Information Technology (CIT), 2010 IEEE 10th International Conference on*, pages 643–650. IEEE.

Oren Zamir and Oren Etzioni. 1998. Web document clustering: A feasibility demonstration. In *Proceedings of the 21st annual international ACM SIGIR conference on Research and development in information retrieval*, pages 46–54. ACM.

Stylometric Analysis of Parliamentary Speeches: Gender Dimension

Justina Mandravickaitė
Vilnius University, Lithuania
Baltic Institute of Advanced
Technology, Lithuania
`justina@bpti.lt`

Tomas Krilavičius
Vytautas Magnus University, Lithuania
Baltic Inistitute of Advanced
Technology, Lithuania
`t.krilavicius@bpti.lt`

Abstract

Relation between gender and language has
been studied by many authors, however,
there is still some uncertainty left regarding gender influence on language usage
in the professional environment. Often,
the studied data sets are too small or texts
of individual authors are too short in order to capture differences of language usage wrt gender successfully. This study
draws from a larger corpus of speeches
transcripts of the Lithuanian Parliament
(1990–2013) to explore language differences of political debates by gender via
stylometric analysis. Experimental set
up consists of stylistic features that indicate lexical style and do not require external linguistic tools, namely the most frequent words, in combination with unsupervised machine learning algorithms. Results show that gender differences in the
language use remain in professional environment not only in usage of function
words, preferred linguistic constructions,
but in the presented topics as well.

1 Introduction

Gender influence on language usage have been extensively studied (Lakoff, 1973; Holmes, 2006;
Holmes, 2013; Argamon et al., 2003) without
fully reaching a common agreement. Understanding gender differences in professional environment would assist in a more balanced atmosphere
(Herring and Paolillo, 2006; Mullany, 2007), however results on extent of variation depending on
context of communication in professional setting
are inconclusive(Newman et al., 2008).

Most studies rely on the relatively small data
sets, or texts of the individual authors are too short

to capture the differences in the language due to
the gender (Newman et al., 2008; Herring and
Martinson, 2004). Some results show that gender differences in language depend on the context, e.g., people assume *male language* in a formal setting and *female* in an informal environment (Pennebaker, 2011). We investigate gender
impact to the language use in a professional setting, i.e., transcripts of speeches of the Lithuanian Parliament debates. We study language wrt
style, i.e., *male* and *female* style of the language
usage by applying computational stylistics or stylometry. Stylometry is based on the two hypotheses: (1) *human stylome hypothesis*, i.e., each individual has a unique style (Van Halteren et al.,
2005); (2) unique style of individual can be measured (Stamatatos, 2009), stylometry allows gain-
ing meta-knowledge (Daelemans, 2013), i.e., what
can be learned from the text about the author
- gender (Luyckx et al., 2006; Argamon et al.,
2003; Cheng et al., 2011; Koppel et al., 2002),
age (Dahllöf, 2012), psychological characteristics
(Luyckx and Daelemans, 2008), political affiliation (Dahllöf, 2012), etc.

Like in most studies of gender and language
(Yu, 2014; Herring and Martinson, 2004), bio-
logical sex as a criterion for gender was used in
this study. We compare differences of the gender related language use at the group level (fac-
tion). Lithuanian language allows easy distinction
between male and female legislators based on their
names in the transcripts.[1]

We investigate several questions: (1) How well
simple stylistic features distinguish genders of
members the Lithuanian Parliament? (2) Which
differences in language use by female and male
Lithuanian Parliament members selected features
and methods are able to capture?

---

[1]Of course, all information about members of parliament
is available on-line.

Proceedings of the 6th Workshop on Balto-Slavic Natural Language Processing, pages 102–107,
Valencia, Spain, 4 April 2017. ©2017 Association for Computational Linguistics

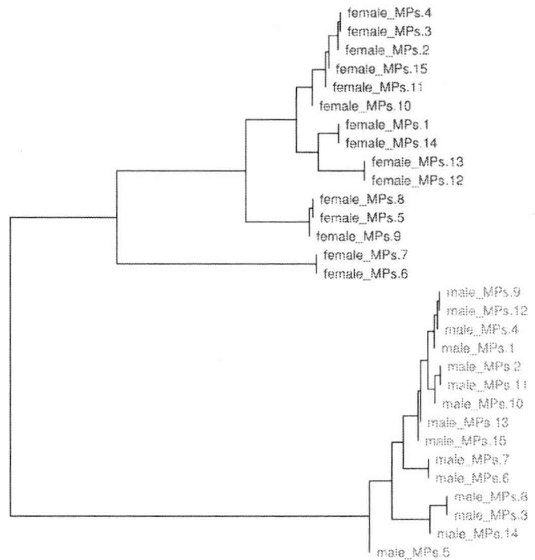

Figure 1: Results with 7000 MFW as features.

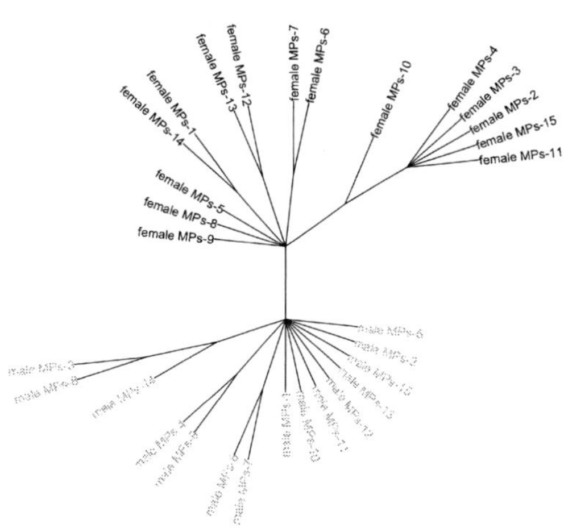

Figure 2: Bootstrap Consensus Tree with Canberra and 100–10000 MFW.

2 Data Set

Corpus of parliamentary speeches in the Lithuanian Parliament[2] is used. It consists of transcripts of parliamentary speeches from March 1990 to December 2013, 10727 of female members of Parliament (MPs) and 100181 of male MPs, overall 23 908 302 words (2 357 596 of female MPs and 21 550 706 of male; see Table 2 for the details). Only speeches of at least 100 words and of MPs with at least 200 of them were included in the corpus (Kapočiūtė-Dzikienė and Utka, 2014). It could have diminished number of female MPs speeches included into the corpus and our analysis as well. However, the choice of unsupervised learning approach downscales class imbalance problem, i.e. significant difference in number of transcribed parliamentary speeches made by female and male MPs.

Lithuanian is a highly inflective language, i.e. nouns have grammatical gender, number and semantic relations between them are expressed with 7 cases; adjectives have to match nouns in terms of gender, number and case; verbs have 4 tenses and particles for each of them, with ending marking its tense, person and number; gender and case for the particles are also marked morphologically

at the ending. All these features produce a substantial number of inflective forms for one lemma. Thus in order to avoid data sparseness we did not lemmatize corpus for our experiments.

To get around of "fingerprint" of individual authorship as much as possible, all the samples were concatenated into two large documents based on the gender, and then were partitioned into 15 parts each. Thus for analysis we had 15 samples of parliamentary speech made by female MPs and another 15 samples – made by male MPs.

3 Stylistic Features and Statistical Measures

We use the most frequent words (MFW) (Burrows, 1992; Hoover, 2007; Eder, 2013b; Rybicki and Eder, 2011; Eder and Rybicki, 2013; Eder, 2013a) (usually, they coincide with function words (Hochmann et al., 2010; Sigurd et al., 2004)), as features, because they are considered to be topic-neutral and perform well (Juola and Baayen, 2005; Holmes et al., 2001; Burrows, 2002).

Stylo package for stylometric analysis using R (Eder et al., 2014) is used for experiments.

Experiments are performed in batches using different number of MFWs, firstly, using the whole corpus, raw frequency list of features is generated, then normalized using *z-scores*, which measure distance of features frequencies in the corpus in terms of their proximity to the mean (Hoover, 2004), where z-scores are defined as $z = \frac{A_i - \mu}{\sigma}$, where A_i is *frequency* of a feature, μ is *mean fre-*

103

MPs by gender	No. of samples	No. of words	No. of unique words
Female	10 727	2 357 596	93 611
Male	100 181	21 550 706	268 030

Table 1: Statistics of Corpus of parliamentary speeches in the Lithuanian Parliament.

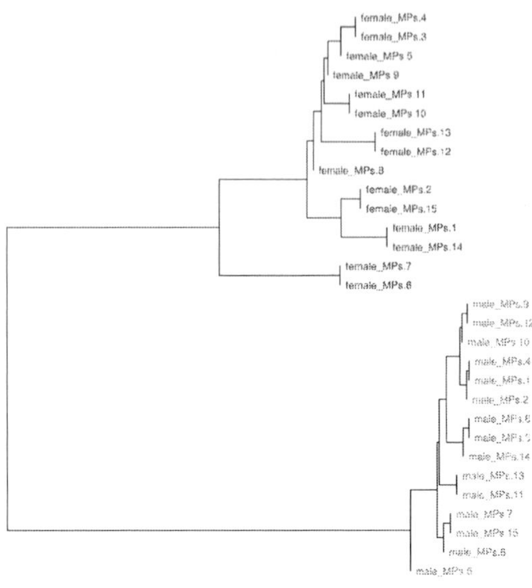

Figure 3: Results with 200 MFW (starting at 6800 MFW).

quency of certain feature in one document, σ is a standard deviation.

Dissimilarity between the text samples is calculated using selected distances (see below), and distance matrix is generated. Then, *hierarchical clustering* is applied to group samples by similarity (Everitt et al., 2011), and dendrograms are used to visualize the results.

Typically Burrows's Delta distance is used for stylometric analysis (Burrows, 2002; Rybicki and Eder, 2011). However, Delta depends on *z-scores*, number of documents and balance of terms in documents, length and number of authors (Stamatatos, 2009). While Burrow's Delta is effective for English and German, it is less successful for highly inflective languages, e.g., Latin and Polish (Rybicki and Eder, 2011). Hence we used Eder's Delta, i.e., a modified Burrows's Delta that gives more weight to the frequent features and rescales less frequent to avoid random infrequent ones (Eder et al., 2014). It was defined to use with highly inflected languages, such as Lithuanian. However, we have achieved the best results

with Canberra distance $\delta_{(AB)} = \sum_{i=1}^{n} \frac{|A_i - B_i|}{|A_i| + |B_i|}$ where n is a number of most frequent features, A and B are documents, A_i and B_i are frequencies of a given feature in the documents A and B in the corpus, respectively (Eder et al., 2014). It was reported to be suitable for inflective languages, albeit it is sensitive for rare vocabulary (Eder et al., 2014), e.g., words that occurred only once or twice.

The goal is identifying stylistic dissimilarities and mapping positions of the text samples in relation to each other, not classifying female/male legislators, hence hierarchical clustering with Ward linkage (it minimizes total variance within-cluster (Everitt et al., 2011)) was chosen. Though it is sensitive to changes in a number of features or methods of grouping (Eder, 2013a; Luyckx et al., 2006), in this study it shows stable results. Robustness of clustering results was examined using bootstrap procedure (Eder, 2013a). It includes extensions of Burrows's Delta (Argamon, 2008; Eder et al., 2014) and bootstrap consensus trees (Eder, 2013a) as a way to improve reliability of cluster analysis dendrograms.

4 Experiments

From 20 to 10 000 most frequent features were used for each experiment. We use hierarchical clustering with Ward linkage and Canberra distance, and visualize results in dendrograms to map positions of the samples in relation to each other.

We focus on identifying variation in female and male parliamentary speech, and do not analyze smaller clusters and dynamics inside them. A more detailed investigation of separate features (e.g., specific words, part-of-speech tags or their sequences) that are characteristic to female MPs and male MPs individually, are part of future plans, while in this paper we focus on the most frequent words.

Experiments with more MFW (from 7000 up to 9910) successfully separated samples of parliamentary speeches by gender, see Figure 1. *Bootstrap Consensus Tree* (BCT) procedure (hierarchical clustering and aggregation of results into con-

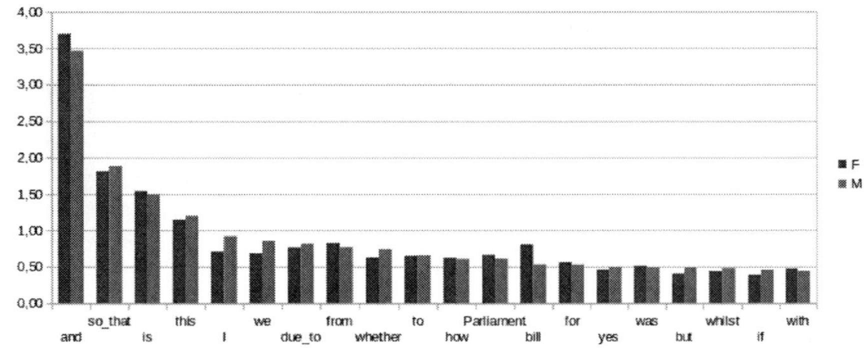

Figure 4: 20 MFW from the beginning with normalized frequencies.

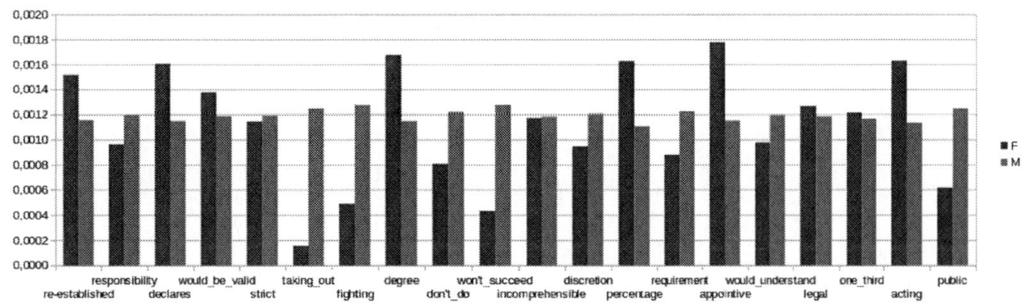

Figure 5: 20 MFW from the range of lesser frequency (6880–7000 MFW).

sensus tree (Eder, 2013a)) was applied to analyze the results. Consensus strength of 0.75 was chosen, i.e., the two documents are related, if they are related in the same proportion in the hierarchical clustering. So, consensus strength 0.75 means that visualized linkages appear in at least 75% of the clusters. See Figure 2 for BCT results for separating male and female legislators in the Lithuanian Parliament.

We needed at least 7000 MFW for clear differentiation of parliamentary speeches by gender in LT parliament. It shows that differences in topics presented as content words are less frequent than function words. To test this assumption, we performed experiments with different number and ranges of MFWs. As Figure 3 shows, less frequent MFWs capture gender variation as well.

The following gender based differences were noted male speeches transcripts (underscores show merge words that are one word in Lithuanian, but are several in English): (1) pronouns *I, we*; (2) demonstratives (e.g. *this*); (3) conjunctions *but, whether, if*; (4) negations (*won't_succeed, don't_do*); (5) *responsibility, public*; (6) *fighting, taking_out*. Some common characteristics of tran-

scripts of female speeches: (1) conjunction *and*; (2) preposition *with*; (3) *parliament, bill*; (4) measurements (*degree, percentage*); (5) parliamentary procedures (*acting, appointive, would_be_valid, legal*). See Figures 4 and 5 for details.

The results show that simple features and methods, such as MFW and hierarchical clustering, perform well with Lithuanian (morphology-rich language with relatively free word order, thus, challenging for many NLP tasks) and identify gender effect on language variation in LT parliament speeches transcripts, and do not require using lemmas (Kapočiūtė-Dzikienė et al., 2014), part-of-speech n-grams (Eder, 2010) and other feature combinations (Argamon et al., 2007; Argamon et al., 2003; Yu, 2014)).

5 Conclusion and Future Work

Results show that MFW and hierarchical clustering with Canberra distance successfully capture variation in transcripts of speeches by female and male MPs, which are clearly visible in dendrograms. Experiments with different ranges of MFW show, that more frequent MFW identify variation in usage of function words, medium frequent MFW reveal variation in topics presented. Thus, for female MPs conjunction *and*, preposition *with*, words *parliament* and *bill*, words for measuring and parliamentary procedures were more characteristic, while male MPs tended to use more first person pronouns, demonstratives, negations, conjunctions *but, whether, if* and words *responsibility, public, taking out, fighting*.

Future plans include experiments with different domain documents, diverse language types (e.g., formal, informal), investigation of other features (e.g., specific words, lemmas, part-of-speech tags or their sequences) that are characteristic to different genders, and other distance measures.

References

Shlomo Argamon, Moshe Koppel, Jonathan Fine, and Anat Rachel Shimoni. 2003. Gender, genre, and writing style in formal written texts. *To appear in Text*, 23:3.

Shlomo Argamon, Casey Whitelaw, Paul Chase, Sobhan Raj Hota, Navendu Garg, and Shlomo Levitan. 2007. Stylistic text classification using functional lexical features. *Journal of the American Society for Information Science and Technology*, 58(6):802–822.

Shlomo Argamon. 2008. Interpreting burrows's delta: Geometric and probabilistic foundations. *Literary and Linguistic Computing*, 23(2):131–147.

John F. Burrows. 1992. Not unless you ask nicely: The interpretative nexus between analysis and information. *Literary and Linguistic Computing*, 7(2):91–109.

John Burrows. 2002. 'Delta': A measure of stylistic difference and a guide to likely authorship. *Literary and Linguistic Computing*, 17(3):267–287.

Na Cheng, Rajarathnam Chandramouli, and KP Subbalakshmi. 2011. Author gender identification from text. *Digital Investigation*, 8(1):78–88.

Walter Daelemans. 2013. Explanation in computational stylometry. In *Computational Linguistics and Intelligent Text Processing*, pages 451–462. Springer.

Mats Dahllöf. 2012. Automatic prediction of gender, political affiliation, and age in swedish politicians from the wording of their speeches - a comparative study of classifiability. *Literary and linguistic computing*, 27(2):139–153.

Maciej Eder and Jan Rybicki. 2013. Do birds of a feather really flock together, or how to choose training samples for authorship attribution. *Literary and Linguistic Computing*, 28(2):229–236.

Maciej Eder, Jan Rybicki, and Mike Kestemont. 2014. Package 'stylo'.

Maciej Eder. 2010. Does size matter? authorship attribution, small samples, big problem. *Proceedings of Digital Humanities*, pages 132–135.

Maciej Eder. 2013a. Computational stylistics and biblical translation: How reliable can a dendrogram be. *The translator and the computer*, pages 155–170.

Maciej Eder. 2013b. Mind your corpus: systematic errors in authorship attribution. *Literary and linguistic computing*, 28(4):603–614.

Brian S. Everitt, Sabine Landau, Morven Leese, and Daniel Stahl. 2011. Hierarchical clustering. *Cluster Analysis, 5th Edition*, pages 71–110.

Susan C. Herring and Anna Martinson. 2004. Assessing gender authenticity in computer-mediated language use evidence from an identity game. *Journal of Language and Social Psychology*, 23(4):424–446.

Susan C. Herring and John C. Paolillo. 2006. Gender and genre variation in weblogs. *Journal of Sociolinguistics*, 10(4):439–459.

Jean-Rémy Hochmann, Ansgar D. Endress, and Jacques Mehler. 2010. Word frequency as a cue for identifying function words in infancy. *Cognition*, 115(3):444–457.

David I. Holmes, Lesley J. Gordon, and Christine Wilson. 2001. A widow and her soldier: Stylometry and the american civil war. *Literary and Linguistic Computing*, 16(4):403–420.

Janet Holmes. 2006. Sharing a laugh: Pragmatic aspects of humor and gender in the workplace. *Journal of Pragmatics*, 38(1):26–50.

Janet Holmes. 2013. *Women, men and politeness*. Routledge.

David L. Hoover. 2004. Delta prime? *Literary and Linguistic Computing*, 19(4):477–495.

David L. Hoover. 2007. Corpus stylistics, stylometry, and the styles of henry james. *Style*, 41(2):174.

Patrick Juola and R. Harald Baayen. 2005. A controlled-corpus experiment in authorship identification by cross-entropy. *Literary and Linguistic Computing*, 20(Suppl):59–67.

Jurgita Kapočiūtė-Dzikienė and Andrius Utka. 2014. Seimo posėdžių stenogramų tekstynas autorystės nustatymo bei autoriaus profilio sudarymo tyrimams. *Linguistics: Germanic & Romance Studies/Kalbotyra: Romanu ir Germanu Studijos*, 66.

Jurgita Kapočiūtė-Dzikienė, Ligita Sarkute, and Andrius Utka. 2014. Automatic author profiling of Lithuanian parliamentary speeches: Exploring the influence of features and dataset sizes. In *Human Language Technologies - The Baltic Perspective -*

Proceedings of the Sixth International Conference Baltic HLT 2014, Kaunas, Lithuania, September 26-27, 2014, pages 99–106.

Moshe Koppel, Shlomo Argamon, and Anat Rachel Shimoni. 2002. Automatically categorizing written texts by author gender. *Literary and Linguistic Computing*, 17(4):401–412.

Robin Lakoff. 1973. Language and woman's place. *Language in society*, 2(01):45–79.

Kim Luyckx and Walter Daelemans. 2008. Personae: a corpus for author and personality prediction from text. In *Proceedings of the Sixth International Conference on Language Resources and Evaluation (LREC'08)*.

Kim Luyckx, Walter Daelemans, and Edward Vanhoutte. 2006. Stylogenetics: Clustering-based stylistic analysis of literary corpora. In *Proceedings of the 5th International Conference on Language Resources and Evaluation (LREC'06), Genoa, Italy*.

Louise Mullany. 2007. *Gendered Discourse in the Professional Workplace*. Communicating in Professions and Organizations. Palgrave Macmillan UK.

Matthew L. Newman, Carla J. Groom, Lori D. Handelman, and James W. Pennebaker. 2008. Gender differences in language use: An analysis of 14,000 text samples. *Discourse Processes*, 45(3):211–236.

James W. Pennebaker. 2011. The secret life of pronouns. *New Scientist*, 211(2828):42–45.

Jan Rybicki and Maciej Eder. 2011. Deeper delta across genres and languages: do we really need the most frequent words? *Literary and linguistic computing*, 26(3):315–321.

Bengt Sigurd, Mats Eeg-Olofsson, and Joost Van Weijer. 2004. Word length, sentence length and frequency–zipf revisited. *Studia Linguistica*, 58(1):37–52.

Efstathios Stamatatos. 2009. A survey of modern authorship attribution methods. *Journal of the American Society for information Science and Technology*, 60(3):538–556.

Hans Van Halteren, Harald Baayen, Fiona Tweedie, Marco Haverkort, and Anneke Neijt. 2005. New machine learning methods demonstrate the existence of a human stylome. *Journal of Quantitative Linguistics*, 12(1):65–77.

Bei Yu. 2014. Language and gender in congressional speech. *Literary and Linguistic Computing*, 29(1):118–132.

Toward Never Ending Language Learning for Morphologically Rich Languages

Kseniya Buraya
ITMO University, Russia
`ksburaya@corp.ifmo.ru`

Lidia Pivovarova
University of Helsinki, Finland
`pivovaro@cs.helsinki.fi`

Sergey Budkov
ITMO University, Russia
`s.a.budkov@gmail.com`

Andrey Filchenkov
ITMO University, Russia
`afilchenkov@corp.ifmo.ru`

Abstract

This work deals with ontology learning from unstructured Russian text. We implement one of the components of Never Ending Language Learner and introduce the algorithm extensions aimed to gather specificity of morphologically rich free-word-order language. We perform several experiments comparing different settings of the training process. We demonstrate that morphological features significantly improve the system precision while seed patterns help to improve the coverage.

1 Introduction

Nowadays a big interest is paid to systems that can extract facts from the Internet (Pasca et al., 2006; Choo et al., 2013; Grozin et al., 2016; Dumais et al., 2016; Samborskii et al., 2016).

The main challenge is to design systems that do not require any human involvement and may efficiently store lots of information limited only by the amount of the knowledge uploaded to the Internet. One of the ways of representing information for such systems is *ontologies*.

According to the famous definition by Gruber (1995), ontology is "an explicit specification of a conceptualization", i.e. formalization of knowledge that underlines language utterance. In the simplest case, ontology is a structure containing *concepts* and *relations* among them. In addition, it may contain a set of axioms that define the relations and constraints on their interpretation (Guarino, 1998). One of the advantages of such structures is data formalization that simplifies the automatic processing. Ontologies are widely used in information retrieval, texts analysis and semantic applications (Albertsen and Blomqvist, 2007;

Staab and Studer, 2013).

In many practical applications, ontological concepts should be associated with *lexicon* (Hirst, 2009), i.e. with language expressions and structures. Even though ontologies themselves contain knowledge about the world, not a language, their primary goal is to ensure semantic interpretation of texts. Thus, *ontology learning* from text is an emerging research direction (Maedche, 2012; Staab and Studer, 2013).

One of the approaches that are used to learn facts from unstructured text is called *Never Ending Language Learning* (NELL) (Carlson et al., 2010a).[1] One of the NELL advantages is its low demand for preprocessed data required for the learning process. Given an initial ontology that contains 10–20 seeds for each category as an input, NELL can achieve a high performance level on extracting facts and relations from a large corpus (Carlson et al., 2010a).[2]

The first implementation of NELL (Carlson et al., 2010a) worked with English. An attempt was made to extend the NELL approach for the Portuguese language (Duarte and Hruschka, 2014). The main result of these experiments was that applying initial NELL parameters and ontology to non-English web-pages would not show high results; initial configuration did not work well with Portuguese web-pages. The authors made a conclusion that in order to extend the NELL approach to a new language, it is necessary to prepare a new seed ontology and contextual patterns that depend on the language rules.

In this paper, we introduce a NELL extension

---

[1] In this paper, we will use term "NELL" to refer both the approach and its implementations since it is traditional for the corresponding papers and the project.

[2] We distinguish two types of concepts: *categories* that are top-level concepts in predefined ontology and *instances*, that are descendants of top-level concepts; instances, apart from small initial seeds, are learned from text.

Proceedings of the 6th Workshop on Balto-Slavic Natural Language Processing, pages 108–118,
Valencia, Spain, 4 April 2017. ©2017 Association for Computational Linguistics

to the Russian language. Being a Slavic language, Russian has a rich morphology and free word order. Thus, common expressions for semantic relations in text have a specific form: the word order is less reliable than for Germanic or Romance languages; the morphological properties of words are more crucial. However, many pattern learning techniques are based on word order of pattern components and usually do not include morphology. Thus, the adaptation of the NELL approach to a Slavic language would require changes in the pattern structure. We introduce an adaptation of NELL to Russian, test it on a small dataset of 2.5 million words for 9 ontology categories and demonstrate that utilizing of morphology is crucial for ontology learning for Russian. This is the main contribution of this paper.

The rest of the paper is organized as follows. Section 2 overviews original NELL approach. Our improvements of the algorithm are presented in Section 3. Section 4 describes our data source, its preprocessing, and experiments we run. Results of these experiments are presented and discussed in Section 5. In Section 6, we give a brief overview of the related papers. We summarize the results and outline the future work in Section 7.

2   Never Ending Language Learner

The NELL architecture, which is presented in Figure 1, consists of two major parts: a knowledge base (KB) and a set of iterative learners (shown in the lowest part of the figure). The system works iteratively: first, the learners try to extract as much candidate facts as possible given a current state of the KB; after that, the KB is updated using learners output. This process is running infinitely, with the current state of KB being freely available at the project webpage.[3]

In this work, we focus on one of the NELL components, namely Coupled Pattern Learner (CPL). CPL is the free-text extractor that learns contextual patterns to extract instances of ontology categories. The key idea of CPL is that simultaneous ("coupled") learning of instances and patterns yields a higher performance than learning them independently (Carlson et al., 2010b).

An expression that matches text in CPL consists of three parts, which must be found within the same sentence:

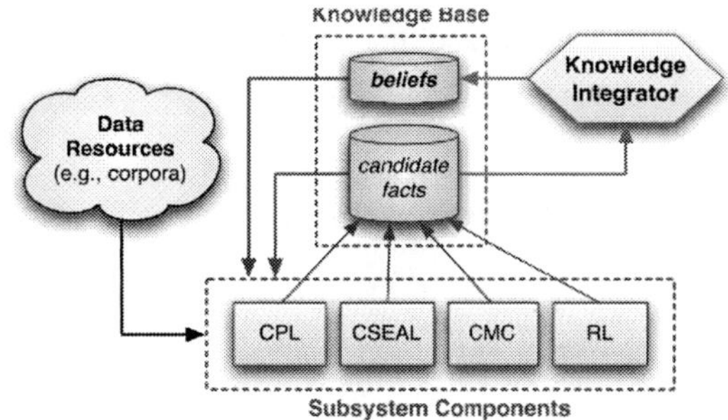

Figure 1: NELL architecture adapted from (Carlson et al., 2010a).

1. Category word. The list of category words is fixed and defined in the initial ontology.

2. Instance extracting pattern. A pattern consists of at most three words including punctuation like commas or parenthesis, but excluding category and instance words.

3. Instance word. At the beginning 3–5 seed instances are defined for each category.

CPL uses two sets: the set of *trusted patterns* and set of *trusted instances*, which are considered to be actual patterns and instances for the corresponding category. Different implementations may or may not exclude patterns/instances from the corresponding sets during further iterations.

The process starts with a text corpus and a small seed ontology that contains sets of trusted patterns and trusted instances. Then every learning iteration consists of the two following steps:

- **Instance extraction**. To extract new instances, the system finds a co-occurrence of the category word with a pattern from the trusted list and then identify the instance word. If both category and instance words satisfy the conditions of the pattern, then the found word is added to the pool of candidate instances for the current iteration. When all sentences are processed, candidate instance evaluation begins after which the most reliable instances are added to the set of trusted instances;

- **Pattern extraction**. To extract new patterns, the system finds a co-occurrence of the category word with one of its trusted instances. The sequence of words between category and instance are identified as a candidate pattern.

---

[3]http://rtw.ml.cmu.edu/rtw/

When all candidate patterns are collected, the most reliable patterns are added to the trusted set.

3 The Proposed Approach

3.1 Adaptation to the Russian Language

Russian patterns should have a specific structure, which should comprise morphological components. Thus we expand the form of the search expression so that case and number are taken into account for both category and instance words.

Let us consider an example, which illustrates importance of including morphology into patterns:

Тренеры знают множество приемов для дрессировки собак, такие как поощрение едой и многие другие.

Coaches know many techniques for training dogs, such as stimulation with food and etc.

This sentence matches *such as* pattern and without morphological constraints that may lead to extracting of wrong relations "**stimulation** *is a* **dog**". If the pattern have specified only part-of-speech rules, then our algorithm would produce a lot of errors. Specification of the arguments (nominative in this example) helps to avoid such false pattern triggering. Another way to avoid such errors would be a syntax annotation of all data and running CPL on top of this annotation; we leave this approach for further research.[4]

3.2 Strategies for Expanding the Trusted Sets

To add new patterns and instances to the corresponding trusted sets, we use *Support* metric. For each category, instances and patterns are ranked separately using the following formulas:

$$Support_c^{(t)}(i) = \frac{\sum_{p \in \text{TruPat}_c^{(t-1)}} Count_c(i, p)}{Count_c(i)}$$

for instances and

$$Support_c^{(t)}(p) = \frac{\sum_{i \in \text{TruInst}_c^{(t-1)}} Count_c(i, p)}{Count_c(p)}$$

for patterns, where i is an instance word, p is a pattern, $Count_c(i, p)$ is the number of cases when i and c match as arguments of p in the corpus related to category c, $Count_c(x)$ is the total number of matches of x in the corpus related to category c, *TruInst* is a set of trusted instances, *TruPat* is a set of trusted patterns, and (t) is an iteration.

Instances and patterns with higher support are considerd to be trusted. To define trusted patterns and istances, we use FILTERBYTHRESHOLD procedure, which is implemented in two versions using two different strategies.

The first strategy uses a certain threshold on *Support* value that is computed after the first iteration for patterns and instances separately. On the first iteration, the filter equals to zero, that means we allow pattern and instance extraction without any limitations. Then the threshold is set as a minimum value of support for all extracted patterns and instances correspondingly. On the next iterations, only the instances and patterns that have *Support* value greater or equal than these thresholds are added to the trusted sets. Note that within this strategy, *Support* value of any pattern and instance does not decrease. We will refer to it as THRESHOLD-SUPPORT. This is the main strategy for CPL-RUS.

THRESHOLD-SUPPORT does not limit trusted elements during algorithm run. It is greedy in sense that it collects all possible instances and patterns that are trusted enough and use them to extract new patterns and instances. Thus, final filtering should be applied in this case after the algorithm stops and the final instances, which has support not less than a certain *minimal support*, should be selected.

The second strategy uses a threshold on a number of elements of the trusted sets. After extracting new instances and patterns, they are sorted with respect to their *Support*, and then 50 most reliable instances and patterns are left in the trusted sets. We assume that this procedure would be able to correct errors made on the earlier iterations, when the algorithm have more evidence. This strategy was used in (Duarte and Hruschka, 2014). We will refer to it as THRESHOLD-50.

3.3 Implementation

Our implementation of CPL component is summarized in Algorithm 1. The algorithm processes each category c separately. It starts with a set of

---

[4]This particular example would probably produce the same error on the English translation, though we believe that such cases should be more rare. Since English has almost no morphology some other mechanism should be used to restrict over-production of patterns; in particular, distinguishing between verb subject and object is easier for a free-word-order language.

Algorithm 1 COUPLED PATTERN LEARNER (CPL-RUS).

Require: set of trusted patterns $\mathrm{TruPat}_c^{(0)}$, set of trusted instances $\mathrm{TruInst}_c^{(0)}$, text corpus T_c

Ensure: $\mathrm{Pat}_c^{(\infty)}$, $\mathrm{Inst}_c^{(\infty)}$

  $t \leftarrow 0$

  repeat

    $\mathrm{CandInst} \leftarrow \mathrm{EXTRACT}(\mathrm{TruPat}_c^{(t)})$

    $\mathrm{TruInst}_c^{(t+1)} \leftarrow \mathrm{TruInst}_c^{(t)} \cup \mathrm{CandInst}$

    $\mathrm{FILTERBYTHRESHOLD}(\mathrm{TruInst}_c^{(t+1)})$

    $\mathrm{CandPat} \leftarrow \mathrm{EXTRACT}(\mathrm{TruInst}_c^{(t)})$

    $\mathrm{TruPat}_c^{(t+1)} \leftarrow \mathrm{TruPat}_c^{(t)} \cup \mathrm{CandPat}$

    $\mathrm{FILTERBYTHRESHOLD}(\mathrm{TruPat}_c^{(t+1)})$

    $t \leftarrow t + 1$

  until $\quad \mathrm{TruInst}_c^{(t+1)} \backslash \mathrm{TruInst}_c^{(t)} \quad \cup$
$\mathrm{TruPat}_c^{(t+1)} \backslash \mathrm{TruPat}_c^{(t)} = \emptyset$

---

trusted patterns, $\mathrm{TruPat}_c^{(0)}$, a set of trusted instances, $\mathrm{TruInst}_c^{(0)}$, and a preprocessed corpus for each c: we use only sentences that contains c lexeme(s) to speed up iterations.

Though this algorithm should run infinitely with more and more data (that is how the original NELL process organized), only small corpora are used in our experiments, and the process stops if no more patterns or instances are found during the previous iteration.

4 Experiments

4.1 Data

We use Russian Wikipedia as the data source due to the convenience of downloading a relatively small corpus devoted to some particular topic (e.g. animals) using Wikipedia categories.[5] However, we do not use a specific Wikipedia structure for anything but corpus collection, thus our method can work with any other source types. Note, that even though the Wikipedia format for articles has its own standards, all of them are written by different people with changing of author style across documents. That makes Wikipedia a good resource to obtain way the data with some varieties in style.

We use Petscan service[6] to download Wikipedia pages that belong to a certain category. For initial experiments, we collect several corpora try-

[5]Wikipedia categories are different from those in ontology though they can be easily matched.

[6]https://petscan.wmflabs.org/

Wikipedia category	Number of pages	Ontology category
ANIMALS	32,412	BIRD FISH MAMMAL REPTILE
COUNTRIES	305,217	COUNTRIES
FOOD	6204	PRODUCTS
VEGETABLES	523	VEGETABLES
FRUITS	329	FRUITS
PRODUCTS	5580	FOOD
SPORT	136,027	SPORT

Table 1: Downloaded Wikipedia pages for CPL input corpus.

ing to select wide but not too general categories. For example, we consider *animals* to be too general and split it into several subcategories, such as *birds*, *fish*, etc. The rational is that too broad categories might be too computationally heavy for initial experiments, while too narrow categories might not contain enough data. In total, we use a corpus of 2.5 million sentences extracted from 7 various categories (see Table 4.1). Then we annotate text with morphological attributes, such as part-of-speech, case, number, and lexeme, using Pymorphy tool (Korobov, 2015).

The results of the processing are lists of extracted patterns and instances for each category.

4.2 Initial Ontology

The initial ontology consists of 9 categories and 41 instances; it is presented in Table 4.2.

Note that FRUIT and VEGETABLE are subcategories for FOOD; we run all three independently that allow us to compare the algorithm performance on more general vs. more narrow categories.

The seed CPL patterns and their morphological constraints are listed in Table 4.2.

4.3 Experiment Design

We run experiments for all categories independently. Then we collect all extracted instances and manually annotate them as correct or incorrect. Then for each category c, we evaluated precision using the following formula:

$$Precision(c) = \frac{CorrInst(c)}{AllInst(c)},$$

Category	Initial instances
BIRD	Robin, blackbird, cardinal, oriole
FISH	Shark, anchovy, bass, haddock, salmon
MAMMAL	Bear, cat, dog, horse, cow
REPTILE	Alligator, chameleon, snake, turtle
GEOGRAPHY	Africa, Canada, Brazil, Iraq, Russia
SPORT	Football, basketball, tennis
FOOD	Pepper, ice, biscuit, cheese, apple
FRUIT	Orange, peach, lemon, kiwi, pineapple
VEGETABLE	Cucumber, tomato, carrot, turnip, celery

Table 2: Seed ontology for Russian CPL (English translation).

Pattern	Arg1, case	Arg2, case	Arg1, num	Arg2, num	Arg1, pos	Arg2, pos
arg1, такие как arg2 arg1, such as arg2	nomn	nomn	plur	all	noun	noun
arg2 являются arg1 arg2 is arg1	ablt	nonm	all	all	noun	noun
arg2 относятся к arg1 arg2 refer to arg1	datv	nomn	all	all	adjf	noun
arg2 относятся к arg1 arg2 refer to arg1	datv	nomn	all	all	noun	noun

Table 3: Initial trusted patterns for Russian CPL for all categories (English translation).

where $CorrInst(c)$ is the number of correct instances extracted for category c, and $AllInst(c)$ is the whole number of instances, that were extracted by CPL for category c.

When we use the THRESHOLD-SUPPORT strategy, we perform a final filtering using different minimal support values. For algorithm comparison, we use values 0.1, 0.5 and 1.0

The main experiment is devoted to CPL-RUS with THRESHOLD-SUPPORT strategy. The algorithm converges after 6–10 iterations depending on category. We run it on all the categories and investigate the dependency of precision on support value used to cut off trusted instances after the algorithm converges.

In addition, we perform a set of smaller experiments to study CPL properties and impact of different parameters. We test: 1) usefulness of morphological features; 2) usefulness of pattern seeds; 3) differences between threshold selection strategies.

In the first experiment, we compare CPL-RUS and a version of this algorithm which do not use morphology (thus, similar to the English CPL). We will refer to the second one as CPL-NOMORPH. We run it on three ontology categories: VEGETABLE, FRUIT, and FOOD. The first run uses morphological constraints and the second allows words in all morphological forms.

In the second experiment, we investigate if the usage of seed patterns can improve the quality of the algorithm; the same experiment was conducted by (Duarte and Hruschka, 2014). As can be seen from the description in Section 2, CPL can learn without seed patterns, relying only on the set of initial categories and instances. However, since the initial ontology is small, this might be not the optimal strategy. We will refer to the second algorithm as CPL-NOPAT. We run the algorithms on the same three categories: VEGETABLE, FRUIT, and FOOD.

In the third experiment, we compare two *Threshold* selection strategies described in Section 3.3: THRESHOLD-SUPPORT, based on minimal *Support* after the first iteration and THRESHOLD-50 that keeps the fixed number of patterns and instances and revise the trusted lists after each iteration.

5 Results and Discussion

5.1 On CPL-RUS

Table 5.1 shows the main results of running CPL-RUS on the whole ontology using seeds.

There is a huge variety in results among categories with COUNTRY and SPORT being the most problematic ones despite the minimum support. FOOD as the more general category performs much worse than more narrow VEGETABLE and FRUIT, though for these categories the number of extracted instances is very low (see Table 5.2).

Interestingly, CPL-RUS with minimal support 0.5 shows better results in terms of precision than with minimal support 1. It means that some false positives have a very high *Support* value.

5.2 On Morphological Constraints

The results of evaluating the importance of including morphological constraints to the Russian CPL are shown in Table 5.2. The precision for all categories, in this case, is much lower, which makes CPL-NOMORPH completely useless. While CPL-RUS can achieve precision 1.0 for VEGETABLE and FRUIT categories, the maximum result for the same categories in unconstrained mode is 0.43.

Table 5.2 presents results on comparison of the learning progress for the three categories with and without morphological constraints. As can be seen, morphological constraints decrease the number of extracted instances and patterns and slow down the training process.

5.3 On Usage of Seed Patterns

Table 5.3 shows the results for running CPL-NOPAT, which does not use any seed patterns. In comparison with CPL-RUS (Table 5.1), this algorithm yields worse precision, especially for the more general FOOD category. Table 5.3 shows the total number of extracted instances in both cases. As can be seen, running algorithm without seed patterns increases its coverage but decreases the resulting precision.

5.4 On Threshold Selection Strategies

Precision for different thresholds of *Support* in CPL-RUS is shown in Figure 2. The numerical values of precision for three minimal support values are shown in Table 5.1.

In our final experiment, we test THRESHOLD-50 strategy that re-arrange patterns and instances on every step and allows only 50 of them to be trusted. The results for four ontology categories are shown in Table 5.4. Precision is better for that strategy, but the number of extracted instances is very small. It means that this strategy yields lower Recall (which is hard to evaluate in exact numbers). This gives us the opportunities for future work to find the way to determine the minimal support value that would satisfy both conditions: the number of extracted instances should not be small, and the precision should be high and does not vary among categories.[7]

5.5 Comparison with Other Approaches

The results of our experiments can be compared with the two previous work on this approach in English and Portuguese languages. Because in this work we extend the basic CPL algorithm only with morphological features of the Russian language, it makes it easy to compare the accuracy of our CPL realizations. The average accuracy for the English CPL version of the algorithm is reported as 0.78 with the minimum as 0.2 for the SPORTS EQUIPMENT category and maximum as 1.0 for the ACTOR, CELEBRITY, FURNITURE and SPORTS LEAGUE categories (Carlson et al., 2010a). The maximum average accuracy for the Russian language is 0.612. As it can be seen, the results for the Russian language also vary between different categories, from 0.16 to 1.0, but the average algorithm accuracy is higher for the English language. The results for the Portuguese version of CPL are presented separately for $5, 10, 15, 20$ iterations of the algorithm (Duarte and Hruschka, 2014). Since we did not run more than 10 iterations of CPL for each category, the most valuable result of comparison of two CPL realizations is to choose the accuracy of 10-iterations of the Portuguese CPL. The results of the average accuracy for the Portuguese CPL is varied from 0.04 to 0.95 (Duarte and Hruschka, 2014).

6 Related Work

In this paper, we focus on coupled pattern and instance learning from the text for ontology learning; the papers related to this topic are briefly

---

[7] One of the reviewers suggested that it may be also useful to use a human-in-the-loop procedure, where a threshold is defined manually after a certain number of iterations using procedure similar to what we used for evaluation.

Category	Number of instances	Precision		
Minimal support		1	0.5	0.1
BIRD	315	**0.875**	0.828	0.707
FISH	731	0.242	0.403	**0.46**
MAMMAL	258	**0.685**	0.619	0.555
REPTILE	42	**0.833**	**0.833**	0.727
COUNTRY	1205	**0.272**	0.244	0.2
SPORT	1356	0.16	**0.17**	**0.17**
FOOD	204	**0.42**	0.41	0.323
VEGETABLE	16	**1.0**	**1.0**	0.9
FRUIT	1	**1.0**	**1.0**	**1.0**
Average		0.610	**0.612**	0.560

Table 4: Results of CPL-RUS.

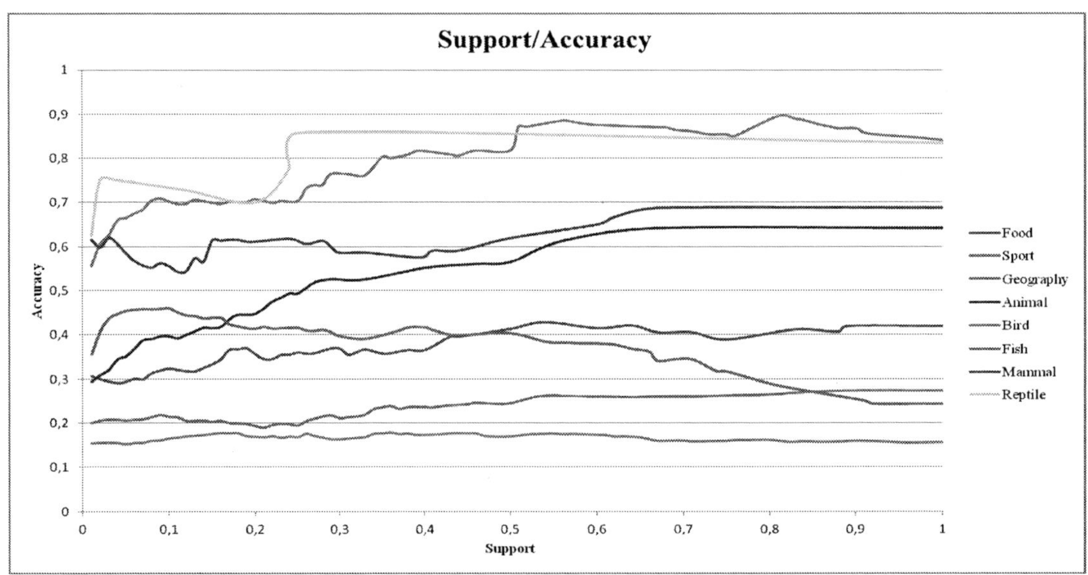

Figure 2: Dependence of CPL-RUS precision on minimal support value.

Category	Number of instances	Precision		
Minimal support		1	0.5	0.1
FOOD	1350	0.14	0.14	0.14
VEGETABLE	335	0.04	0.06	0.06
FRUIT	10	0	0	0.43

Table 5: Results of CPL-NOMORPH.

overviewed in this section. More general introduction to NELL and its predecessors can be found in (Carlson et al., 2010a).

Bootstrapping is well-known as a method for semi-supervised pattern learning. It was initially proposed for Information Extraction, that is for the traditional setting when the event templates are given beforehand (Riloff et al., 1999; Agichtein and Gravano, 2000; Yangarber, 2003). Bootstrapping for ontology learning from text has been applied, for example, by (Liu et al., 2005; Paliouras, 2005; Brewster et al., 2002).

Later the same principle was adapted for Open-Domain Information Extraction, aiming at discovering entity relations without any restrictions on their type (Shinyama and Sekine, 2006; Banko et al., 2007; Wang et al., 2011).

The idea of automatic extracting of domain templates from large corpus has been extensively studied, for example, by (Filatova et al., 2006; Chambers and Jurafsky, 2011; Fader et al., 2011). Thus, pattern-based information extraction as re-

Iteration/ Category	FRUIT		VEGETABLE		FOOD	
	inst	pat	inst	pat	inst	pat
1	0/2	10/13	0/3	42/139	2/7	37/154
2	1/3	7/10	7/158	50/548	8/416	59/2264
3	0/5	10/10	4/121	42/475	29/696	37/1227
4	0	0	1/43	9/233	39/143	78/0
5	0	0	0/9	0/87	21/63	163/0
6	0	0	0/1	0/14	17/22	213/0
7	0	0	0	0	36/3	131/0
8	0	0	0	0	26/0	72/0
9	0	0	0	0	9/0	101/0
10	0	0	0	0	13/0	53/0

Table 6: Number of extracted instances and patterns in case of using/non-using morphological constraints.

Category	Number of instances	Precision		
Minimal support		1	0.5	0.1
FOOD	262	0.07	0.09	0.17
VEGETABLE	12	0.75	0.86	0.73
FRUIT	1	1	1	1

Table 7: Results for CPL-NoPat.

Category	with seeds	without seeds
BIRD	551	652
FISH	731	890
MAMMAL	264	267
REPTILE	45	45
COUNTRY	1204	1276
SPORT	1358	1412
FOOD	204	273
VEGETABLE	16	20

Table 8: The number of extracted instances for each category with/without seed patterns.

Category	Number of instances	Precision
BIRD	3	1.0
FISH	1	1.0
MAMMAL	50	0.96
REPTILE	4	0.95

Table 9: Results for running CPL-Rus with THRESHOLD-50.

these works assumed that the KB is rather big (such as Freebase).

As far as we aware, this is the first work on the application of pattern learning techniques for the Russian language, despite general interest in Information Extraction (Starostin et al., 2016) and building of linguistic resources (Loukachevitch and Dobrov, 2014; Braslavski et al., 2016). Bocharov et al. (2010) and Sabirova and Lukanin (2014) used rule-based approach to extract taxonomic relations from text. Kuznetsov et al. (2016) applied a number of machine learning techniques to automatic relation extraction from the Russian Wikipedia but their method depends on the specific structure of Wikipedia.

search field becomes closer to ontology learning and knowledge-base population, though the latter task might be more difficult since it requires cross-document inference (Ji and Grishman, 2011).

The idea of simultaneous (coupled, joint) learning of both instances and relation have been justified. Li and Ji (2014) argued that though these two tasks are traditionally broken down into separate components, this is a rather artificial division leading to over-simplification and error propagation from the earlier tasks to the later steps.

Using a knowledge base to extract relations has been previously proposed as a distant supervision approach by, among others, (Mintz et al., 2009; Surdeanu et al., 2012; Riedel et al., 2013), though

7 Conclusion

In this work, we made the first attempt to adapt the NELL approach to the Russian language. We changed CPL component, so it can work with morphology. We conducted several experiments with the extended version, CPL-Rus algorithm on the corpus containing over 2.5 million sentences. Our main findings are the following:

- it is possible to adapt CPL for Russian with relatively little efforts;

- the morphological constraints are crucial for Russian pattern learning;

- a small set of manually compiled seed patterns increases CPL accuracy;

- the obtained results vary for different categories; that probably means that the algorithm settings should be optimized independently for each category.

This work leaves a room for further experiments. We plan to run CPL on much bigger datasets, including the whole Wikipedia corpus and other web-pages. This would require an expansion of the seed ontology and, probably, a construction of seed patterns individually for each category or a group of categories.

We will also continue working on threshold selection strategies. Another line of research is to run CPL on top of syntactic annotation; in principle, this should increase precision though some amount of errors might be introduced by syntax parser itself.

Acknowledgments

Authors would like to thank Maisa Duarte and Estevam Hrushka for assistance during experiments preparation and for giving examples of initial ontology for CPL algorithm. This research is supported by the Government of Russian Federation, Grant 074-U01.

References

Eugene Agichtein and Luis Gravano. 2000. Snowball: Extracting relations from large plain-text collections. In *Proceedings of the fifth ACM conference on Digital libraries*, pages 85–94. ACM.

Thomas Albertsen and Eva Blomqvist. 2007. Describing ontology applications. In *European Semantic Web Conference*, pages 549–563. Springer.

Michele Banko, Michael J. Cafarella, Stephen Soderland, Matthew Broadhead, and Oren Etzioni. 2007. Open information extraction from the web. In *IJCAI*, volume 7, pages 2670–2676.

Victor Bocharov, Lidia Pivovarova, Valery Rubashkin, and Boris Chuprin. 2010. Ontological parsing of encyclopedia information. In *International Conference on Intelligent Text Processing and Computational Linguistics*, pages 564–579. Springer.

Pavel Braslavski, Dmitry Ustalov, Mikhail Mukhin, and Yuri Kiselev. 2016. Yarn: Spinning-in-progress. In *Proceedings of the 8th Global WordNet Conference, GWC 2016*, pages 58–65.

Christopher Brewster, Fabio Ciravegna, and Yorick Wilks. 2002. User-centred ontology learning for knowledge management. In *International Conference on Application of Natural Language to Information Systems*, pages 203–207. Springer.

Andrew Carlson, Justin Betteridge, Bryan Kisiel, Burr Settles, Estevam R. Hruschka, and Tom M. Mitchell. 2010a. Toward an architecture for never-ending language learning. In *AAAI*, volume 5, page 3.

Andrew Carlson, Justin Betteridge, Richard C. Wang, Estevam R. Hruschka, and Tom M. Mitchell. 2010b. Coupled semi-supervised learning for information extraction. In *Proceedings of the third ACM international conference on Web search and data mining*, pages 101–110. ACM.

Nathanael Chambers and Dan Jurafsky. 2011. Template-based information extraction without the templates. In *Proceedings of the 49th Annual Meeting of the Association for Computational Linguistics: Human Language Technologies-Volume 1*, pages 976–986. Association for Computational Linguistics.

Chun Wei Choo, Brian Detlor, and Don Turnbull. 2013. *Web work: Information seeking and knowledge work on the World Wide Web*. Springer Science & Business Media.

Maisa C. Duarte and Estevam R. Hruschka. 2014. How to read the web in Portuguese using the never-ending language learner's principles. In *2014 14th International Conference on Intelligent Systems Design and Applications*, pages 162–167. IEEE.

Susan Dumais, Edward Cutrell, Jonathan J. Cadiz, Gavin Jancke, Raman Sarin, and Daniel C. Robbins. 2016. Stuff I've seen: a system for personal information retrieval and re-use. In *ACM SIGIR Forum*, volume 49, pages 28–35. ACM.

Anthony Fader, Stephen Soderland, and Oren Etzioni. 2011. Identifying relations for open information extraction. In *Proceedings of the Conference on Empirical Methods in Natural Language Processing*, pages 1535–1545. Association for Computational Linguistics.

Elena Filatova, Vasileios Hatzivassiloglou, and Kathleen McKeown. 2006. Automatic creation of domain templates. In *Proceedings of the COLING/ACL on Main conference poster sessions*, pages 207–214. Association for Computational Linguistics.

Vladislav Grozin, Kseniya Buraya, and Natalia Gusarova. 2016. Comparison of text forum summarization depending on query type for text forums. In *Advances in Machine Learning and Signal Processing*, pages 269–279. Springer.

Thomas R. Gruber. 1995. Toward principles for the design of ontologies used for knowledge sharing? *International journal of human-computer studies*, 43(5):907–928.

Nicola Guarino. 1998. Formal ontology and information systems. In *Proceedings of FOIS*, volume 98, pages 81–97.

Graeme Hirst. 2009. Ontology and the lexicon. In *Handbook on ontologies*, pages 269–292. Springer.

Heng Ji and Ralph Grishman. 2011. Knowledge base population: Successful approaches and challenges. In *Proceedings of the 49th Annual Meeting of the Association for Computational Linguistics: Human Language Technologies-Volume 1*, pages 1148–1158. Association for Computational Linguistics.

Mikhail Korobov. 2015. Morphological analyzer and generator for Russian and Ukrainian languages. In *International Conference on Analysis of Images, Social Networks and Texts*, pages 320–332. Springer.

Artem Kuznetsov, Pavel Braslavski, and Vladimir Ivanov. 2016. Family matters: Company relations extraction from wikipedia. In *International Conference on Knowledge Engineering and the Semantic Web*, pages 81–92. Springer.

Qi Li and Heng Ji. 2014. Incremental joint extraction of entity mentions and relations. In *ACL (1)*, pages 402–412.

Wei Liu, Albert Weichselbraun, Arno Scharl, and Elizabeth Chang. 2005. Semi-automatic ontology extension using spreading activation. *Journal of Universal Knowledge Management*, 1:50–58.

Natalia Loukachevitch and Boris Dobrov. 2014. Ruthes linguistic ontology vs. Russian wordnets. In *Proceedings of Global WordNet Conference GWC-2014*, pages 154–162.

Alexander Maedche. 2012. *Ontology learning for the semantic web*, volume 665. Springer Science & Business Media.

Mike Mintz, Steven Bills, Rion Snow, and Dan Jurafsky. 2009. Distant supervision for relation extraction without labeled data. In *Proceedings of the Joint Conference of the 47th Annual Meeting of the ACL and the 4th International Joint Conference on Natural Language Processing of the AFNLP: Volume 2-Volume 2*, pages 1003–1011. Association for Computational Linguistics.

Georgios Paliouras. 2005. On the need to bootstrap ontology learning with extraction grammar learning. In *International Conference on Conceptual Structures*, pages 119–135. Springer.

Marius Pasca, Dekang Lin, Jeffrey Bigham, Andrei Lifchits, and Alpa Jain. 2006. Organizing and searching the world wide web of facts-step one: the one-million fact extraction challenge. In *AAAI*, volume 6, pages 1400–1405.

Sebastian Riedel, Limin Yao, Andrew McCallum, and Benjamin M. Marlin. 2013. Relation extraction with matrix factorization and universal schemas. *NAACL HLT 2013*, pages 74–84.

Ellen Riloff, Rosie Jones, et al. 1999. Learning dictionaries for information extraction by multi-level bootstrapping. In *AAAI/IAAI*, pages 474–479.

Kristina Sabirova and Artem Lukanin. 2014. Automatic extraction of hypernyms and hyponyms from Russian texts. In *Supplementary Proceedings of the 3rd International Conference on Analysis of Images, Social Networks and Texts (AIST 2014)/Ed. by DI Ignatov, MY Khachay, A. Panchenko, N. Konstantinova, R. Yavorsky, D. Ustalov*, volume 1197, pages 35–40.

Ivan Samborskii, Andrey Filchenkov, Georgiy Korneev, and Aleksandr Farseev. 2016. Person, organization, or personage: Towards user account type prediction in microblogs. In *Proceedings of First New Zealand Text Mining Workshop (TMNZ) in conjunction with the 8th Asian Conference on Machine Learning (ACML 2016)*, pages 1–13.

Yusuke Shinyama and Satoshi Sekine. 2006. Preemptive information extraction using unrestricted relation discovery. In *Proceedings of the main conference on Human Language Technology Conference of the North American Chapter of the Association of Computational Linguistics*, pages 304–311. Association for Computational Linguistics.

Steffen Staab and Rudi Studer. 2013. *Handbook on ontologies*. Springer Science & Business Media.

Sergey Starostin, Viktor Bocharov, Svetlana Alexeeva, Anastasiya Bodrova, Alexander Chuchunkov, Irina Efimenko, Dmitriy Granovsky, Vladimir Khoroshevsky, Irina Krylova, et al. 2016. Factrueval 2016: Evaluation of named entity recognition and fact extraction systems for Russian. In *Computational Linguistics and Intellectual Technologies. Proceedings of the Annual International Conference «Dialogue»(2016)*, number 15, pages 702–720.

Mihai Surdeanu, Julie Tibshirani, Ramesh Nallapati, and Christopher D. Manning. 2012. Multi-instance multi-label learning for relation extraction. In *Proceedings of the 2012 Joint Conference on Empirical Methods in Natural Language Processing and Computational Natural Language Learning*, pages 455–465. Association for Computational Linguistics.

Wei Wang, Romaric Besançon, Olivier Ferret, and Brigitte Grau. 2011. Filtering and clustering relations for unsupervised information extraction in open domain. In *Proceedings of the 20th ACM international conference on Information and knowledge management*, pages 1405–1414. ACM.

Roman Yangarber. 2003. Counter-training in discovery of semantic patterns. In *Proceedings of the 41st Annual Meeting on Association for Computational*

Linguistics-Volume 1, pages 343–350. Association for Computational Linguistics.

Gender Profiling for Slovene Twitter Communication: The Influence of Gender Marking, Content and Style

Ben Verhoeven
CLiPS Research Center
University of Antwerp
Prinsstraat 13, Antwerp, Belgium
ben.verhoeven@uantwerpen.be

Iza Škrjanec
Jožef Stefan International Postgraduate School
Jamova cesta 39, Ljubljana, Slovenia
skrjanec.iza@gmail.com

Senja Pollak
Department of Knowledge Technologies
Jožef Stefan Institute
Jamova cesta 39, Ljubljana, Slovenia
senja.pollak@ijs.si

Abstract

We present results of the first gender classification experiments on Slovene text to our knowledge. Inspired by the TwiSty corpus and experiments (Verhoeven et al., 2016), we employed the Janes corpus (Erjavec et al., 2016) and its gender annotations to perform gender classification experiments on Twitter text comparing a token-based and a lemma-based approach. We find that the token-based approach (92.6% accuracy), containing gender markings related to the author, outperforms the lemma-based approach by about 5%. Especially in the lemmatized version, we also observe stylistic and content-based differences in writing between men (e.g., more profane language, numerals and beer mentions) and women (e.g., more pronouns, emoticons and character flooding). Many of our findings corroborate previous research on other languages.

1 Introduction

Various computational linguistic and text mining tasks have so far been investigated for Slovene. Standard natural language processing (NLP) tools have been developed, such as preprocessing tools for lemmatization (Juršič et al., 2010), tagging (Grčar and Krek, 2012; Ljubešić and Erjavec, 2016) and parsing (Dobrovoljc et al., 2012), more recently adapted also for preprocessing nonstandard texts, such as historical or computermediated Slovene (Ljubešić et al., 2016). However, not much attention has been paid to computational stylometry. While Zwitter Vitez (2013)

applied authorship attribution, author profiling received nearly no attention. Recently Ljubešić and Fišer (2016) have addressed the classification of private and corporate Twitter accounts, while – to the best of our knowledge – we are the first to address gender profiling.

Author profiling is a well-established subfield of NLP with a thriving community gathering data, organizing shared tasks and publishing about this topic. Author profiling entails the prediction of an author profile – i.e., sociological and/or psychological characteristics of the author – based on the text that they have written. The most prominent author profiling task is gender classification, other tasks include the prediction of age, personality, region of origin, and mental health of an author.

Gender prediction became a mainstream research topic with the influential work by Koppel et al. (2002). Based on experiments on a subset of the British National Corpus, they found that women have a more relational writing style (e.g., using more pronouns) and men have a more informational writing style (e.g., using more determiners). Later gender prediction research remained focused on English, yet the attention quickly shifted to social media applications (Schler et al., 2006; Burger et al., 2011; Schwartz et al., 2013; Plank and Hovy, 2015). In the last few years, more languages have received attention in the context of author profiling (Peersman et al., 2011; Nguyen et al., 2013; Rangel et al., 2015; Rangel et al., 2016), with the publication of the TwiSty corpus containing gender information on Twitter authors for six languages (Verhoeven et al., 2016) as a highlight so far. We aim to contribute to the language diversity of this research line by looking at Slovene.

Proceedings of the 6th Workshop on Balto-Slavic Natural Language Processing, pages 119–125,
Valencia, Spain, 4 April 2017. ©2017 Association for Computational Linguistics

Slovene belongs to languages with a pronounced morphology for gender. Nouns (and personal pronouns) have a defined grammatical gender (feminine, masculine, and neuter) in agreement with which other parts of speech can be inflected. Some of those structures allow for the identification of the author's gender in self-referring context. For example, the author's gender can be reflected in corresponding self-describing noun forms, e.g., *učitelj/učiteljica* (teacher$_{male/fem}$), and even more frequently in agreements of adjectives, e.g., *lep/lepa* (beautiful$_{male/fem}$), and non-finite verb forms, such as l-participles,[1] e.g., *sem delal/delala* (I worked$_{male/fem}$), which makes these markings a potentially useful feature for gender identification. As the inflected gender features might overshadow other relevant features, such as content and style, we investigate not only a token-based, but also a lemma-based approach. Disregarding easily manipulatable gender features (e.g., grammatical gender markings) can be seen as a first step towards an adversarial stylometry system, where we assume that the writer might not be who they claim to be. A second step would be to disregard content features, which can be easily manipulated as well. The lemma-based approach also allows for meaningful results to contribute to the field of sociolinguistics.

For our research in Slovene, findings in author profiling for related languages are of interest, especially with regard to feature construction due to morphological richness. Kapočiūtė-Dzikienė et al. (2015) predicted age and gender for Lithuanian literary texts. Lithuanian parliamentary texts were used to identify the speaker's age, gender and political view in Kapočiūtė-Dzikienė et al. (2014). A study of Russian showed there is a correlation between POS-bigrams and a person's gender and personality (Litvinova et al., 2015). Another relevant contribution to the field for Russian was the interdisciplinary approach to identifying the risk of self-destructive behavior (Litvinova and Litvinova, 2016). Experiments for gender identification for Russian show the advantages of grammatical features. Sboev et al. (2016) removed topical and genre cues from the corpus of picture descriptions and personal letters in Russian and ran tests for various features and machine learning algorithms to find the combination of grammatical information (POS-tags, noun case, verb form, gender, and number) and neural networks performed best. As far as we know, no gender classification of tweets in these languages has been presented.

The present paper is structured as follows: in Section 2, we describe the Janes Tweet corpus and its modification for the experiments, which are presented in Section 3. In Section 4, we discuss the results in terms of performance and feature interpretation, while in Section 5 we conclude our study and propose further work.

2 Corpus Description

For our experiments, the Janes corpus (Erjavec et al., 2016; Fišer et al., 2016) of user-generated Slovene was adapted to match the TwiSty corpus setting (Verhoeven et al., 2016). We will first introduce the Slovene source corpus and then describe our reformatting of it for the current research.

The Janes corpus was collected within the Janes national research project[2] and consists of documents in five genres: tweets, forum posts, news comments, blog entries, and Wikipedia user and talk pages. The Twitter subcorpus is the largest Janes subcorpus. The tweets were collected using the TweetCat tool (Ljubešić et al., 2014), which was designed for building Twitter corpora of smaller languages. Employing the Twitter Search API and a set of seed terms, the tool identifies users writing in the chosen language together with their friends and followers. The tool outputs tweets together with their metadata (tweet ID, time of creation and retrieval, favorite count, retweet count, and handle). In total, the corpus includes tweets by 8,749 authors with an average of 850 tweets per author.

The authors were manually annotated for their gender (female, male and unknown) and account type (private and corporate). Personal accounts are considered as private account types, while companies and institutions count as corporate ones. The gender tag was ascribed based on the screen name, profile picture, self-description ('bio') and – in the few cases that this was not sufficient – the use of gender markings when referring to themselves. The account type was annotated given the user name, self-description and (typically impersonal) content of tweets. Since the focus of our study

---

[1] Verb l-participles is the name for the Slovene participles that end in letter 'l' in the masculine form and can be used for past, future and conditional constructions.

[2] http://nl.ijs.si/janes/

	WRB	MAJ	Accuracy	Precision	Recall	F1-score
Token	56.9	68.5	92.6	92.7	92.6	92.6
Lemma	56.9	68.5	87.9	87.9	87.9	87.9

Table 1: Results of gender prediction experiments based on tokenized text and on lemmas. Abbreviations: WRB = Weighted Random Baseline, MAJ = Majority Baseline. Precision, Recall and F1-score are averaged over both classes (since both classes matter).

was the binary prediction of female or male gender, only private male and female accounts were considered in the experiments.

Given the multilingual context of user-generated content, each tweet had to undergo language identification. For this the `langid.py` program (Lui and Baldwin, 2012) was used. The identified language tags were additionally corrected with heuristics resulting in four possible tags for the entire corpus: Slovene, English, Serbian/Croatian/Bosnian, and undefined (Fišer et al., 2016).

This subcorpus of Janes was reformatted to resemble the TwiSty corpus in order to address the same task of author profiling. There are however a few differences that we should mention for completeness. The Janes corpus does not have the personality type information available for the users and the language identification was performed in a different way.

3 Experiments

The experimental setup of this research is largely based on the TwiSty experiments (Verhoeven et al., 2016). We will briefly describe this approach and explain our additions.

First of all, to ensure comparability of instances, we construct one instance per author by concatenating 200 language-confirmed tweets. Authors with less than 200 tweets are discarded. All user mentions, hashtags and URLs were anonymized by replacing them with a placeholder token to abstract over different instances to a more general pattern of their use. The final dataset contains 3,490 instances with more men (68.5%) than women (31.5%), see Table 2.

The gender prediction task is set up as a two-class classification problem with classes *male* and *female* in a standard tenfold cross-validation experiment using the LinearSVC algorithm in `scikit-learn` (Pedregosa et al., 2011). We used n-gram features on both word ($n = [1, 2]$) and character ($n = [3, 4]$) level. We did not perform

	Count	Percentage
Male	2,391	68.5
Female	1,099	31.5
Total	3,490	100

Table 2: Corpus statistics: male and female private Twitter users represented by 200 tweets per author.

any feature selection, feature weighting or parameter optimization.

The experiment was performed in two different settings: on tokenized text,[3] and on lemmatized text. The lemmatized text is available in the Janes corpus (for lemmatization process see Ljubešić and Erjavec (2016)). The results of these experiments can be found in Table 1 and will be discussed in Section 4.

We also performed the experiment on a normalized version of the text that was available in the Janes corpus. This means that substandard spellings were corrected to the standard form, especially including the restoration of diacritics. Our expectation was that standardizing the text would allow for 1) certain features to cluster together and get stronger and thus more generalizable; and 2) disambiguation of certain words due to diacritics restoration. However, the results of this experiment were near-identical to the experiment on tokenized text, so we will not further discuss this here.

4 Discussion

Our experiments show a very high and interpretable result. Using tokenized text clearly outperforms the use of lemmas by around 5%, but both systems appear to work really well, significantly outperforming both the weighted random baseline (WRB) and majority baseline (MAJ).

Interestingly, our results are higher than the state-of-the-art results for the different languages

---

[3]Using the `happierfuntokenizing` script by Christopher Potts (`http://wwwbp.org`), as also used by Verhoeven et al. (2016).

in TwiSty. The most comparable language in data size would be Portuguese, which achieves 87.6%, while we achieve 92.6% for Slovene. As our feature analysis below will show, the difference lies in the gender markings.

Slovene encodes gender more extensively than Romance languages do. Especially the frequently used verb l-participles are important features for gender profiling, because a gender marking for the author is present every time the author is the subject of the past and future tense and conditional verb mood that are expressed by the auxiliary and the participle. Although agreement is partly informative also in other Romance languages, i.e., through participle agreement in French, e.g., *je suis allé/allée* (I went$_{\text{male/fem}}$), Italian, e.g., *io sono andato/andata* (I went$_{\text{male/fem}}$), Spanish, e.g., *yo fui invitado/invitada* (I was invited$_{\text{male/fem}}$), or adjectival agreement in French, e.g., *je suis heureux/heureuse* (I am happy$_{\text{male/fem}}$) or Spanish, e.g., *yo soy viejo/vieja* (I am old$_{\text{male/fem}}$), the gender markings are much less frequent than in Slavic languages, such as Slovene.

By lemmatizing the text, we remove this effect and we observe the performance of the system to lower to 87.9% which is very comparable to that of Portuguese and Spanish in the TwiSty paper (Verhoeven et al., 2016).

We also investigated the most informative features that `scikit-learn` outputs when retraining the model on the entire dataset (i.e., no tenfold). We extracted a ranked list of the 1,000 most informative features per class[4] and were able to make a comparison between the genders and between the token- and lemma-based approaches.

The most informative features of the token-based approach confirm very clearly our explanation of the higher performance of this approach compared with the lemma-based approach. The bulk of the most informative features can be related to gender markings on verb l-participles (e.g., MALE: *mislil* (thought), *bil* (been), *vedel* (known), *gledal* (watched); FEMALE: *mislila* (thought), *dobila* (gotten), *rekla* (said), *videla* (seen)), as well as feminine adjective forms (e.g., *ponosna* (proud), *vesela* (happy)).

The informative features for the lemma-based approach contain almost no gender markings. However, many interesting stylistic and content-based features become apparent, some of them also occurring lower on the ranking with the token-based approach.

We found several word and character features associated with the use of profane language that are strongly linked to the male category, e.g., *jebati* and *fukati* (to fuck), *pizda* and *pička* (cunt), *rit* (ass), *srati* (to shit), *kurec* (dick), *joške* (boobs). Another characteristic distinctive of the male class is non-alphabetical symbols including symbols for euro (€) and percent (%), and numerals (as digits) – the latter were also found to be more indicative of male authors and speakers in an English corpus of various genres (Newman et al., 2008) and the spoken part of BNC (Baker, 2014). Interestingly, vulgar expressions do not occur among the most informative features of the female category, while a small number of numerals can be found. The female category is distinguished by the use of emoticons (;3, :*, :), ♥), however the emoticon with tongue (:P) is related to the male category. Among the most informative features on both lemma- and token-level various interjections often combined with character flooding occur in the female category: *(o)joj* (oh), *oh* (oh), *ah* (oh), *ha* (ha), *bravo, omg, jaaa* (yaaas), *aaa* (argh), *ooo* (oooh), *iii* (aaaw). The female category further displays linguistic expressiveness in intensifiers (*ful* (very), *čist* (totally)) and adjectives and adverbs denoting attitude (*grozen* (horrible), *lušten* (cute), *gnil* (rotten), *čuden* (weird)), but these require further support in analysis.

A strong stylistic feature of the female category is referring to self with personal and possessive pronouns in first person: *jaz* (me), *zame* (for me), *moj* (my/mine) on the lemma-level, and *meni* (to me), *moje* (my/mine), *mene* (me$_{\text{accusative}}$) on the token-level with some of these features on both levels occurring within word bigrams (*biti_moj* for be_mine). Referring to others is also more present in the female category, namely with possessive pronouns for third person singular (*njen* (her/hers), *njegov* (his)) and first person plural (*naš* (our/ours)). This corroborates prior findings for English where women also use more pronouns than men (Schler et al., 2006).

A minor feature that requires further analysis is the use of diminutive endings in the female category (*-ček* and *-kica*).

The lemma-based approach provides insight into interesting tendencies regarding the content.

---

[4]These lists are available online at: `https://github.com/verhoevenben/slovene-twisty`.

The topics in the male category are associated with drinking (*pivo/pir* (beer), *bar*; *piti* (to drink) in the token-based list), sports (*tekma* (game), *šport* (sports), *fuzbal* (football), *zmaga* (win)) and motoring (*guma* (tire), *avto* (car), *voziti* (to drive/ride)). In the female category, a topic on food and beverages is also present, but with a different focus (*hrana* (food), *čaj* (tea), *čokolada* (chocolate), *sladoled* (ice cream)). Both female and male authors refer to other people, but they focus on different agents. Referring to women (*ženska*), men (*moški*), kinship (*starš* (parent), *mami* (mom), *otrok* (child), *babica* (grandma), *teta* (aunt)), female friends (*prijateljica*) and female colleagues (*kolegica*) relates more with the female category, while we can find references to wives (*žena*), male colleagues (*kolega*) and male friends (*prijatelj*) in the male category.

The token- and lemma-based levels of both categories display various modality markers: *marati* (to like), *ne_moči* (not_able), *zagotovo* (definitely), *želim* (I wish) for the female category, and *rad* (like/want_male), *verjetno* (probably), *hotel* (wanted_male), *želel* (wished_male), *potrebno* (necessary) for the male category.

It is interesting to note that these stereotype-confirming gendered features strongly resemble earlier results on social media data for English. In their research on Facebook text, Schwartz et al. (2013) also found men to use more swear words and women to use more emoticons. Similarly, according to a study by Bamman et al. (2014) on English tweets, emoticons and character flooding are associated with female authors, while swear words mark tweets by male authors. Again, both groups use kinship terms, but with a divergence similar to our finding.

5   Conclusions and Further Work

We conclude that the classification of Twitter text by gender works very well for Slovene, especially when the system can use the gender inflection on the verb l-participles, but also in a lemmatized form where the system can use stylistic and content features.

Should one wish to use gender classification in an adversarial setting – i.e., when you take into account people trying to actively mislead a reader by posing as a different person or gender – the content features should also be removed from the experiment as they too can be easily manipulated. Func-

tion words and POS-tags are the best features in this setting, as they are not under conscious control (Pennebaker, 2011). Slovene would be an interesting language to research this for, as pronouns – which are considered to be very salient author profiling features – are often not explicit.

Acknowledgements

The work described in this paper was partially funded by the Slovenian Research Agency within the national basic research project Resources, Tools and Methods for the Research of Nonstandard Internet Slovene (J6-6842, 2014-2017). The first author is supported by a PhD scholarship from the FWO Research Foundation – Flanders.

References

Paul Baker. 2014. *Using Corpora to Analyze Gender*. Bloomsbury, London.

David Bamman, Jacob Eisenstein, and Tyler Schnoebelen. 2014. Gender identity and lexical variation in social media. *Journal of Sociolinguistics*, 18(2):135–160.

John D. Burger, John Henderson, George Kim, and Guido Zarrella. 2011. Discriminating gender on Twitter. In *Proceedings of the Conference on Empirical Methods in Natural Language Processing*, EMNLP '11, pages 1301–1309, Stroudsburg, PA, USA. Association for Computational Linguistics.

Kaja Dobrovoljc, Simon Krek, and Jan Rupnik. 2012. Skladenjski razčlenjevalnik za slovenščino. In Tomaž Erjavec and Jerneja Ž. Gros, editors, *Zbornik 15. mednarodne multikonference Informacijska družba - IS 2012, zvezek C*, pages 42–47. Institut Jožef Stefan, October.

Tomaž Erjavec, Jaka Čibej, Špela Arhar Holdt, Nikola Ljubešić, and Darja Fišer. 2016. Gold-standard datasets for annotation of Slovene computer-mediated communication. In *Proceedings of the Tenth Workshop on Recent Advances in Slavonic Natural Languages Processing (RASLAN 2016)*. Brno, Češka.

Darja Fišer, Tomaž Erjavec, and Nikola Ljubešić. 2016. Janes v0.4: Korpus slovenskih spletnih uporabniških vsebin. *Slovenščina 2.0*, 4(2):67–99.

Miha Grčar and Simon Krek. 2012. Obeliks: statistični oblikoskladenjski označevalnik in lematizator za slovenski jezik. In T. Erjavec and J. Žganec Gros, editors, *Proceedings of the 8th Language Technologies Conference*, volume C, pages 89–94, Ljubljana, Slovenia, October. IJS.

Matjaz Juršič, Igor Mozetič, Tomaž Erjavec, and Nada Lavrač. 2010. LemmaGen: Multilingual lemmatisation with induced ripple-down rules. *J. UCS*, 16(9):1190–1214.

Jurgita Kapočiūtė-Dzikienė, Ligita Šarkutė, and Andrius Utka. 2014. Automatic author profiling of Lithuanian parliamentary speeches: Exploring the influence of features and dataset sizes. In *Human Language Technologies The Baltic Perspective, Proceedings of the Sixth International Conference Baltic HLT 2014*. Kaunas, Lithuania.

Jurgita Kapočiūtė-Dzikienė, Andrius Utka, and Ligita Šarkutė. 2015. Authorship attribution and author profiling of Lithuanian literary texts. In *Proceedings of the 5th Workshop on Balto-Slavic Natural Language Processing*. Hissar, Bulgaria.

Moshe Koppel, Shlomo Argamon, and Anat Rachel Shimoni. 2002. Automatically categorizing written texts by author gender. *Literary and Linguistic Computing*, 17(4):401–412.

Tatiana Litvinova and Olga Litvinova. 2016. Authorship profiling in Russian-language texts. In *Proceedings of the 13th International Conference on Statistical Analysis of Textual Data (JADT)*. Nice, France.

Tatiana Litvinova, Pavel Seredin, and Olga Litvinova. 2015. Using part-of-speech sequences frequencies in a text to predict author personality: a corpus study. *Indian Journal of Science and Technology*, 8(9):93–97.

Nikola Ljubešić and Tomaž Erjavec. 2016. Corpus vs. lexicon supervision in morphosyntactic tagging: the case of Slovene. In *Proceedings of the Tenth International Conference on Language Resources and Evaluation (LREC 2016)*, Paris, France, may. European Language Resources Association (ELRA).

Nikola Ljubešić and Darja Fišer. 2016. Private or corporate? Predicting user types on Twitter. In *Proceedings of the 2nd Workshop on Noisy User-generated Text*, pages 38–46.

Nikola Ljubešić, Darja Fišer, and Tomaž Erjavec. 2014. Tweetcat: A tool for building Twitter corpora of smaller languages. In *Proceedings of the 9th Language Resources and Evaluation Conference (LREC 2014)*. ELRA, Reykjavik, Iceland.

Nikola Ljubešić, Katja Zupan, Darja Fišer, and Tomaž Erjavec. 2016. Slovene data : historical texts vs. user-generated content. In Heike Zinsmeister Stefanie Dipper, Friedrich NeuBarth, editor, *Proceedings of the 13th Conference on Natural Language Processing (KONVENS)*, pages 146–155.

Marco Lui and Timothy Baldwin. 2012. langid.py: An off-the-shelf language identification tool. In *Proceedings of the ACL 2012 system demonstrations*, Jeju, Korea. ACL.

Matthew Newman, Carla Groom, Lori Handelman, and James Pennebaker. 2008. Gender differences in language use: An analysis of 14,000 text samples. *Discourse Processes*, 45(3):211236.

Dong Nguyen, Rilana Gravel, Dolf Trieschnigg, Theo Meder, and C-M Au Yeung. 2013. TweetGenie: automatic age prediction from tweets. *ACM SIGWEB Newsletter*, 4(4).

Fabian Pedregosa, Gael Varoquaux, Alexandre Gramfort, Vincent Michel, Bertrand Thirion, Olivier Grisel, Mathieu Blondel, Peter Prettenhofer, Ron Weiss, Vincent Dubourg, Jake Vanderplas, Alexandre Passos, David Cournapeau, Matthieu Brucher, M. Perrot, and Edouard Duchesnay. 2011. Scikit-learn: Machine learning in Python. *Journal of Machine Learning Research*, 12:2825–2830.

Claudia Peersman, Walter Daelemans, and Leona Van Vaerenbergh. 2011. Predicting age and gender in online social networks. In *Proceedings of the 3rd international workshop on Search and mining user-generated contents*, pages 37–44. ACM.

James W. Pennebaker. 2011. *The Secret Life of Pronouns: What Our Words Say About Us*. Bloomsbury USA.

Barbara Plank and Dirk Hovy. 2015. Personality traits on twitter -or- how to get 1,500 personality tests in a week. In *Proceedings of the 6th Workshop on Computational Approaches to Subjectivity, Sentiment and Social Media Analysis (WASSA)*. Lisbon, Portugal.

Francisco Rangel, Fabio Celli, Paolo Rosso, Martin Potthast, Benno Stein, and Walter Daelemans. 2015. Overview of the 3rd author profiling task at pan 2015. In *CLEF 2015 Working Notes*. CEUR.

Francisco Rangel, Paolo Rosso, Ben Verhoeven, Walter Daelemans, Martin Potthast, and Benno Stein. 2016. Overview of the 4th author profiling task at pan 2016: cross-genre evaluations. In *CLEF 2016 Working Notes*. CEUR-WS.org.

Aleksandr Sboev, Tatiana Litvinova, Dmitry Gudovskikh, Roman Rybka, and Ivan Moloshnikov. 2016. Machine learning models of text categorization by author gender using topic-independent features. In *Proceedings of the 5th International Young Scientist Conference on Computational Science*. Procedia Computer Science, Krakow, Poland.

Jonathan Schler, Moshe Koppel, Shlomo Argamon, and James W Pennebaker. 2006. Effects of age and gender on blogging. In *AAAI Spring Symposium: Computational Approaches to Analyzing Weblogs*, volume 6, pages 199–205.

H. Andrew Schwartz, Johannes C. Eichstaedt, Margaret L. Kern, Lukasz Dziurzynski, Stephanie M. Ramones, Megha Agrawal, Achal Shah, Michal Kosinski, David Stillwell, Martin E.P. Seligman, and Lyle H. Ungar. 2013. Personality, gender, and age in the language of social media: The open-vocabulary approach. *PloS one*, 8(9).

Ben Verhoeven, Walter Daelemans, and Barbara Plank. 2016. TwiSty: a multilingual Twitter stylometry corpus for gender and personality profiling. In *Proceedings of the 10th Language Resources and Evaluation Conference (LREC 2016)*. ELRA, Portorož, Slovenia.

Ana Zwitter Vitez. 2013. Le décryptage de l'auteur anonyme : l'affaire des électeurs en survêtements. *Linguistica*, 53(1):91–101.

Author Index

Association for Computational Linguistics
209 N. Eighth Street
Stroudsburg, Pennsylvania 18360

ISBN 978-1-5108-3862-8

9 781510 838628